THE

OTHER SIDE

OF

THE RECORD

THE

OTHER SIDE

of the

RECORD

By *Charles O'Connell*

◇◇◇

GREENWOOD PRESS, PUBLISHERS
WESTPORT, CONNECTICUT

TO

David

MY SON

CONTENTS

Contents

⋞ Prelude: ⋟

and a Personal Theme

AT FIVE o'clock of a December morning, not long ago, a quartet of people who had obviously been out all night sat round a table in a restaurant on New York's 59th Street and ordered double brandies. I cannot identify the restaurant because the brandy was ordered, delivered, and imbibed after the legal closing hour; but I can, at least a little vaguely, identify the quartet. The seventy-three inches (perpendicular) of South American beauty was a lady who a few weeks before had pleaded self-defense to a charge of murdering her wealthy husband, and had been acquitted on this ground. (This must have been the chivalrous South American way of paying tribute to beauty, since the gentleman was shot in the back.) The second lady at the table, no less lovely in a North American way than the first, was a famous star of motion pictures. The third member of the quartet was one of the world's greatest musicians. The fourth was myself.

The party had begun at five o'clock in the evening of the preceding day, with a round or two of cocktails at somebody's apartment on Park Avenue. Later there was dinner at the Madison Hotel. A late arrival at *Life with Father*. An interlude of seeing and being seen at El Morocco, then one of Dwight Fiske's séances of slick and simpering insinuations at the Savoy-Plaza; one more nightclub, and finally the little tableau

I have sketched above. At five o'clock in the morning I was tired. Tired of music, bored with musicians, surfeited with beauty, despoiled of conversational ideas—and the brandy was neither cognac nor armagnac nor good.

All this, I thought, *in the name of a job.* And in the course of five minutes I reflected upon the things I had been required to do and to suffer, and the years I had consumed in doing and suffering them, as part of my duty as musical director of RCA Victor. I had played ping-pong most of the night with Jascha Heifetz (a good player and a bad loser); jumped naked and shivering into Albert Spalding's icy pool at 7 A.M.; listened to Toscanini's jokes, comprehensible only in their earthiness; labored (successfully) to bring a smile to the dour visage of Rachmaninoff; soothed the childish rages of Iturbi; endured the vulgarity and din of "The Stork" to entertain Artur Rubinstein; softened and diverted the bovine stubbornness of Flagstad; ignored Pons's sulks and Moore's tantrums, and so on, *ad infinitum* and *ad nauseam*. All this in the interest of a commercial organization that should be, has been, and may again be one of the most distinguished, productive, and useful institutions of its kind. *What doth it profit a man*, I wondered. So at 5:05 that morning I actually, if only mentally, resigned.

I had been for nearly twenty years in the service of Victor and recorded music. First it was the old Victor Talking Machine Company, and then through the successive metamorphoses of that honorable institution—the Audio-Vision Appliance Company, the RCA Victor Company, the RCA Manufacturing Company, Inc., and the RCA Victor Division of the Radio Corporation of America. The last thirteen of those years were occupied with the duties of music director for Victor Red Seal records, a term which, though outlined poetically in Holy Writ (see page xiii), in view of what follows in this book, I must explain. During the term extending from 1930 to April 1, 1944, I was solely responsible for virtually every Red Seal record made in America. My duties were to engage all Red Seal artists, deciding what new ones should be added to our list and which names should be subtracted; to negotiate recording contracts with the artists and their managers; to choose the repertoire to be recorded by each artist; to supervise musically all important Red Seal recordings and sometimes to conduct the orchestral accompaniments as well; to pass upon the musical viability of the records after they were made, and to get the artists' approval of them; to decide the content of each month's issue of records; to prepare descriptive and analytical notes on major works; to revise and in the main rewrite *The Victor Book of the Opera;* to extract from the corporation enough money for advertising Red Seal records in order slowly to rebuild them to their once favorite place with the musical public; finally, and this is the chief explanation for this book and the little scene that inspired it, I was required to maintain at all times and against all comers the forever precarious relations between musical artists and my employers.

Many friends have regarded my job, with all its varied and heavy responsibilities, as the most fascinating and one of the most important musically, in the world. It often was; too, it was and is enormously gratifying to have a hand in making beauty immortal and in bringing it to ever-increasing numbers of people. *"I gat me men singers and women singers. . . . So I was great."* Then why abandon this unique and fascinating occupation? There were many reasons—too many and too varied responsibilities, too many plots and counterplots by the ignorant, the stupid, the malicious; but most of all, too little music and too much business.

I was busy. I have no more than the normal individual's objection to work, but over the years I have developed a passionate antipathy toward useless, trivial, misdirected, and unworthy work, and much of mine up to April 1, 1944, could be so described. *After all, I thought, this isn't the work for you. You are a musician and not a diplomat, lawyer, businessman, father-confessor, or professional hand-holder. You play the pipe organ well enough to have appeared in the most distin-*

guished of musical company. You play the piano well enough
to make the Victor Red Seal label. You have conducted successfully and repeatedly every first-class symphony orchestra
on the American continent. You have two successful books to
your credit. And you're nearly forty-three years old. Time you
did something that's more fun than brandy for breakfast.
Time you got acquainted with your children and perhaps even
with your wife. Time you chose your companions and your
friends. Time you did some of the things you want to do, and
fewer of those which lead to nothing but disappointment, dis-
illusion, and ingratitude. Time for a release, a katharsis.

This book is it.

You may deduce that during the period of my musical directorship I had more than a little to do with the great ones of
music. The brandy-for-breakfast incident was typical of thousands—ridiculous, amusing, amazing, disillusioning perhaps—
but often entertaining. I will tell you of some of them, and
something of the people concerned, in the following pages. In
doing so I want to avoid as far as possible two things: malice
and musical criticism. The first I shall restrict to the normal
limits permissible to a naturally amiable soul such as myself;
the second I wish to reserve to another time and place where
it might appear more properly and with more interest to the
reader. I must emphasize here too that when I resigned from
Victor, I, like the character in *La Bohème*, was able to say
"*addio senza rancor*"; I left the association of a good many
friends reluctantly and with bitterness toward no one.

I have another reason for writing this book. For years I have
been bored, irritated, and sometimes infuriated by the endless
stream of cheap and incredible nonsense that has been published about musical matters and about noted performing musicians. I speak not only of the outgivings of the press agent,
but of the obscene rot that has been peddled to publishers by
the sycophant, the hero-worshipper, and the third-rate critic.
I do not want to disparage, denigrate, or debunk anyone, but
would like rather to add a third dimension to the somewhat

flat and distorted pictures of certain notable musical people and musical events that have been presented to the public.

I suppose no one really believes everything he sees in print simply because it is in print; yet it seems to me that a man who aspires to have his words broadcast either by the magic of the press or the miracle of radio should have some concern with the truth. Dates and documents, except as they are expressly called to your attention, are of little interest or importance to this record; as Dr. Johnson remarks, if a man could say nothing (for or) against a character, but what he can prove, history could not be written. The truth, as set forth here, may occasionally be disagreeable to some of my musician friends, and incredible to their admirers. Let them all console themselves with the thought that I could have told "the whole truth," but being familiar with the quality of mercy, I will not. I promise to tell, rather, "nothing but the truth." Who rightfully may resent that?

CHARLES O'CONNELL

I gat me men singers and women singers. . . . So I was great. . . . I withheld not my heart from any joy; for my heart rejoiced in all my labour: and this was my portion of all my labour.

Then I looked on all the works that my hands had wrought . . . and behold, all was vanity and vexation of spirit, and there was no profit under the sun. . . .

Then said I in my heart, As it happeneth to the fool, so it happeneth even to me; and why was I then more wise? . . . For there is no remembrance of the wise more than of the fool for ever; seeing that which now is in the days to come shall all be forgotten. . . .

Therefore I hated life. . . . Yea, I hated all my labour . . . because I should leave it unto the man that shall be after me.

And who knoweth whether he shall be a wise man or a fool? Yet shall he have rule over all my labour wherein I have laboured. . . .

For what hath man of all his labour, and of the vexation of his heart, wherein he hath laboured under the sun?

For all his days are sorrows, and his travail grief; yea, his heart taketh not rest in the night. . . .

There is nothing better for a man, than that he should eat and drink, and that he should make his soul enjoy good in his labour. . . . For who can eat, or who else can hasten hereunto more than I?

Ecclesiastes ii: 8–25

The devil can cite Scripture for his purpose.

Shakespeare: The Merchant of Venice: Act 1, Sc. 3

He will give the devil his due.

Shakespeare: King Henry IV, Part I: Act 1, Sc. 2

GRACE MOORE

❦ Grace Moore* ❧

"The lady doth protest too much,

methinks"

OVER a period of years I have had many opportunities for in-
dulging myself in a harmless and fascinating pastime—the
making of motion picture films, mostly in color, and I have
acquired a not extensive, quite expensive, and select collection. The locale of these pictures varies from the beaches of
Cape Cod to Harbor Island at Balboa, California; the subject
matter includes such items as Stokowski doing a comic bit
with a tall and glamorous lady—his wife Evangeline; Toscanini
mugging through a piano duet with me at my home in Philadelphia; Artur Rubinstein miming a Jewish story to the evident amusement of Bill Primrose, Emanuel Feuermann,
Jascha Heifetz, and myself at Heifetz's seagirt California
home. Not long ago I resurrected some of these films with
which to while away the tedious hours one must spend in
bed during a pneumonia convalescence, and suddenly the sun-

---

* This chapter was written nearly two years before the tragic death of Miss
Moore. The admonition *"de mortuis nil nisi bonum"* is not one that Miss
Moore approved or observed, and after reflection the author feels no compulsion to apply it in her case. Grace Moore was basically and naturally honest
and candid. It seems to the author that her memory is better and more re-
spectfully served by preserving those qualities in dealing with her. Consequently, what has been written about her stands exactly as when it was written
and she was alive. It has been read and approved by one of her warmest
admirers and closest personal friends.

lit and flower-starred acres of Far Away Meadows, embraced
by Connecticut's loveliest hills, came to life before me. Against
the background of Grace Moore's charming old house and the
pool that reflects the summer sky and the color of Grace's eyes,
moved such arresting figures as Helen Hayes and Désiré
Defrère, Hilda Burke and Val Parera, Gilbert Miller and Elsa
Maxwell, Jean Dalrymple, sweet as honey, hard and brilliant
as diamond; and finally Grace herself, relaxed in slacks, a blue
bandeau binding her windblown blond hair, and a real, warm,
sunny smile bringing to her face an engaging quality that her
dear public never sees. I am happy that I have even this vital-
ized shadow (in technicolor) of Grace in one of the comparatively rare moments when she is herself. Here she was at home
and among friends—not the meretricious ones who forgather
so often to drink her Scotch, mock her French, and arouse her
Irish, but those who sense behind her pretentiousness, snob-
bism, self-delusion, and capricious temper a warmly human
and basically simple, honest, and lovable personality.

Grace has the mind of an exceedingly shrewd, precocious,
and confused child. She is almost completely uneducated. If
this sounds harsh, let me add at once that I do not mean to
imply that she is ignorant in the ordinary sense of the word,
uninformed, unworldly, or stupid. I prefer to use the word
"educated" in the Jesuitical and strict sense—that is, "drawn
out" or "developed." This lady is by no means lacking in intelligence, keenness of perception, basic honesty, or native
talent, but she has never thoroughly exploited or developed
her capacities in any direction, musical or other. Hers is not a
full-flowered, a rounded personality. Except for certain rough
spots that have been sloughed off through the natural effect
of the frictions which she herself has often created, she is an
unlicked cub. Her personality is asymmetrical; of gemlike substance, but amorphous in structure and development.

Miss Moore's book [1] and a letter from the author came to

---

[1] *You're Only Human Once*, Doubleday, Doran & Co., Inc., 1944.

my hands, by a curious coincidence, the very day after I had revived my feature picture starring Grace and her friends. Both the book and the letter are revealing. The contents of the letter I may not disclose, but the book, to anyone who knows Grace and can read between the lines, is a devastating exposure. Whoever wrote it managed, consciously or otherwise, to give an interlinear portrait-etching of Grace that is uncharitably accurate. The average reader will not be able to see this because the portrait presented in the book must be held up to the mirror of Grace's personality as it actually is before it becomes clear. I understand that the book has been very successful, and naturally so, I suppose, for it superficially presents Grace as the public would like her to be and, I dare say, as Grace would like herself to be. I have been unable to find in it a single expression characteristic of Grace.

It is obvious from Grace's biographical sketch that she was one of those obnoxious little girls, congenitally exhibitionist, for whom some sort of career that would keep her before the public gaze was inevitable. I suppose a very high percentage of adolescent girls decide on the theater as a career. Few of them, happily, realize their ambitions in this direction. A career in the world of entertainment isn't accomplished by wishful thinking. It requires, in various proportions, talent, determination, courage, ability and willingness to work and to endure almost intolerable drudgery, and, vitalizing all, an intense, constant, enduring, and insuperable love of the art one has chosen to serve. Grace Moore has some of these qualifications. Most musicians with whom she has worked deny that she has musical talent, but they are wrong. Grace is gifted with a voice of marked natural beauty and considerable power. It has some really lovely tones and though it is quite variable through its range, it is almost always of an agreeable timbre. When musicians say that Grace isn't musical they mean, I think, that she is musically undeveloped and insecure. This applies to her voice as well as to her general musicianship. Her sense of time values is rudimentary, her sense of rhythm quite defective, her concept of orchestral values limited to the idea that an orchestra is something used as background for a voice. Her sense of pitch, which, as with the vast majority of musicians, is relative rather than absolute, doesn't come below the level of the average. Her temperament is passionate without tenderness. I think there are many people with talents equal or superior to Grace's who have never approached and never could approach success because they lack the second qualification I have mentioned, which Grace possesses in a truly extraordinary degree. That is determination.

If Grace's determination had been as wisely directed as it is powerful, I think she would be today one of the most interesting artists in the world of entertainment. But Grace did not determine first and foremost to become a great musician or to exploit to their limits the talents nature has given her. No, I think Grace determined rather that she would wear pearls and precious stones and decorations; that she would receive on the stage of the Metropolitan the homage of an audience always fashionable, always distinguished, always befurred and bejeweled—an audience

> Ermined and minked and Persian-lambed,
> Be-puffed (be-painted, too, alas!)
> Be-decked, be-diamonded—be-damned!
> The women of the better class.

I think she determined that she would meet as an equal in achievement the great ones of the world, or at least those she considers great. But the facile friendship and easy admiration and voluble flattery of these people—mostly the frothy people who come to the surface of that curious and sometimes noisome mixture called café society—have deflected her determination from (if indeed it was ever focused upon) the idea and the ideal of developing artistic completeness and integrity. No, Grace was not lacking in determination, and her determination has brought her exactly what she wanted. I assert that it could have just as readily brought her to more marked artistic distinction.

Grace has the capacity but not the willingness to work where music is concerned. She has never in her life, so far as I can discover, worked persistently, seriously, or intelligently at music as such. Grace cannot be taught by anyone or anything except experience and imitation. Such development as her voice reveals has been accomplished not by teachers or coaches but by Grace herself, her observations of more finished artists, and her varied experience. One of her teachers tells how hopeless it was. She would work with him through lesson after lesson and come back and do things exactly as she had done them before, rationalizing her unwillingness to change or to accept the instruction of anyone by claiming: "Well, I sang it for Messager and he liked it this way," or "I have always done it so and it seems to have gone over all right." In line with this is the amusing remark she made to me one night at dinner after having discussed her resounding success in a certain performance. Knowing the music and privately considering it not within Grace's powers, I asked (slyly, I thought), "And how were the reviews, Grace?" and she answered, "Lousy, of course, but my dear Mr. O'Connell, don't you know that I have made my career on bad notices?"

I conducted a pair of concerts with the Cincinnati Orchestra early in 1944 at the invitation of Eugene Goossens, who had been asked to take over temporarily in Cleveland. I had Grace as soloist. Among other items on her part of the program was a kind of scena from *Goyescas*, which I had permitted to be included at Grace's urgent request. This music is not too simple, and I took the precaution of rehearsing it thoroughly with the orchestra prior to Grace's arrival. When Grace did come, everything went well until we came to the *Goyescas*. At this point Grace informed me that she had sung it not long before with Hans Kindler and the National Symphony in Washington, and that Mr. Kindler had given her *two whole rehearsals* just on this one number! This

sounded pretty ominous to me, but we went to work hopefully. We went through the number once, encountering quite
a few rough spots, which we cleaned up as we went along. We
played it again, pretty smoothly, but by no means perfectly.
A singer never understands that an orchestra, involving the
time-reactions of perhaps a hundred men, can never be as
flexible and as quick in following the aberrations of a solo
voice as can a piano accompanist. Grace, who never sings
anything twice the same way, became quite impatient and
told me that if she had to go on singing so much, she would
not have any voice left for the concert the following evening
and certainly none for her *Tosca* performance in New York,
which was more than half a week away. I pointed out that she
would have to work with us, and really rehearse if she expected to do this number; that if Hans Kindler had required
her to rehearse it for two hours or for two rehearsals, which-
ever it was, she could hardly expect that we could do as well
in ten minutes. All this, I must say, was perfectly in good
nature. I added that if she did not want to continue to rehearse and give us a chance to anticipate at least some of the
details of her highly personal interpretation we simply
wouldn't perform the *Goyescas*, though it appeared on the
printed program. Well, Grace wouldn't rehearse, so I
wouldn't perform; and we did our program minus what
should have been the most interesting number in the soloist's department. Nobody was disagreeable about it.

This hasn't always been the case when Grace and conductors have disagreed, as they have very frequently. Grace's
arrogance and contrariness are often merely a cover for her
musical insecurity. Not many of her associates quite understand this, and they ascribe to a natural bitchiness her occasional scenes with conductors and other musicians. I don't
think this is the case at all. I think Grace is naturally amiable,
but resorts to the traditional humors of the prima donna to
distract attention from certain musical shortcomings. But

I am sure she thought she was right when she turned on Fritz Reiner in front of the orchestra at a Ford broadcast rehearsal and demanded, "Who the hell do you think you are to tell me how to sing *Carry Me Back to Old Virginny?*" Personally, I think Fritz Reiner is qualified to tell pretty nearly anybody how to sing pretty nearly anything, and if he had difficulty in accompanying Grace even in so simple a little song, I am not at all surprised.

There was another incident connected with my Cincinnati appearance with Grace that not only amused me a great deal but also indicates Grace's determination and courage. The concerts we did were on Saturday and Sunday nights. About noon on Sunday Grace phoned me at the Netherland-Plaza Hotel and informed me in a voice of tragedy that she couldn't possibly go on at Sunday night's concert. She couldn't speak above a whisper, let alone sing. So much rehearsal had worn out her voice; and she proceeded to hold forth on this subject for a good half hour, and not exactly in a whisper. I knew there was an Ethiopian concealed somewhere about the wood-pile and so I listened patiently until the aborigine revealed himself. Suddenly Grace said, "Have you seen the morning papers?" I said, "No." She said, "Why, you should see those reviews." "Aha," ι thought, "this is it." If I remember correctly, there is only one paper published in Cincinnati on Sunday, and that is the *Enquirer*. It happened that a season or two before Grace had been rather difficult with the critic of the *Enquirer*, and apparently it was now the critic's turn. At any rate, the review was the reason for Grace's refusal to go on for the second half of our engagement. I was considerably upset because I felt that the orchestra stood to lose a lot of money—indeed had already done so, as we didn't draw a particularly large audience the first night and had serious competition for the second. I was not able to persuade Grace, but got her to agree to phone me again in an hour or two. Perhaps then she would be feeling better. It happened that James

Melton was singing a recital in Cincinnati that Sunday afternoon. I located Melton, explained the situation, and asked
him if he would go on in Grace's place that night. He was
reluctant, first because his afternoon recital would naturally
use up a good part of his vocal energy, and second because
he didn't want to hurt Grace's feelings. On the other hand,
he is a good friend and a good trouper, and finally he agreed
that if Grace would not appear, he would. This intelligence
was communicated to Miss Moore by Mr. O'Kane, manager
of the Cincinnati Orchestra, and it wasn't long before she
phoned me and told me that she had had some coffee, was
feeling much better, and felt that she could go on as scheduled. She did, and with resounding success.

I must add that I have never seen the *Cincinnati Enquirer*
review of these concerts, but if it was unkind to Grace, then
it must also have been unjust, because she sang beautifully
at both concerts of the pair.

I have mentioned as a requirement of the great artist deep
love for the art one serves. This, I am afraid, is a qualification
that Grace doesn't possess. In the first place, she doesn't really
love music, and in the second, she has no willingness to serve
music; she rather expects it to serve her, as indeed it has done
and done well. Fundamentally Grace is not concerned with
artistic achievement per se. She is interested in it only insofar
as it contributes incidentals. She feels, as she sets forth explicitly in her book, that there is a distinction between an
artist and a human being, that the two are incompatible, that
the artist who strives for perfection is necessarily isolated from
human contacts and quarantined from human life and living.
Thus she rationalizes her own preoccupation with frivolity,
with the "smart world," with the charms of the Lido and the
Riviera and 52nd Street, as if these morbid manifestations of
human life had any connection with essential humanity.
Grace wants to wear the diamonds and sables of a prima
donna, but she doesn't want to go straight home after the

show, take them off, drink a glass of warm milk,[2] and go to bed. The brummagem brilliance of Broadway is her *summum bonum* and her métier. That she has had the kind of success that she wanted in opera and concert is not because of any extraordinary talent for music, but rather because of really egregious boldness, resolution, and determination.

I do not know and I do not think that Grace has any stable set of values, human or artistic. As I have said before, I think she is confused. She is impressed, and easily impressed, by the most obvious flattery and *blague*. The horde of pansies, phonies, and other epiphytes who beset the entertainment business find her engaging, responsive, and impressionable— at least temporarily. No one is quicker to spot a fake or a faker; but Grace likes a good fake even though she knows it's a fake. She will tolerate pretension even when she knows it's pretension. I have often resented, because I am truly fond of her, the fact that she will waste her time, her talents, her charms, her good mind, her warm and honest nature, so often upon the trash of the human race. A person whose name gets into the papers is to Grace an important person; and to be

---

2 Perhaps after the opera Grace will prefer champagne, but following the exhausting efforts of a recording session she once introduced me to an extraordinary potation. I had escorted her from our studios to the Ritz-Carlton, where she was then staying. Knowing she was tired and more than a little under tension, I suggested that a cocktail might be relaxing. She agreed, with enthusiasm, and we went into the rather prissy bar at the Ritz. Grace informed me on the way that she was going to have a Bloody Mary. I had to confess no acquaintance with this tyrant among drinks, and I made a bet with Grace that neither would the waiter know what entered into its formula. Whereupon, as we sat down and the waiter approached, Grace ordered, in a voice that could be heard all over the room, "I want a Bloody Mary." Everyone jumped, but the waiter calmly said, "Yes, Miss Moore," lost my bet for me, and presently produced a concoction truly sanguinary in color and murderous in effect. It was served in an eight-ounce glass and contained one third vodka, two thirds tomato juice, a dash of Worcestershire, and a few drops of lemon juice. Shake well before using, and you will certainly shake afterward. However, the taste is so innocent that I once inveigled George Marek, music editor of *Good Housekeeping*, who is a total abstainer, into drinking a Bloody Mary under the impression that it was spiced tomato juice. Along about ounce number seven George got wise, but manfully finished it without any apparent ill effect.

received cordially at a 52nd Street ex-speakeasy has real importance in her eyes. Paradoxically, at the same time Grace
was not perverting the truth when she made it clear that
she likes self-made people. She knows the real thing when she
sees it, but sometimes seems to prefer the counterfeit. She
will, on occasion, be pretentious herself, but can laugh at
herself for doing it. She can be the most unholy snob and the
most delightful human being in the world.

Grace has generous impulses and not infrequently is moved
by them. Just as frequently she repents them, in which case
she will either take back the generous gift or, if it is irretriev-
able, poison it with malice. She is most likely to behave this
way toward people of whom she is really fond and who are
devoted to her, or to whom her favor is in some degree important. During that famous summer on the Riviera which
she describes so amusingly in her book, she was wearing on
the beach an old batik robe that once had been very handsome, but which showed evidence of having been thoroughly
used as contributory negligee to her briefly summerized beach
costume. Or perhaps Grace was just tired of it; so she generously presented it one day to her secretary. This young
woman is much too fastidious a person to have worn the
robe in its rather unattractive condition, and also too appreciative of a beautiful thing to discard it. She consequently
took it to an expert French cleaner, had its pristine loveliness
restored by *nettoyage à sec*, and appeared on the beach in it,
whereupon Grace suddenly appreciated its beauty all over
again and demanded, and obtained, its return. Grace once
gave her publicity representative an unusual and attractive,
though not costly, piece of jewelry that she had tired of. When
she saw it on the girl, however, it began to look attractive again
and Grace retrieved it. I think these performances are simply,
amusingly childish, but I think it was not at all kind of Grace
to refer as she did in her book to the wedding present she
gave Dorothy Kirsten. Grace had been taking unto herself
a good deal of credit, during some months prior to Dorothy's

wedding, for having out of the greatness of her heart and her desire to help other musicians, financed this young girl's musical training. She was in truth furious, for reasons of her own, when Dorothy announced her marriage; and I think Grace's crass announcement that "I gave her as a wedding present complete clearance of all her debts to me" was noxious.

Once we entertained Miss Moore, together with Vladimir Golschmann and his lovely wife, at our home in Philadelphia after a concert they did with the Robin Hood Dell Orchestra. Grace was marvelously gowned and wore, I suppose, fifty thousand dollars worth of jewels. It was necessary for her to leave our house shortly after twelve o'clock, as she had engagements the following morning in New York. There was only one available train, leaving Philadelphia at 12:20 A.M. and carrying nothing but sleepers, which were sold out, and day coaches, which were thronged with soldiers. I explained the situation to Grace, and instead of being dismayed she was delighted. She would not even permit me to drive her to the station, but took a taxi alone, and spent a good two hours hobnobbing with a day coachful of soldiers. Having the attention simultaneously and personally of eighty-three young men would, I am sure, appeal to Grace, but I am willing to gamble that she put herself out to be charming, friendly, and a pal to every one of these boys during that ride to New York; and they must have enjoyed it as thoroughly as Grace did.

It is such things as this which make me impatient with Grace's occasional pretentiousness. I wish that she wouldn't insist on being a lady. If Grace says she is a lady—and she does, in various ways, too often and too emphatically—I'll agree; not only to preserve my time-ravaged locks, but because I have no clear concept of "lady" or "gentleman," and apparently she has. Grace seems to define these terms as describing people who "have acquired or kept good manners"; but this is hardly satisfactory and she can't possibly mean it. There must be more to the title than this, else no one so familiar with

the mordant lexicon of the mule skinner, or who brightly con-
fesses to letting another lady "have one" right across the
puss, can establish claim to it.

Grace reminds me, at moments, of a delightful young
friend I once had in Philadelphia—an artist who lived in one
of those fascinating old buildings, remodeled into studio apart-
ments which line one side of Washington Square and look
defiantly or hopefully across to the "modernistic" pile of N.
W. Ayer, or toward the monumental home of the Curtis Publishing Company directly to the north—the frigid north. Ruby,
like most of us who at the time inhabited Philadelphia's version of Greenwich Village, occasionally had difficulties with
the public utilities. One day she had a phone call from one
of the Bell Telephone Company's most polished bill collectors, and I had the pleasure of listening to her end of the
conversation. Omitting the details, the nature of which you
may guess, let me report the climax:

"What? . . . who didn't? . . . some dumb bookkeeper . . .
charge so much for the service on this unprintable telephone?
. . . in your hat! . . . a what? . . . a lady? . . . you're goddam right
I'm a lady!"

LILY PONS

◦§ Lily Pons ≈◦

An essay in astro-economics
with special reference to
the Kostelanetz constellation —
Lily, André, Coq d'or, Coca-Cola,
and Chrysler

ASTRO-ECONOMICS is a very abstruse science, of which I am neither a professor nor a very close student. I am, however, familiar with its basic thesis, which is, stripped of detail, simply this: if one star can make a lot of money, two stars in conjunction can make a lot more. Some pairs of stars, especially those who know the uses of that adversity which descends upon us all on March 15 annually, make money that can be represented only by appropriately astronomical figures.

There have been some remarkable partnerships in the arts and sciences. One may think of Tchaikovsky and Mme von Meck, Marie and Pierre Curie, Clara Wieck and Robert Schumann, Richard and Cosima Wagner, Elizabeth Barrett Fontanne and Robert Browning Lunt, Charles and Mary Beard; but for complete, rounded perfection and effectiveness there is, there has been, no astral conjunction quite in a class with the constellation of the planets, Lily Pons and André

Kostelanetz. I shouldn't refer to these stars as planets, I suppose, because (and this is without checking up on my celestial
physics) planets shine only by reflected light; and though it
is true that André and Lily glitter with uncommon brilliance
under the fierce light of publicity in which they live and
breathe and have their being, it would be grossly unfair to
deny either or both of them the extraordinary talents that are
theirs.

These talents are by no means entirely musical. Pons, in
addition to being a coloratura soprano of notable accomplishments, has studied a charming role and acts it to perfection
every day of her life. She has a flair for the extraordinary and
fantastic in *couture*, and with unerring acumen ferrets out
those productions and those producers that are the most sensational; and she wears her remarkable clothes with a manner.
The association of the coloratura soprano voice and the sounds
—I will not call them songs—of birds is a "natural" for the
publicity man; and Lily readily admits a passion for our feath-
ered friends, especially the rare and costly varieties. In her
New York apartment I have often observed a cage full of the
creatures, which, happily, were never vocal when I was present. The bird motif is worked pretty hard. Indeed, I recall a
cocktail party that Lily and André gave for the unveiling of
one of her many portraits, which—surprise!—represented her
with an archæopteryx, or something, perched prettily on her
finger. I almost expected to see a caption under it—"Can
you sing?"

You could not be with Lily very long without observing
evidence of her well-publicized superstition concerning the
number thirteen. Most people who have any superstition
about this mystic number regard it as unlucky. Obviously,
for Mme Pons, in whose life nothing average or ordinary
has ever happened except birth, it would have quite the
opposite significance. Thirteen has many a happy association for her. It appears, together with the initials LP, on the
license plate of her car; and just to be a spoil-sport, let me add

that in the "Nutmeg" state you too could have your initials for a license number if you are well-behaved. In the state of Connecticut, the Utopia [1] of so many tax-conscious professional people, where Lily has a charming house, anybody may have his initials or any reasonable arrangement of figures or letters on his license plate as long as he obeys the motor laws. Thus the LP13 on Lily's Brewster-bodied Ford. But thirteen is even more important for Lily. According to the press agents, Mr. Kostelanetz proposed thirteen times before she bestowed her hand.

Lily claims the south of France as her birthplace, but it remained for U.S., long before she became a citizen, to name a post office, Lilypons, Maryland, after her.[2] It is related that she first studied piano with a career in prospect, and that her remarkable voice was discovered quite by accident. I hope she and her admirers will forgive me if I cannot wax enthusiastic about Lily's voice, for the reason that the coloratura type has absolutely no appeal for me as a musician. I have admired only one, and that one not for its coloratura qualities but for its remarkable rather sultry sweetness and lyrical loveliness. That was the voice of Galli-Curci. The singing of a coloratura is a cross between a cackle and a whistle, and performers on the vocal high wire and trapeze are utterly devoid of musical interest to me. As coloratura voices go, I think that Miss Pons has one of the best extant. She has extraordinary range, some warmth in the lower register, and she often negotiates the inhuman difficulties of the great coloratura arias with quite accurate intonation.

I remember when Lily first came to this country as the pupil and protégée of Maria Gay and Giovanni Zenatello—not as the pupil of Alberto de Gorostiaga, as was intimated in the authorized article in the *Saturday Evening Post*. She looked then

---

[1] Charming country, readily accessible from New York—and no state income tax.

[2] Another distinction is, I believe, that she is the first Metropolitan prima donna to display her umbilicus in that fortress of propriety. The costume was for *Lakme*.

essentially very much as she does now, except for the color of
her hair, which has always been variable. At that time it was
quite black. She is very short in stature; this she compensates
by wearing the highest of high heels. I think this is not so
much that she wishes to be tall, since diminutiveness is one
of the attributes her press agent so enthusiastically dotes on.
I think it is rather to distract the eye from rather generous
dimensions in the horizontal planes.[3] Miss Pons has the
swarthy skin of the Mediterranean peoples, but unusually generous and skillful *maquillage* obscures her natural epidermal
tint and texture. Her legs are so frail as to be almost birdlike,
and her feet, the tiniest I have ever seen on a mature person.
She wears such extraordinarily short-vamped and high-heeled
shoes that she must perforce walk almost on the balls of the
toes. The effect is certainly to make her feet seem tinier than
they actually are; it also suggests to unbeglamored and disil-
lusioned eyes a case of *talipes equinus*.

If these remarks seem unchivalrous or malicious, let me say
at once that they are not so to be construed. No one on the
operatic stage and few in any theater anywhere can look so
delectably young, or radiate more bewitching charm, or seem
so precious, so fragile, so completely and perfectly fashioned
by some kind of magic, out of zephyrs and flowers of spring. If
it is true that Lily's magnetism for an audience is a work of
artfulness, it is likewise true that it could never be convincing
if it did not originate fundamentally in a warm, simple, sunny
nature. I have known the lady for quite a few years, offstage
and on, at work and at play, and sometimes under circumstances both trying and unflattering, and in all my acquaintance with her, she has invariably been *"gentile, aimable, et
douce."*

---

[3] I once knew a music critic who lost his job when one of his readers got
out the dictionary to discover what the critic meant by a certain expression in
his review, to wit: "the steatopygous Schumann-Heink." I think that I would
be on safe ground, however, if I content myself with the word "kallipygian"
which must be complimentary since a smart Fifth Avenue women's shop not
long ago spent a great deal of money in selling the idea to its clientele.

WORKING WITH LILY

I am happy to have had some influence in bringing about Pons's engagement for Victor records, and this, incidentally, was tantamount to gambling a lot of Victor's money, for she had at the time made no appearances in the United States and had no public here. Though I was not then directly concerned with the production·of Victor records, I was consulted in this particular matter and on hearing an extraordinary recording of Miss Pons's voice which Mme Gay presented, I, with a group of other Victor people, recommended a contract for Miss Pons. I did negotiate subsequent contracts with her, always without difficulty, until the last time the contract was up for renewal, when I was outbid by Columbia. This was a matter of regret to me and to my employers, who valued Miss Pons very highly as an artist, though on a purely dollars-and-cents basis her services were never, for us, a good investment. I do not believe they are profitable to Columbia either, although sales of Pons's records have been substantial. That they were profitable to Miss Pons, both in cash guarantees or advances against royalties and in a great deal of costly advertising, goes without saying.

It has always been very pleasant to work with Lily. She is a good musician, she is always well prepared, and never, so far as I can recollect, has had to cancel or interrupt a recording session because of any vocal indisposition. She is amiable, docile, co-operative, and gracious. Usually I engaged Wilfred Pelletier to conduct for her, and that assured an agreeable situation—which was by no means true later on when we were required to engage Kostelanetz.

Here was a rather awkward situation. I had three reasons for not wanting André to conduct for Victor recordings, and I could not with discretion discuss them with Lily. The first reason was that I wanted an abler conductor. I do not mean

to disparage André at all, for he is a first-class workman; but
we were doing opera, not the Coca-Cola hour, and I wished
to have not only a first-class operatic conductor but one associated with the Met, as Lily was, and one reasonably con-
versant with the opera. Secondly, Kostelanetz was, at the time,
rising as the bright particular star of our competitors, and
I didn't warm to the idea of advancing the prestige of a Columbia artist at the expense of Victor. Finally, André required an orchestra so large as to be unreasonably expensive,
actually impracticable in relation to the size and acoustic
character of our studio, and in bad taste musically. We finally
decided, nevertheless, to accede to Lily's wishes and engage
Kostelanetz. The results were not too happy. The records were
fair, but the incident brought to a crisis a situation which had
been existent for some time between Lily and André. He
may have used it to give extra pressure to the influence he was
bringing to bear on Lily to transfer her devotion from Victor
to Columbia. This she was quite unwilling to do, but André,
wisely as it turned out, eventually persuaded her. Furthermore, André, who is as touchy as "the fretful porpentine,"
was deeply offended when I protested what seemed to me the
senseless waste of time and talent in recording, for which he
was directly and solely responsible by reason of his grossly
inflated orchestra and the agonizing slowness of his recording
methods. He retired into typical Russian sullenness for a day
or two and then, as a final expression of pique, warned us
solemnly that we must not use his name as conductor on the
records. I was only too willing to be restrained by this prohibition.

"TO HELL WITH MR. O'CONNELL!"

Lily, as I have said, is quite amiable, and furthermore, I
suspect her of having a sense of humor. I am sure she enjoyed,
as I did myself on reflection, the most embarrassing moment
of my life. It happened like this:

The Democratic National Convention which nominated Franklin D. Roosevelt for his second term met at Philadelphia. The climax planned for the convention was to come on the last night, when Roosevelt was to appear at Franklin Field, the stadium of the University of Pennsylvania, to make his speech of acceptance. Immediately preceding the President's appearance there was to be an hour's concert by the Philadelphia Orchestra with a soloist. Mr. Stokowski discreetly declined an invitation to conduct this concert, but very considerately suggested me as a substitute, and Reggie Allen, then manager of the orchestra, engaged me as conductor and Lily Pons as soloist. It had rained most of the day, but as concerttime approached the Pons luck asserted itself, the skies cleared, and we rushed to Franklin Field, where 110,000 wild-eyed Democrats awaited the arrival of our Chief Executive. I was mightily excited—by the character of the occasion, the imminent appearance of the President, the sight of the multitudinous audience, the knowledge that every radio station in the United States would be tuned in, the pleasure of conducting the Philadelphia Orchestra, and by no means least, the honor of conducting for Miss Pons. Besides, she called me *"Maestro"!*

The inimitable *sang-froid* of Jim Sauter, who was in charge of entertainment and probably of everything else at the Democratic Convention, calmed me down somewhat and I went to work with a will. I might as well have stayed home. I assure you that 110,000 people can make more noise than 110 musicians, and there were moments during that concert when I literally could not hear the orchestra; in fact, when I had finished conducting the "Rhumba" movement from Harl McDonald's Second Symphony the trombones still had a couple of bars to go. As nobody heard them, it didn't matter much except to the trombones and myself.

When the soloist appeared, however, the audience quieted as if by magic, and in ten seconds Lily had them in the hollow of her little hand. I don't remember all we did, but among

other things there was Bishop's *Lo, Here the Gentle Lark.*
The solo flute, John Fischer of the Philadelphia Orchestra,
the solo soprano, the orchestra, and myself managed to finish
neatly together. This was Lily's concluding number, and when
the applause quieted, Mr. Sauter, master of microphones, delivered himself of an announcement. "And now," he cried
into the enormous void of silence, "and now the Philadelphia
Orchestra will play Beethoven's *Consecration of the House,*
under the direction of Mr. O'Connell." Whereupon an anonymous Stentor, in a voice far-carrying as a coyote's on the plains,
perfectly audible to 110,000 Democrats and via radio to
110,000,000 other citizens, gave out with "To hell with Mr.
O'Connell; give us some more Lily Pons!" Lily was sweet
enough not to want to laugh and gave me a most sympathetic
look, but when she saw that both Sauter and I were in con-
vulsions she had a good laugh out of it too. Later there were
tragicomic happenings of one sort or another, including the
difficulties of getting the orchestra started at the right moment
on *Hail to the Chief*—but we were talking about Lily and
André.

SUPER-SALESMAN

André is the shrewdest man in the music business. No one
can match him at capitalizing an asset or suppressing a lia-
bility. He is possessed of a ferocious acquisitiveness, yet has
the courage to spend money in great amounts in order to make
money in greater. If the money is supplied by a radio sponsor
or a recording company, so much the better. Indeed, it is the
investment of such money in André's unique talents that has
made him a very wealthy man. I am sure he earns more from
radio and record royalties than any conductor in his or any
other field. He has surely, shrewdly, and cautiously developed
and impressed on the public mind the Pons-Kostelanetz association, each of the two artists edging over little by little from

his and her respective side of the tracks, until ultimately, like all parallel lines, they will seem to converge; merge in that wonderful common ground of music, the musical *pons asinorum* traversed by the low-highbrows, the high-lowbrows, and the myriad middlebrows.

To this numberless mass André is the master musician of all time, and therefore, he has doubtless been to Chrysler what he was to Coca-Cola—the master salesman. Like all good salesmen, he knows how to work both sides of the street and across the tracks too. He knows, as few musicians or even businessmen know, the uses and the value of exploitation, promotion, and, above all, publicity. He knows what is to be exploited and what shouldn't be; that Lily's French accent is cute and that his own, which is of the Gregory Ratoff variety, might be regarded as funny; that Lily's diminutive charm and glamorous stage appearance are assets, whereas his own personal charms are perhaps less obvious. He knows that Main Street likes to read of Lily's mink and sable and chinchilla, and that such luxuries are really not luxuries at all, but useful and convincing "props" and sound investments from any viewpoint. Furthermore, he knows music. He knows how to arrange it, beglamorize it, conduct it, and sell it, because he knows up to forty decimal places the common denominator of musical taste in the radio audience. The Pons-Kostelanetz combination has been mutually advantageous and fantastically profitable. Lily brings to it the glamour of the Metropolitan, a touch of what the lowbrow thinks is highbrow, a picturesque personality, vocal fireworks, and musical talent of no mean order. André contributes really sound musicianship, extraordinarily shrewd commercial sense, crafty showmanship, sometimes good and often cheap music, but all of it, always, hand-decorated and chromium-plated.

André, deplorably, is showing signs of going "longhair" —figuratively, of course. This comes about, I think, partly because of suppressed desires, partly from much the same impulse that underlies a rich brewer's donation of stained-glass windows to the church, and partly out of financial considerations. Many a millionaire gets religion after he's got enough money to afford it. André can afford it. André has doubtless made all the money that he wants, or at least all that he can use; and it would perhaps bring our symbols *Coq d'or* and Coca-Cola a little closer into line if he were to graduate into the symphonic field. This no doubt would be attended with some difficulty for any man so long and intimately associated in the public mind with crass commercialism and with what, in the sense that it appeals to the mass, one may call vulgate music. But I think André will be able to wangle it by judicious application of the assets at his disposal; and indeed he has already made moves in this direction. There have been discreet offers, to various of the major orchestras during their summer season and to at least two of the major orchestras in their winter season, of the services of Lily as soloist, *and at very special fees, but necessarily, of course, with André conducting.*

Pension funds and pension-fund concerts are likely to benefit from the ministrations of André and his partner—that is, the pension funds and the pension-fund concerts of the more prosperous and more important orchestras, whose names will bring new prestige to Kostelanetz publicity. I shall be surprised if he does not accept, at least for what part of the season he can spare from the more remunerative commercial field, the co-conductorship of an American symphony orchestra.

When I juxtaposed *Coq d'or* and Coca-Cola I was, of course, speaking figuratively. I meant to indicate that the conjunction of two stars in their respective fields results in a combination for money-making unparalleled even in these mad years; that the combination of what Lily has, plus what André has, plus André's knowledge of how to exploit what they both have, is invincible.

André's musical background is obscure. I have been told that he was an opera conductor in Russia prior to his taking up residence in the United States, but this I do not believe.

If we are to take at face value the assertions of all the
émigré musicians and refugeniuses, it must be that Italy, Central Europe, and Russia were populated exclusively by conductors. I know more than one imported musician who made
a precarious living as a *chor-répétiteur* or accompanist in some
provincial European opera house but who on arriving here at
once has achieved a nice fat job on the basis of having been
a well-known European opera conductor.

This was not the case with André. Whatever his European
background, the experience and the practical musical education that developed him into the excellent musician that he is
were gained in this country. He had valuable and ultimately
highly profitable experience as a routine arranger and transcriber for the Judson Radio Company, forerunner of the
Columbia Broadcasting System, where Eugene Ormandy was
at the same time principal conductor. I am given to understand, by an unimpeachable authority, that André learned what
he knows about conducting from Mr. Ormandy. This would
hardly be surprising, since Mr. Ormandy is technically one
of the soundest and most expert men ever to lift a baton in
this country, and both able and generous in helping other
musicians in their work.

HOW TO MAKE MUSIC BETTER
THAN IT IS

If you had been accustomed to listening to André's Coca-
Cola hour via radio and had later been present in the broadcasting studio, you would probably have been startled to find
that the live orchestra doesn't sound at all like what goes out
on the air. So many microphones, echo chambers, and every
other electronic and mechanical gadget that can be employed
come between the actual performance and the broadcast that
the finished product you hear via radio really has little resemblance to the raw material developed in the studio. André has

skillfully and with imagination, if not always with good taste, exploited every resource that radio science can offer. The extraordinary clarity which is sometimes noticed in the Kostelanetz strings is accomplished, first, by the curious style of Kostelanetz orchestration, which so often requires all the strings to play in unison in the upper register; and secondly, by an electromechanical operation which gives the sound a floating and spacious quality. The whole orchestra is treated not as a unit but as a number of small groups, each with its own microphone, each controlled more by the flow of electric current than by the baton. I do not like, nor can any musician of cultivated tastes like, the character of the orchestrations which André has had made for him, but I do admire their cleverness and adroit employment of orchestral color and the skill with which the type of orchestration and the mechanical gadgets are made to operate together to produce a unique effect. As I have pointed out, André is keenly aware of every possible detail that can be used to make his work distinctive and popular. The question of his taste is not at issue. I dare say he is not playing to satisfy *his* taste but rather to tickle that of a certain broad level of the listening public. Whether that is good or bad is probably of no interest to the conductor so long as he satisfies it.

The techniques of recording have been employed to the great advantage of Lily also—though no more so than with other singers who have appeared in the movies. Sound-film recording is a priceless boon to any performing musician because it makes it possible that the public will never hear any but the artist's best—and there is no reason why the public should ever hear any but an absolutely perfect performance. The reason for this is that ten or a dozen or a hundred sound film recordings can be made, and indeed are made sometimes, of each selection. These can be synthesized into one finished recording by the simple expedient of cutting up the film and pasting one hundred or one thousand fragments together to make a perfect whole. "A good note here, a good note there;

here a note, there a note, everywhere a good note!" A perfect performance in public almost never happens, but even if it does happen, it is lost forever. In film recording perfect performances can be and are manufactured out of dozens or scores of imperfect performances, each one of which has something in it that is good. That is why movie crowds are so impressed and concert audiences so often disappointed when singing stars of the films appear in person. The various vital helps that the film record can give are absent. A voice that seems full and resonant on the screen may actually be small, pinched, and cold. There may be in reality a few or many lapses from pitch, but on the screen there are none. Film recording is the great deceiver, but I don't know that we should quarrel with it if its only crime is making things better than they are.

The versatility of film recording was rather amusingly demonstrated when Deanna Durbin was making the picture *100 Men and a Girl*. The orchestral recordings were all to be made in the Academy of Music in Philadelphia, where a very elaborate multi-channel film-recording system had been set up. Mr. Stokowski was to conduct the accompaniments for Miss Durbin. The day came for Deanna to record her songs with the orchestra, and it happened that the young lady was indisposed and decidedly not in good voice. In addition, she was scared to death. The recorders were nothing daunted. They recorded the accompaniments anyway and later on recorded the solo voice in Hollywood, combining the two in a final "dubbing," or re-recording, for the finished film. If you saw the picture, you heard Deanna singing in Hollywood and her accompaniment being played in Philadelphia.

I have been told that over a hundred "takes" were made on one number which Lily Pons sang in her last film. I don't know that this is true, but it could be, as this is common practice. I did not see or hear the film and consequently don't know the results from personal experience, but I am sure they were perfect.

SOMETHING FOR THE BOYS

I was personally disappointed in the wartime activities of many musicians. At least as far as those in the upper brackets are concerned, their USO activities were often conditioned upon their estimate of their tax situation or of the amount of exploitation that could be applied to their camp appearances. A good many singers and instrumentalists have achieved those income brackets where it is determined that additional earnings will be unprofitable. Entertainment at camps, with all expense paid and all transportation provided to remote corners of the world, with the opportunity for subsequent, impudent advertisement of patriotic effort and uproarious success among the boys, suggested to many wealthy entertainers a handy way of continuing to work, to keep in the limelight, to have the extraordinary experience of visiting war theaters in wartime, and to avoid additional taxes.[4]

I do not, of course, mean to suggest that all the musicians who have given their talents to entertain the armed forces have been actuated by such sordid motives. A few fine artists who happened to be of draft age went to their military duties without protest, deferment, or lamentations;[5] and I must cite in this connection the most honorable of them all—Albert

---

[4] New Delhi, India, Oct. 24 (U.P.)—The British Army newspaper *Contact* today praised its American counterpart, the *C.B.I. Roundup*, for criticizing Hollywood entertainers who find the Far Eastern theater too "rugged," and asserted that the same criticism applies to many British stage, screen and radio performers. Like the *C.B.I. Roundup*, *Contact* agreed that entertainers have done a great deal in this war. But it also agreed that they had no right to make undeserved publicity out of their trips to the front at a time when men were risking their lives fighting the enemy in Europe and the Far East.

Philadelphia Inquirer, Oct. 25, 1944

[5] Nevertheless, there were a surprising number of able-bodied young orchestra players who managed, after being drafted or enlisted, to establish themselves in sinecures in and about New York, in the Army, Navy, Coast Guard, and Maritime Service; and to make about as much money as ever from radio and recording dates. Sometimes they were in uniform, sometimes not.

Spalding, the American violinist, veteran of the air force in the first World War and in his fifties, who without fanfare, without the specious pretext of entertaining the soldiers, undertook a man's job with the armed forces and disappeared completely from the concert stage. Spalding, rather than accept a factitious commission, rather than pose in uniform or perform as a player, joined the armed forces under an assumed name. His identity was not disclosed until May 6, 1945, after a broadcast of the program called *We the People*, during which his work in Italy was described—his daily broadcasts to the Italian people, his instructions for sabotaging German installations, secreting food, equipment and arms from the enemy, and other such matters.

THE PONS THAT DEPRESSES

It was inevitable that André and Lily would eventually, sometime before the end of the war, do something romantic and spectacular—for the boys. I am sure that with their usual thoroughness they overlooked no angle. Iran, from whence we had heard no harrowing tales of bloodshed or hardship, was chosen as the locale most in need of the services of the conductor and the coloratura. I know of no other instance where the appearances of a radio performer for the entertainment of our soldiers were exploited through a commercial radio hour, as happened in the case of André. "On tour with the armed forces," Coca-Cola repeatedly told us. Some people were critical of the exploitation—first of their camp shows and then of the retaking of Paris—which was engineered when they returned to New York on August 23, 1944. With customary foresight, an interview had been arranged at Lily's suite in the Waldorf. Photographers were on the job; and the *New York Herald Tribune* and other newspapers printed a two-column cut of the returning ambassadors of music, both in the slickest of uniforms, Lily modestly confining the num-

ber of decorations in her lapel to four. The press reported Lily
"in ecstasy" and already planning concerts for Paris. "Everything in my home is Paris and everything in my heart is
French," she cried, "and now we do not have the feeling of
captivity any longer." A rather startling statement, I thought,
for one whom America has kept for years in fabulous luxury
and whom France scarcely knew at all before the war; one
to whom America has provided everything she has, including
recently obtained citizenship with its freedom, and a refuge.
Lily added that she couldn't go to France for at least three
months for "she must sing the opera in New York and San
Francisco" (advt.) "because I am the American too."

But nothing that publicity agents have ever accomplished
could have pleased them as much as what happened on the
editorial page of the *New York Herald Tribune* the following
day. This was, I suppose, fortuitous, and without the collaboration of press agentry. In one column the *Herald Tribune*
excoriated the publicity seekers of our own Ninth Air Force,
and in the adjoining column, under a headline that included
Miss Pons's name, gave the lady and her husband the benefit
of a pontifical editorial—the most astonishing piece of free
publicity I have ever seen.

Even this was not the climax. Ten days later the *Saturday
Evening Post* in the issue dated September 2, 1944, with an
article entitled "Main Street Moves to Amirabad" printed a
picture two thirds of a page wide and six inches deep, purport-
ing to show "Appreciative soldiers of the Persogulf Command
raising the roof after some high-grade warbling by little Lily
Pons. André Kostelanetz conducted the 46-Yank orchestra."
This photograph, you will note, appeared less than ten days
after Pons-Kostelanetz returned from their Persian campaign.

The *Post* goes to press from four to six weeks in advance of
publication date. Making due allowance for time consumed
by travel and by mails, André must have had this picture made
almost the instant he set foot on Persian soil. Of course, the
interviews, news stories, and editorials, timed with the return

of Pons and retaking of Paris, the ready suite at the Waldorf capable of accommodating a sufficient number of the press and supplying them with entertainment (though Lily's apartment a few blocks further north might have served the purpose) and finally the *coup de grâce* of a feature picture in the *Saturday Evening Post*—all this may have been a series of coincidences and not a prelude to André's and Lily's reappearance on the Coca-Cola hour the next Sunday afternoon, September 3; but to me it seemed like insensitive commercial exploitation of our young fighting men for the benefit of those very American darlings of the American public who can say to that American public: *"Everything in my home is Paris and everything in my heart is French."*

JOSÉ ITURBI

⋘ José Iturbi ⋙

"So prime, so swell, so nutty and so knowing"

BYRON: *Don Juan*, CANTO xi, STANZA 19

A TELEPHONE LINE is a snare, and if it terminates at your bedside, where you will have put it with the idea that it will in any way save you trouble and annoyance, it is likewise a delusion. I have two such tyrants on my night table, one of which is a listed number on which anyone can call me, and the other an unlisted number on which everyone does. José Iturbi was not among the most frequent callers, but he did sometimes call at inopportune moments. Mr. Stokowski developed a distressing habit of calling me about 9:30 Sunday morning; Mr. Ormandy would phone at any hour of the day or night, and his conversations average forty minutes in length. Mr. Iturbi would call when the spirit moved him, and his conversations were brief, to the point, and usually productive of results—the results being something that José wanted or thought he wanted urgently.

José is an impulsive chap. One morning my phone rang and it was he calling. "Charlie," he said at his most rapid-fire pace, "willyoudomeafavoransweryesorno?" I was hardly awake and somewhat staggered by this verbal blitz; I hemmed and hawed a bit, but then, knowing José, said, "Why yes, of course I will. What is it?" José said, with a chuckle of devilish satisfaction, "You are conducting my orchestra in Rochester next Saturday night. What is your program?"

Well, my program for that particular Saturday night did *not* involve a trip to Rochester or the rehearsing and presentation of a program. But one's plans have a way of undergoing drastic revision when Mr. Iturbi is in the neighborhood. I hurriedly put together a program suitable for a summer concert, got a train to Rochester, and found that there were no arrangements whatever for rehearsal or for the time or even the location of the concert. The only really definite fact that I could excavate from this situation was that there was no fee involved, but I didn't expect that anyway and under the circumstances was happy to contribute what I could to the organization of a summer season operated by the personnel of the orchestra. I shall never forget the concert. It was given at a forgotten lake resort a dozen miles or so from Rochester, in a little grove surrounding a summer hotel. The grove, I think, was the general headquarters of all the mosquitoes in western New York. A one-armed paperhanger was never as busy as I was, trying to conduct and to get some of the mosquitoes off my face at the same time. I did my best to ignore them, but they were not to be ignored, and I remember taking one swipe at my own jaw that resulted in a gory spray disfiguring the white shirt of my good friend Harold Paley, leader of the second violins and organizer of the summer concerts. We staggered through the program somehow, and as I came off the stage finally, José met me in the wings. His first utterance was: "What is your program for next Saturday night?" I really thought this was a little unfair, but José is hard to resist, and when he added that his sister Amparo, who is one of the most charming people in the musical world as well as a distinguished pianist, was to be soloist, I must confess that I accepted José's further commands with equanimity. The next concert was performed under much more favorable auspices, and, no doubt because of Amparo's beautiful playing, was successful in every way.

José is one of the most entertaining, ingratiating, and irritating personalities in the world of music. He has a genuine Spanish wit, mordant, ironical, and barbed; and he turns it upon all, friend and foe, with equal enthusiasm. He has a distinct gift for irritating and antagonizing people, particularly his friends, and an even more potent faculty of charming and enslaving them all over again. He has managed to infuriate the left-wingers who accused him of being a Fascist, women musicians who felt he was unreasonably opposed to their admittance into symphony orchestras, lovers of American popular music and popular artists when he refused to conduct a program of Herbert, Gershwin, and other music in similar style and to appear on the same platform with Benny Goodman. This last indiscretion was especially sinful since José has not hesitated to perform on radio programs like Jack Benny's or Bing Crosby's, and furthermore, makes quite a point of playing Gershwin's *Rhapsody in Blue*. There are those who do it better.

I have never known anyone so indifferent to money per se, so extravagant in its use. He has earned a handsome income for many years, yet has often been literally without funds, for he keeps no account of what he spends and has been known to spend so wildly that his entire bank balance was liquidated and then some. Even in such circumstances, however, a frantic wire to his management would always put at his disposal any number of dollars he might require, for the management not only had confidence in José's earning power, but was nicely protected by contracts and things like that. Iturbi would buy a house or a five-thousand-dollar automobile or a much more costly airplane as casually as I might buy an emergency packet of handkerchiefs. In fact, he might buy several houses at once and set about building a swimming pool for one of them, as he did in California. Heifetz, Rubinstein, Melchior—they each had a house in California—why shouldn't José have several? Besides, he long entertained plans concerning the movies—plans which have now very definitely materialized.

The line I have quoted from George Noel Gordon, Lord Byron, must be accepted as subject to my particular interpretation for the purposes of this book. José is certainly "prime," that is to say, first-class, in many respects; "swell" in the American slang sense; "nutty," that is to say, somewhat eccentric; and "knowing" in everything that concerns his multitudinous and simultaneous purposes. That the quotation happens to be from *Don Juan* is not inappropriate, in view of the fact that one of the newspaper columnists recently listed José as "one of the ten wolves of Hollywood." He has a degree of Spanish cruelty, a cold, ultra-refined, devious, and irrefragable logic that the most devout student of Loyola—I mean the saint and not the school—might envy. On the opposite side of the ledger, he is fantastically generous, which, perhaps, is likewise Spanish. One curious incident that befell me in this connection is worth relating, and I hope José will forgive my mentioning it. A few years ago I permitted myself the fantastic notion that, at depression prices, even I might become the owner of a plot of ground and some day might even erect a shelter on it. In the course of a mission for Victor I had discovered, in the Berkshire Hills not far from Stockbridge, just about what I was looking for—a rough, rock-strewn, but picturesque abandoned farm with what, to me, is the loveliest prospect in the eastern United States; "distant, secluded, still," yet accessible from every place I am likely to be. Not long thereafter I learned, in the course of a casual conversation with José, that he too was looking for a country place, perhaps in Connecticut. I told him, with a certain enthusiasm, of the discovery I had made, and he seemed very interested, even to the point of asking how much such a place would cost. The land I had my eye on was for sale at two thousand dollars.

"Charlie," he said, "I want you to have the place." I replied that I wanted very much to have it but saw no immediate prospect since I could not instantly lay hands on two thousand dollars at the time and, indeed, had very seldom been able to do so. But José could, and did; in half a minute he had written out to me a check for two thousand dollars, which he insisted on my accepting. I was deeply touched, of course, and I was also deeply embarrassed. I tried to explain to José that I could not accept such a gift from anyone under any circumstances, and above all I could not accept any favors of any kind from a friend with whom I had business, professional, and personal relations. José was hurt, and the shadows that can so quickly and easily gather in his normally genial face, gathered, but presently were dissipated by the impact of a new idea: I should accept the two thousand dollars as a loan and pay it back whenever I could afford it or, better still, never. This proposition, of course, was equally impossible, and I finally succeeded in turning the conversation to other matters. This interview, I might add parenthetically, took place in the bedchamber of a suite of enormous rooms in the old Great Northern Hotel, with José sitting in bed, completely engulfed in papers, coffeepots, a bottle of armagnac, two complete and untouched breakfasts, several scores, and a few other odds and ends. In order to get a good look at him I had to perch at the foot of the bed. My briefcase was among the impedimenta that surrounded him, and presently I extricated it, closed it up, concluded the interview, and went home. Next day when I went through my briefcase at my office in Camden, New Jersey, I found in it the check for two thousand dollars signed by José Iturbi. Here was a situation. I had exhausted myself with protestations, I had refused gift, loan, and every other consideration, at the same time maintaining, by what I thought was skillful tightrope walking, José's amiable mood, and here he had gone right back to the beginning. After some reflection I felt there was only one thing to do, and reluctant as I was to have either José or myself embarrassed by revealing the details of this situation, I laid the whole matter before Mr. Edward Wallerstein, then my chief and now president of Columbia Records, Inc. I asked him to take note of the fact that I was returning the check to José by registered mail in care of my dear friend and his, Ruth M. O'Neill. Ruth is an official of the Columbia Concerts Corporation, and I don't know anyone who won't call her darling and mean it; more important, however, she had always interested herself rather maternally and very extensively and ably in José's complicated affairs; she knew him, sympathized with him, and had his confidence.

Before you do either José or me the injustice of entertaining for a moment the idea that this gesture was anything other than pure and sincere generosity, let me add that during our debate whether or not I should accept José's check, he pointed out, not without some really blistering Spanish profanity, that I needn't think this gift had anything to do with my official position, that he would make just as many records and record exactly what he wanted, when he wanted, and how he wanted, whether I was Victor's musical director or a street-cleaner, and that if I thought he was offering me a bribe he would punch me in the jaw. I have no doubt that he would and could, or that I would have deserved it.

José is very exacting of his friends and associates. He asks, I think, too much of human patience. I do not mean that he requires help or favors from anyone, but he does demand for his own thoughtlessness and eccentricities indulgence that sometimes puts too great a strain on the endurance of normal people. When he toured with the Philadelphia Orchestra as co-conductor with Eugene Ormandy a few years ago, I know the management was in a continual tizzy because of Iturbi's contempt for the virtue of punctuality. I do not accuse him of being late for a concert or a train connection, but he was continually so nearly late that Reggie Allen, manager of the orchestra, Louis Mattson, assistant manager, Phil Beard, representative of the Pennsylvania Railroad, and others connected with operating the tour returned not three or four weeks but ten or fifteen years older.

In recording he was always difficult to deal with as a pianist and never difficult as a conductor. I do not know the explanation of this, and it is indeed rather paradoxical. José has various ways of aggravating the difficulties of recording his work. He makes quite an act out of simultaneous playing and conducting—an act which, since he began to display it some years ago, has been emulated by Bruno Walter and, more recently, Dimitri Mitropoulos. People who go to concerts have regarded this as something quite marvelous, unknowing or forgetting that not so long ago it was a very common, and indeed a standard, practice. José usually does a Mozart concerto in this way, and I suppose Mozart always did his own concertos similarly. I feared that sooner or later José would insist on playing and conducting in his records, and eventually he did, my protests notwithstanding. Although he told me that this was the only occasion when he ever had had satisfactory accompaniment, I can hardly agree with him; nor would some of his colleagues who have conducted for him feel particularly flattered by this assertion. Excellent though the accompaniment is, one can hardly avoid noticing the imperfections of ensemble, the infinitesimally small but damaging inaccuracies of attack, and other defects probably inseparable from performances made under these circumstances. They would not occur, and indeed have not occurred, in performances when Iturbi played and an able man conducted.

Recording piano music with this man has given me some very bad moments, hours, days, and weeks. José intensely dislikes being bound by agreements respecting a date, an hour, and a minute, and sometimes the necessity for keeping a recording engagement would irritate him excessively. On some such occasions he has come to the studio in so black a humor that I knew instantly on seeing him that there was no hope of recording that day. He would, however, go through the motions of making a record and finally blame the piano for his inability to get the effect he wanted. He would then depart in a storm of Iberian blasphemy. Hibernian blasphemy also has a certain eloquence.

Once I thought I would put one over on José. I waited

until we had a good solid agreement that he would record at a certain time. He warned me I was to be certain to have a good and proper piano in the studio for him. He formerly had used the Steinway piano in the studio, but shortly before this date had switched his allegiance to the Baldwin. Consequently, I hatched up a little plot with Johnny Ortez, manager of artist relations for the Baldwin Piano Company, and he delivered to us three Baldwin concert grands, each of which was tuned and regulated the very day of the recording by Iturbi's own tuner. I put every other piano out of the studio and arranged for unlimited studio time for José. About two hours before he was expected at the studios he phoned to tell me that he would like to make some harpsichord records also and would I be sure to have a fine harpsichord, perfectly in tune, along with the piano. I haven't the faintest personal interest in harpsichord records, and the enthusiasm of the company as well as that of the public had always been kept rather well under control. However, as a placebo to José I agreed to have a harpsichord, although at the moment I hadn't the faintest idea where I was to get one. Furthermore, I knew that if you brush one of these reprehensible instruments with a feather duster it will instantly get out of tune and out of adjustment. Finally, I had never thought that an instrument that suggests the amplified sound of a June bug walking on a screen door was worth the trouble it takes to make it, tune it, adjust it, play it, or listen to it. So I wasn't very happy at this point.

When José arrived at the studio slightly under two hours late, the three magnificent Baldwins stood neatly lined up and ready for action, and over to the side was the harpsichord of a misguided friend of mine, who had lent it in this crisis. José's own tuner, who has worked devotedly and exclusively with the pianist for God knows how many years, had just put the finishing touches on the pianos and had manipulated the harpsichord into what I considered perfect playing condition. I think José was angry because he was late, and therefore he was in a rather bad humor. He walked over to the first Baldwin, struck a thunderous chord out of which he selected one note to pound with machine-gun rapidity and violence; after which he slammed down the lid, turned to me apparently speechless with rage, and went on to the next piano, where the same thing occurred. He walked to the third piano, delicately touched one note, spat contemptuously, and went to the harpsichord. I did not suppose so frail a mechanism could withstand his assault, but it did. There were no records made that day.

But when José did play the piano, for records or elsewhere, it was heavenly, and it still is. He was one of those who taught me that we Americans generally entertain very erroneous ideas about Spanish music and Spanish musicians. I think we expect either wild abandon or exaggerated Latin romanticism from Spanish musicians, and as far as instrumentalists are concerned this is utterly wrong. It seems to me that the Spaniard is the most meticulous, literal, logical interpreter of music, and I think this applies to Iturbi as it does to Casals and as it does to Andrés Segovia. The only man I have ever heard play Spanish music on the piano with the sentiment and freedom—and perhaps I should say the exaggeration—that we laymen expect from Spanish musicians, was George Copeland. (George was born in Boston, has lived a long time in France, where he was a favorite pupil of Debussy, but he found his spiritual home, I think, in Spain. He had a lovely villa in Mallorca, which he abandoned rather hurriedly just before the outbreak of the revolution in Spain when one morning he found the head, and only the head, of one of his Loyalist servants in his patio.)

It is the Spaniard's insistence upon clarity, precision, and vitality that contributes so much, I think, to Iturbi's incomparable playing of Mozart and other so-called "classic" composers. It is these same qualities that make it possible for Segovia to etch with the steel-pointed tone of his guitar the fabulous miniatures of the great Bach works. It is again these qualities that make Casals's playing of the Bach Suites one of the noblest achievements in the history of interpretive music. Within the boundaries of certain musical territory I have no hesitation in associating the names of Iturbi, Segovia, and Casals.

José is very enthusiastic about the movie career that he has inaugurated. As a friend and admirer, I want to see this venture succeed. It is difficult to avoid reflection, however, that few motion pictures which centered around a "long-haired" musician have been successful except, perhaps, financially and temporarily for the "long-haired" musician. _Fantasia_ was a _succès d'estime_, but in this the sound track was the hero. Lily Pons's pictures were unsuccessful from a boxoffice point of view even though Lily has a singular attraction for those who particularly want to see rather than hear. Heifetz's _They Shall Have Music_ was handsomely profitable to Heifetz, but not, I understand, to anyone else. Grace Moore's _One Night of Love_ certainly was a success, and I do not mean to detract from Grace's part when I say that the success could be attributed to a combination of many factors, including the comparative novelty of good sound on film. In any case, it was hardly a "long-hair" job. José, however, has told me that his pictures have vastly increased interest in his appearances as a concert pianist, and if they have this effect, more power to them; for José as pianist is a rare and wonderful artist, and the more people who hear him, the better for them, for music, and for José.

José's disarming smile alone should captivate his movie audiences. When he smiles his whole face is illumined, not omitting his fine dark eyes and brilliant white teeth, which shine the more brightly because of his round-the-clock five o'clock shadow. Everything about José is solid and strong. He is a little bit chubby, but his roundness is exceedingly deceptive, for under it he has the muscular equipment of a prizefighter. Incidentally, José is a genuine _aficionado_ of the ring. I attended the fights in Hollywood—under pressure—with him and Preston Sturges, his good friend, and I judged from his expression that José took exactly the same kind of pleasure in them as he might in a bullfight. His hands, wrists, arms, and shoulders are enormously powerful, though they look merely fat. He is short, jug-shaped, and is acquiring, unhappily I suppose, a certain secretarial spread. I dare say this is an occupational disease with pianists. He customarily wears an astonishing collection of medals, scapulars, crosses, amulets, and other objects of veneration, each no doubt with its special protective powers. José must have given St. Christopher many an anxious moment, for prior to the war and the suppression of civil aviation he flew his own plane expertly and quite madly. I have traveled more than a hundred thousand miles by plane and have been in two minor accidents without having been terrified as yet, but his invitation to fly with him was the only request I ever was able to deny him. He drives his car much in the same manner as he flies his plane, but this has no particular terrors for me as I have driven with such madmen as Bill Primrose, such nerve-wreckers as E. Power Biggs, demon chauffeurs like Eugene Ormandy, and curiously inexpert ones like Leopold Stokowski. José is a sedate driver by comparison.

It is curious that Iturbi, with his intense, almost clannish family spirit, has remained unmarried so long. He is a widower, a father, and a grandfather—and extremely devoted. He is notably attractive to women, adores children, and dotes on his grandchildren. He has a fierce family pride—a characteristic which drove him, with what agonies one may only surmise, to bring suit against his own daughter in the California courts to obtain custody of her children when he felt that he could manage matters better than the children's mother. This is not to indicate that there was any antipathy between him and his daughter, for indeed there was not; they were in each other's arms in the courtroom, and not long after the trial José bought and equipped a charming house in Beverly Hills for his daughter and his grandchildren. Such gestures on José's part could not dispel the melancholy that seemed to becloud his daughter's life—a life that became so intolerable that she ended it by her own hand.

José likes good food and drink, though not with any special enthusiasm: I have on occasion held *kaffee-klatsch* with him until far into the night—and it wasn't entirely coffee—but I have never known him to be in the slightest degree affected except to become somewhat more amiable even than usual; nor will he permit himself any commerce with demon rum when there is work to be done. He smokes gigantic cigars usually; occasionally a cigarette, but when he unlimbers that pipe the effect is really overpowering. This weapon is approximately the size and shape of what we call in New England a summer squash, and I firmly believe that it is charged with macerated shoe-findings. Like so many men of short stature, Mr. Iturbi loves everything that is big, or oversize, or rugged. The most hirsute tweeds, the quart-capacity fountain pen, the block-long, four-ton sedan-limousine, the inch-thick soles (they add a bit to the height too), and the blackest-rimmed of horn-rimmed spectacles (or to be contrary, a delicate pince-nez)—these are some of José's trade-marks.

Mr. Iturbi keeps a *pied à terre* at the Lotos Club in New York, as I do myself. This has brought us together frequently and casually and pleasantly. He always leaves word for me when he is there, but the announcement of his presence that I enjoy most is to be awakened in the morning, or more likely, around lunchtime, by cascades of glittering notes descending from the gallery on the sixth floor where José is wont to practice. Next to that, I like to hear my phone ring—believe it or not—if on the other end I hear a voice say, "Charlie, I am here. Come down and have breakfast in my room." There is likely to be brandy for breakfast too, though God knows I prefer to do without it until after dinner. However, it's hard to resist José.

EUGENE
ORMANDY

⇜§ Eugene Ormandy §⇝

And . . . came forth a little horn, which waxed
exceeding great, toward the south, and toward the
east, and toward the pleasant land . . . and it cast
down some of the host and of the stars to the ground,
and stamped upon them. Yea, he magnified himself
even to the prince of the host.

DANIEL: viii: 9–11

WE ARE LED to believe that after the war, native American wines like the Rhin of Chile, the Great Western of New York, or the Christian Brothers of California will supplant such exotic potions as Berncastler Doktor and Pol Roger and Lagrima Cristi; that the Oka of Quebec, the Liederkranz of the Middle West, and the less odoriferous lactic ferments of Wisconsin will capture the American market from Roquefort, Pont l'Eveque, and Parmigiano; nylon will replace the silk of Japan, and alcohol or hydrocarbons give forth synthetic rubber more useful than the natural latex. "A consummation devoutly to be wished," for among these necessary luxuries we have in our own land treasures often as precious as their European counterparts. It required a world-wide war to bring about their discovery, but we are learning.

Neither the war nor any other influence seems powerful enough, however, to persuade our public, our symphony orchestra boards of directors, or the managers who control the destinies of symphony conductors, that a conductor is not necessarily an imported luxury. All our major orchestras—the least of them better than any abroad—are directed by men whose cultural roots are impacted in the various soils of Europe. As I write, we have a Russian, a Pole, an Italian, a Hungarian or two, a Dutchman, a Belgian, several Frenchmen, and a Greek; on occasion we have had a Finn, an "Argentine" from Germany, a "Cuban" from Italy, a Mexican, a Negro, a Japanese, and a child. I do not think that the engagements of Carlos Chávez, Dean Dixon, and Lorin Maazel signify anything. Chávez was given a few concerts not because he is a North American or a conductor, but in recognition of him as a composer, an organizer, and a pioneer. Dean Dixon was not engaged only because he is an able conductor and an American, but also because he is a Negro. Lorin Maazel was exhibited before the NBC Orchestra and others not because he is a native with conducting talent, but because he is a little boy. Edwin McArthur acquitted himself nobly when, through Flagstad's influence, he was given certain opportunities, and Charles O'Connell has repeatedly conducted nearly all the major orchestras, but in these cases there were special circumstances both as powerful and as irrelevant as the facts that Dixon is a Negro and Maazel a child. Only Arthur Fiedler, conductor of the magnificent Boston "Pops," Alfred Wallenstein of the Los Angeles Philharmonic, and Werner Janssen, who is wealthy enough to subsidize his own orchestra and talented enough to conduct it, have as native sons been given a reasonable opportunity. I define no civil or political distinction among native or naturalized, white or black, Christian, Jewish, Buchmanite or Unitarian, agnostic or atheist citizens, and I have both admiration and warm personal feelings for most of our conductors. I am indicating a condition that is changing with respect to other luxuries and necessities (classify conductors as you like) and expressing a wish that in music we should look more frequently, and with more confidence, to our own.

Of course, all our important conductors, with the exception of Arturo Toscanini, are American citizens. Technically, no foreign-born musician—other than NBC's conductor—can get a job playing in or directing an orchestra unless he has at least taken the first step toward becoming an American citizen. The American Federation of Musicians sees to that. To do justice to my conductor friends, however, I must say that most of them became citizens out of conviction and with enthusiasm. Three of them seem to me most thoroughly, intelligently, and genuinely American: Stokowski, Kindler, and Ormandy, and of the three Ormandy should perhaps be mentioned first. I do not for a moment disparage the standing as citizen, or the sincerity or patriotism of any of our conductors; nor in estimating Ormandy's position among the group of three do I mean to minimize the intense, the passionate devotion to this country of Stokowski or Kindler. These men, loving our country as they do, have rather a philosophical and cosmopolitan viewpoint—Stokowski through his world-wide travels and interest in every people, every land, Kindler perhaps because of a cultivated European background and years of international associations in Washington. Ormandy comes nearer to being an average, even a parochial and therefore typical, American.

Eugene speaks Hungarian well, I suppose: it is his native tongue. His German is fair; his English when he isn't self-conscious about it is not heavily accented and is happily free from that rhotacism characteristic of both the Viennese and the Parisian and which, to my ears at least, is quite painful; his American slang, which he uses frequently and with facility though not always with point, is good and corny. The tensions and pressures and haste and confusion of his first years in America's musical madhouses—the movie theater, radio, the "transcription" business—and his years of living and working in the Midwest probably did much to develop a peculiarly American vocabulary, to cultivate certain American habits, and to erase many a mark of the Central European.[1] You can always identify a Continental by a certain spurious elegance in the cut of his clothes. Mr. Ormandy wears strictly American clothes, and the most conventional; only by a slickness and too-tightness in them will you suspect the foreigner. With his rufous hair, expanding tonsure, pale blue eyes, and rhinocerical profile, he sometimes suggests a burlesque Irishman in his Sunday suit.

He has acquired many American characteristics, not all of them desirable. Sensitive about his stature (5 feet 4 inches), he has had, nevertheless, the sense to discard the "elevator" shoes he formerly wore, because they hurt him. Actually he is a splendid physical type, a kind of miniature giant. A rather handsomely V-shaped torso, remarkably muscular in the chest, arms, and shoulders, narrows down to slim hips and straight, well-proportioned legs. His hands and feet are small and delicate; in action he is quick, agile, vigorous, and often graceful. He has a super-abundance of energy that the demands of conducting, exigent though they are, cannot consume; and this, I think, is one of the reasons for his restlessness and certain nervous habits that are rather disconcerting at times.

Gene has an American's indifference to sophisticated food, though his own home, especially when he lived in Minneapolis, has often provided it. His diet by preference is confined to a few commonplace dishes that he has probably eaten every day of his life. Like Toscanini, he hates strange food. I remember a little party we had for him at our house, and we thought that having him as guest provided a good excuse for terrapin à la Maryland—a dish we cannot often afford, but regard as rather celestial. Gene with politeness and obvious suspicion accepted his portion, tasted it, decided that he liked it, and

---

[1] Mr. Ormandy is not related to Guy Ormandy, dance-band leader, but is a brother of Martin Ormandy, cellist in the Philharmonic Symphony of New York.

was progressing very happily until he discreetly inquired of Steffy, his wife, what it was he had been eating. When she told him—not, I suppose, without a certain connubial malice—that it was turtle, he put it aside with haste and horror. I don't believe he has had food in my home since.

Ormandy doesn't use alcohol or tobacco, nor has he any understanding of people who do. His "party" drink is a Hungarian raspberry syrup diluted with seltzer. It isn't bad. I often drink it myself, rather than the more potent waters that are always available and always offered a visitor in the Ormandy household. Like so many people who don't drink, he thinks everyone who does is a drunkard; and if you accept the drink that he will offer you, even though, as discretion would indicate, you confine yourself to one, any remark you make thereafter is attributed either to alcoholic geniality or alcoholic malice. For that reason I have cultivated a taste for Hungarian raspberry syrup and soda water—in self-defense. I once regarded Gene's loyalty to his friends as one of his notable and endearing characteristics, but his naïveté sometimes permits him gossipy and guileless indiscretions that can be quite distressing and even harmful. He has a *cacoethes loquendi*, "a rage for saying something when there is nothing to be said," that none of his friends who drink, even in their most unbuttoned moods, would or could match. When this madness is upon him he may discuss musicians with a critical candor that has embarrassing potentialities, for in such moments he has occasionally "cast down some of the host and of the stars to the ground, and stamped upon them." They might not like this.

Mr. Ormandy is much given to flattery and is woefully susceptible to it. Indeed, he will believe almost anything. He is as easily influenced by the malicious and lying tongue of meretricious friendship as by the candor of those who truly and unselfishly wish him well. Since he appears to have convictions about nothing, he can be temporarily convinced of anything; but a conniving blackguard is more persuasive than a time-proven friend. He has a curious, distressing mental hyperopia that permits him to see evil if it is sufficiently farfetched but blinds him to it when it is under his nose.

As infant prodigies have nowadays become so numerous, their press agents are making them more infantile and more prodigious. It has been revealed that Eugene Ormandy was born with a violin in his hand, and it has been seriously asserted that he could distinguish, at the age of eighteen months, one recorded symphony from another. I don't think the one less probable than the other. Passing over the problems of obstetrics involved in the first precious bit of publicity, the second is the kind of stupid stuff for which elsewhere in these pages I have indicated a certain dislike. The truth is that in 1901, when Gene was eighteen months old, recording was so crude that even the people who made the records could not recognize them; and Maestro Ormandy was eighteen years, not months, old, when the first symphony was recorded. I can and gladly do testify to his prowess as a violinist.

In a conversation one night at his house, then at Gladwynne, near Philadelphia, I was indiscreet enough to tease Gene about his claims to violinistic virtuosity, and succeeded only in eliciting stronger claims. Finally Gene, somewhat nettled, offered to show me, and I took him up on it. He excavated a violin—and a beautiful one too—from an old trunk in his bedroom, tuned it, tucked it under his chin, and said with a malicious gleam in his eye, "What will you have?" Actually I didn't want any fiddling at the moment, and thinking I could call his bluff safely I suggested the Bach Chaconne. I know no music for the violin that so thoroughly and cruelly exploits the resources of the instrument and still remains noble and profound music.

Mr. Ormandy without hesitation dug into that instrument and gave a performance that, under the circumstances, was dazzling. I knew he hadn't played for years. I knew of course that he must have been at least a good violinist, but I wasn't, up to that moment, convinced that he had ever been a great one. I am now. I have heard performances by current geniuses of the instrument that weren't as good as Gene's. It wasn't perfect, to be sure; who ever played the Chaconne perfectly? But it was sure and sound and brilliant and thoughtful; even the man who quietly joined us while Gene played concurred in my opinion. He can play the Chaconne too. His name: J. Heifetz.

Mr. Ormandy, born Jenö Blau, has, I am told, forsworn the faith of his fathers to accept that of a Protestant sect. I think it is the sect which, having a famous "American" church in Paris and a "National Cathedral" in Washington, must be very American indeed. I suppose that like the usual convert Eugene accepts all of the Church's admirable precepts; but I have very definite and personal knowledge that he subscribes, with enthusiasm tantamount to mania, to the assertion: "It is better to give than to receive." I have never known anyone so willing, indeed so eager, to give of himself, his time, his effort, his hospitality, and his substance, and who was also so determined in his refusal to accept similar gifts from his friends. His giving is impulsive, his gifts of outrageous magnificence. I myself have been the beneficiary of the most valuable things in his power to give—his help and his friendship. What little I know of the technique of conducting I learned from him, and there never has been a time in our acquaintance when he would not interrupt his own work or study to give me help that I needed. Indeed he even put at my disposal, that I might hear some music I had orchestrated, the Minneapolis Symphony Orchestra, the first full-scale orchestra I ever conducted. He has been similarly generous to other friends, and more than one prosperous radio conductor of the moment owes a good part of his success to Ormandy's technical and professional help.

The generosity toward his friends that Ormandy has so frequently exhibited has been extended not merely occasionally or frequently, but constantly and expensively, toward direct and collateral relatives and *their* friends. Any man would provide for the comfort and security of his aging parents, as Gene has done; but not every man would undertake to keep in luxury a tribe of relatives and friends, some of them quite able to take care of themselves, and few of them appreciative either

of the material benefits or, what is more important and more
difficult to achieve, the opportunities for benefiting themselves that Ormandy's open hand and persistent effort conferred on them.

His interest in the refugee problem, just before and during
the early months of the war, was not confined to sentiment
and sympathy: he did something about it. He did so much, in
fact, especially in posting cash bond of many thousands of dollars for these unfortunate people, that he embarrassed himself
financially—in spite of an income not very far from $100,000
annually. I have dined at Ormandy's house—aptly named, for
his refugee guests at least, "Journey's End"—with fourteen
people at table, and all but Steffy, Eugene, and myself were
people whose escape from the hell of Europe he had brought
about. Every one of them was sheltered in that house—men,
women, and children. Schools, music lessons, much needed
medical care, clothing, even motorcars were provided. The
connections established by the conductor of the Philadelphia
Orchestra are many, varied, and interesting. Ormandy unhesi-
tatingly capitalized these, and presently his dependents had
opportunities for work that few Americans ever get: one to be
a physician at the Mayo Clinic, at Johns Hopkins, at a famous
Boston hospital; another, professor at the University of Pitts-
burgh; another, sales executive with a great oil distributor;
another, teacher in a noted school of music. It seemed strange
to me that these people, living on his bounty and under his
roof and most of them related to him by blood or marriage,
did not always accord him ordinary courtesy, and occasionally
found it unnecessary even to speak to him. I never heard Gene
utter a disparaging or critical word about them; on the contrary, he never tired of advertising their charms and their talents. There have been moments when an unworthy, cynical,
and, I hope, unjust suspicion arose in my mind, and I questioned within myself whether or not pure generosity and
Christian charity could account for such incredible kindness;
whether or not it could be traced to a desire to seem and to be,

in the eyes of a horde of dependents, the *grand seigneur*, the *grosse Kanone*, the little boy who "made good." Then I would remember Ormandy's love of giving, his detestation of accepting; in this there can be no question of his sincerity.

I recall a trivial but significant incident corroborating this. It occurred during my first visit with the Ormandys in Minneapolis twelve years ago. I was their house guest, which I assure you is a pleasant privilege. One night after dinner a magnificent basket of fruit was brought in, and Gene, who hadn't eaten much of dinner (he doesn't like stylish cooking), fell upon the fruit with a kind of dainty ferocity, for he could live exclusively and happily on such things. He complimented Steffy on having provided so welcome and beautiful a dessert, whereupon she hastened to explain that she wasn't responsible for it. The basket had been sent round by one of the directors of the Minneapolis Symphony. Gene instantly put down the succulent pear on which he had been operating, invoked the maledictions of Saints Stefan and Elisabeth upon the innocent head of the donor, and ordered the basket given at once to his chauffeur.

I defied the lightning myself on a few occasions, one of which particularly amused us both—Gene because he thought it gave him an opportunity to embarrass me, myself because the denouement exposed his unfamiliarity with certain little details of pleasant living. It happens that I have a weakness for fine shirts particularly, and for related things like hose and handkerchiefs and cravats, and I have the shirts made by a very good *chemisier*, likewise an expensive one. Gene noticed a shirt I was wearing, became quite lyrical about it, in fact. Thinking that at last I had discovered a gift I could provide that would really please him, and at the same time would be beautiful and useful, I secretly procured one of his shirts that really fit him, took it to my shirtmaker, and had one like mine made to Gene's dimensions. He seemed really pleased with it, but a week later phoned and began to torment me about having given him such a cheap shirt. Now this shirt was made of something called taffeta flannel—paper-thin, featherweight, yet opaque and wonderfully soft and pliable. I was offended at Gene's use of the word "cheap." Pressing for details, I finally elicited the information that the shirt had shrunk in laundering so that he couldn't get into it. I explained haughtily that one doesn't send such a shirt to the family wash, or out to a Chinese laundry; it must be dry-cleaned. "Dry-cleaned," he fairly screamed, "and pay thirty-five cents every time I wear it?" I think Gene still believes I tried to deceive him with a cheap shirt because it shrank in the wash, and that if I didn't, I am a damned fool for paying a lot for *that* shirt. At any rate, I know he is pleased that my little but probably detested gift didn't work out.

It must be American to enjoy giving, and certainly any European must know that. But Gene has other rather American characteristics. He is normally quite observant of the decencies of human intercourse, but put him behind the wheel of a motorcar and like most of us he forgets his manners. He drives with reckless skill, and with little consideration of his passengers or other drivers, yet manages to stay within the law. He is American in that he is deeply impressed by titles, wealth, and material success, but European in his confusion of unctuous manners with breeding. He is American in his mental agility and innocence, his acquisitiveness, his complete candor and integrity in financial matters, his eagerness to like people and to be liked; un-American, I think, in his suspicion of strangers and lack of confidence in himself, the last perhaps negatively indicated by his naïve boastfulness. Mr. Ormandy never lies when he boasts, or indeed at any other time; rather, he has no hesitation in quoting—accurately—those who say flattering things about him, and they are many. Among those who know and understand and love the man, Ormandy's willingness to affirm his own genius with such candor is disarming and harmless to him, particularly as many of us know that his not always modest self-estimates are by no means without foundation, but I have often feared for the impression that he might make on new friends and acquaintances who would not at first understand his childlike and uninhibited self-approval. He is American, I am afraid, in his restlessness, his nervousness, his lack of poise, inability to relax or to divert, entertain, or amuse himself outside of his work. He has no use for leisure because he knows no use for it. I wish he could be convinced, with Rossetti, that

> Unto the man of yearning thought
>   And aspiration, to do nought
> Is in itself almost an act,—
>   Being chasm-fire and cataract
> Of the soul's utter depths unsealed.

Mr. Ormandy is somewhat addicted to the American vice of hero-worship. Since his whole life is devoted to making successful music, and music successful, logically his deified heroes are Arturo Toscanini and Arthur Judson. In Judson he confides as in a father, and this has been to their mutual profit; for A. J. is lord of all conductors (except two or three) and wisely chose, years ago, to put golden opportunities in Eugene's way. These have paid, and still pay, both conductor and manager. But Maestro Toscanini is Ormandy's supreme deity.

I remember when, quite a few years ago, Ormandy looked upon Toscanini certainly with admiration, but with a suspicious and resentful and even fearful eye. He had substituted for the old maestro, and the mischievous gossips infesting the orchestral world were quick to carry to Gene fantastic tales of Toscanini's resentment and contempt. These tales were, I know, absolutely without foundation then, but they worried Gene who, unacquainted with the great man, was foolish enough to believe them. Later, knowing of the frequency and degree of intimacy of my contacts with Toscanini, Gene harassed me for months with questions as to what Maestro had said about him. I could not convince the man that Toscanini had said nothing disparaging, had, furthermore, never in my hearing (up to that time) so much as mentioned Ormandy's name. Gene seemed to be a little disappointed. Again, when there was talk of Toscanini as guest-conductor of the Philadelphia Orchestra, Mr. Ormandy's god seemed to totter on his pedestal; I, who was negotiating the arrangements, could say nothing to allay the worshipper's fears. With the *fait accompli* confronting him, however, Gene warmly welcomed the maestro, for it gave him his opportunity to "magnify himself even to the prince of the host." He hung on Toscanini's every word, dogged his footsteps night and day, entertained him within an inch of his life, had him X-rayed, medicated, massaged, fed, feted, soothed, and sympathized with by everyone within reach. Maestro found the treatment so beneficent that for a while he seriously threatened to move to Philadelphia or its suburbs.

The thing that has established Mr. Ormandy most securely as "one of us" is something that he perhaps does not know about, an accolade conferred by American boys and men only upon one who is really accepted and well liked. He has won a nickname, to wit, "The Jeep." If "Gene the Jeep" sounds a little disrespectful, Doctor Ormandy has no one but himself to blame. When I first knew him in Minneapolis, he was a martinet, aloof, severe, and moderately terrifying to the men of the orchestra. When he came to Philadelphia he not only permitted but encouraged familiarity, either because of an exaggerated eagerness to ingratiate himself with the personnel of that peerless band or because, having worked with many of the men on various occasions through the years, he couldn't, any more than they could, be brought suddenly into a formal relationship. Nevertheless, here he courted a grave danger, one that could and should have been eliminated once and for all with a single firm insistence at his first rehearsal upon respectful attitudes and firm discipline. Difficult as this might seem to be for any conductor succeeding Stokowski, and more difficult for a conductor who in remarkably few years had come up from the ranks, it was not impossible. Eugene has chosen to accomplish it by degrees, "cutting off the dog's tail an inch at a time." He has made progress painfully, and the end is not yet.

As for "The Jeep": I think Gene, who until he sees these lines perhaps has not heard his nickname, should not resent it. What is a jeep? Surely there's nothing more American, and no product of our industrial civilization held in more esteem, even in affection. It's an American thing; it's small, busy, active, powerful; it cheerfully carries a heavy burden; it will go anywhere to do its job, and does its job superlatively well. That is a fair description of a jeep, and if the same description is applied to Mr. Ormandy by his men, he should feel complimented indeed, certainly more so than by the epithets applied to him by the men of the Minneapolis Orchestra, which he overheard just after one of his most touching farewell speeches. This so disconcerted him that before leaving to conduct a guest appearance in Philadelphia he frantically wired his manager, Arthur Judson, to meet him there as he had tidings of the gravest import to discuss. Eugene himself related to me how he met Judson, struggled unhappily through lunch, and finally, under Judson's skillful prodding, revealed the grave matter on his mind. "A. J.," he said, "I must resign, and resign at once." Judson, accustomed to the aberrations of musicians in general and conductors in particular, was not particularly excited but brusquely asked, "What's the matter with you now?" Gene, in humiliation and pain, confessed: "I overheard some of the men in the orchestra call me a little son-of-a-bitch." At this, Judson, instead of thundering anathemas or even mildly sympathizing, laughed one of his rare hearty laughs, clapped Gene on the shoulder and said: "Congratulations, old man, now you're a *real* conductor!"

Mr. Judson was right when he implied that any conductor worth his salt is regarded by some and referred to by many of his men as an illegitimate son or the offspring of a female canine. Even the revered Toscanini, the magnetic Stokowski, and the terrifying Koussevitzky have, in my hearing, been so described by their men a thousand times. This does not in-

dicate any lack of respect or even of affection, but is merely a
healthily vulgar Americanism that relieves the pressure of constant tensions and irritations inseparable from the work of preparing symphony programs.

Mr. Ormandy seems to derive a certain amusement from
this episode when he relates it now, which makes it the more
difficult for me to understand why he took so seriously a report
from one of his more malicious informers that he was commonly described, in recording circles generally and particularly
by me, as "that little bastard." I have never heard anyone at
Victor refer to Mr. Ormandy by this or any other disrespectful
term. As for myself, my vocabulary of abuse is sufficiently extensive, my acquaintance with the subject sufficiently intimate,
to suggest epithets much more precise, descriptive, and imaginative than "bastard." When Gene complained tearfully
about this matter, I tried to explain it by pointing out the re-
grettable but harmless freedom and the absence of malice with
which the average American uses ugly terms. It was difficult to
convince him even when, in the course of the same conversation, he himself casually referred to one of his most distinguished colleagues as "that son-of-a-bitch."

Mr. Ormandy has a second nickname, the implications of
which are less flattering than "The Jeep"—"Little Caesar."
Gene occasionally demonstrates the exaggerated assertiveness
often characteristic of little people, but with a difference; he is
inclined to be overbearing with those whom he regards as his
inferiors, and correspondingly unctuous with those who, he
senses, are his superiors. He is rather difficult with secretaries,
orchestra librarians, and servants, and with the last-stand players in the orchestra. The orchestral virtuosos can do no wrong,
or if they do are gently admonished with nothing more emphatic than an indulgent smile. Let an obscure and earnest
fiddler make a noticeable error and he is flayed and thrown to
the lions. Here Eugene does not imitate his hero Toscanini,
who is much more likely to excoriate the fine players when
they fail in a delicate nuance than to reprove the incompetent

for obvious vulgarisms. His cruel humiliation of a man in the NBC Symphony, a player of wonderful technique, fastidious taste, and exquisite sensibility who not long ago was one of Ormandy's Philadelphia men, is an example of a peculiar musical sadism. Perhaps the fact that Ormandy was present on this occasion lent added savor to Maestro Toscanini's savage satisfaction.

The most important and effective contribution to the resuscitation of recorded music about thirteen years ago was made by Arthur Judson, Eugene Ormandy, and myself—through Judson's shrewdness, Ormandy's skill, and my good luck. When I undertook the position of musical director for Victor, my job really was not so much to develop the record business as to extricate the company from it. RCA had bought the old Victor Talking Machine Company, or as one of Victor's publicity men inadvertently put it,[2] Victor had been "sold out" to RCA. How true! RCA had no faith or interest in recorded music, then at the nadir of its popularity, though I think that the present attitude of the holding corporation is drastically different. RCA might have abandoned the record business when it bought the old Victor Company had it not fallen heir to a number of long-term contracts with accompanying obligations. My first duty as musical director was to help the vice-president and general counsel, Mr. Lawrence B. Morris, talk certain of the Victor artists out of the financial obligations Victor owed them, because there were insufficient sales to support them. We made some progress in this direction, but even while carrying out orders along this line I was convinced that recorded music need not die and, properly directed, could again be vital and successful. I knew that the company was not willing to make any investment in new recordings unless contracts absolutely and irrevocably required it, and yet I felt also that new and good recordings were

---

[2] *Life*, October 9, 1944.

the only possible starting point for the rebuilding of the record business. I was more than interested, therefore, when in the course of a casual conversation on this subject, Arthur Judson suggested that it might be wise for me to look into the situation of the Minneapolis Orchestra and Eugene Ormandy, who had a very curious and old-fashioned arrangement with the musicians' union. Accepting Mr. Judson's suggestion, I did investigate the matter and found that the contract between the men and management of the Minneapolis Orchestra provided, with union approval, that for their stated salary they were obliged to give a certain number of hours per week, which time could be employed in rehearsals, in concerts, in broadcasting, or in recording, as the management should elect. This meant in effect that the orchestra could be employed for recording without extra compensation, the union thoroughly approving. I lost no time in getting in touch with the Minneapolis authorities and with Mr. Ormandy, and we joined in a contract. We got an enormous group of recordings, made with the most extraordinary skill, sureness, and celerity; and we acquired them virtually for nothing. They paid the Minneapolis Orchestra $163,362.58 up to November 1, 1944 (and to Mr. Ormandy not so much as a dollar). The deal convinced me that for once in my life I had been a smart businessman. The record business gained an infusion of new blood that ultimately resulted in its complete and vigorous recovery.

I have said that Mr. Ormandy was not paid for his heroic efforts in connection with the Minneapolis recordings. "Remuneration! O, that's the Latin word for three farthings"— but it was not exactly a case of love's labor lost. Indeed, he was not compensated in cash, but the records won for him nationwide attention and were largely responsible, in combination with the efforts of Samuel R. Rosenbaum, Arthur Judson, and myself, for bringing about his eventual appointment as conductor of the Philadelphia Orchestra. That, I suppose, was sufficient compensation.

We had started the ball rolling, and we went back to Minneapolis a second year. After the blood-sweating sessions of the first recording period with Mr. Ormandy, I did not have the heart to ask the Minneapolis men to go through another hellish week of recording without compensation, though with respect to union requirements and my arrangement with the orchestra management I was perfectly entitled to require this. I extracted $2500 from RCA Victor, Eugene and Steffy Ormandy matched this with another $2500, which I suspect came largely from their own pockets, and we paid $5000 to the Minneapolis men for another hectic period of recording. It was as successful and as profitable to the company as the first; perhaps more so, since record sales in the interim had begun to show a very substantial increase. The talent cost for these recordings was, as I have indicated, $2500 so far as the company was concerned. If they were made today the same records would cost approximately $80,000 for orchestral talent alone.

I was for a time quite puzzled, because after Mr. Ormandy's appointment in Philadelphia I was not permitted to renew the contract with Minneapolis. Of course, by this time the union had awakened to the situation, and had we again recorded with Minneapolis we should have had to pay the standard union rate. Although we would not have gotten as much for our money, either in quantity or quality, as we had gotten for nothing, it would have been a good investment. This orchestra had by now been thoroughly established on records, and to pay the union rate would not have been a hardship for Victor, and indeed a renewal of the contract would have been dictated by the logic of the situation. Mr. Edward Wallerstein, at that time my superior and head of Victor's recording activities, did not agree. When he later resigned to organize the Columbia Company, where he had complete authority and a free hand, he immediately made a contract with Minneapolis.

When Mr. Stokowski decided to withdraw himself from the Philadelphia Orchestra, the need of a conductor to share the season was acute. This orchestra has the highest payroll of any in the world. Its operating expenses are, I believe,

greater than those of any other major orchestra, though because of astute management its administrative expenses are
lower than most. To compensate for its huge payroll the
orchestra has depended for years upon income from records.
This income is very substantial and at times has been reckoned annually in six figures. It was fairly obvious that anyone
who shared the conductorship with Stokowski, and who might
ultimately take over as principal conductor, should be a man
who could sustain this vital income for the orchestra. I had
firm confidence in Ormandy, first as a musician, then as a man
willing to co-operate in all good and practical things; so when
I was approached by certain of the directors of the Philadelphia Orchestra as well as by Mr. Judson, the then manager,
for my ideas as to who the new conductor should be, I could
think of no one but Eugene. My suggestion and the reason for
it were given serious consideration. Naturally I discussed the
matter with Mr. Stokowski, and while he was not at all dis-
posed to dictate either his associate or a possible successor, he
was most generous in his comment on Mr. Ormandy and quite
agreeable to the association's choice. Ormandy was appointed
associate conductor, later conductor, and more recently, musical director.

ORMANDY AND THE PHILADELPHIA ORCHESTRA

In the technical sense Ormandy is, normally, the equal of any
living conductor and superior to most. I say normally because
lately he has shown a lamentable tendency, in the matter of
stage deportment, to play the sedulous ape to Toscanini. This
is neither becoming nor effective, but slightly ridiculous.
When he is himself, Ormandy's beat is absolutely clear, firm,
and incisive, his feeling for rhythm and tempo unerring, his
sense of pitch phenomenally acute.

I once had striking evidence of this. Mr. Ormandy had recorded with the Philadelphia Orchestra the Fourth Symphony of Brahms. When he heard the proof pressings of these records, he thought that they were remarkably good except in one respect: they were almost a quarter tone higher than the key of E minor, in which the symphony actually was played. I couldn't believe this and suggested that possibly the turntable of Mr. Ormandy's phonograph was revolving at a rate of speed slightly higher than normal. This, of course, would raise the pitch as well as increase the tempo. Mr. Ormandy said that his turntable's speed was correct. Still incredulous, I produced another recording of the Fourth Symphony of Brahms and compared it with Mr. Ormandy's as to pitch. They agreed absolutely. Mr. Ormandy was not at all disconcerted by this and still insisted that his recordings were perhaps a quarter of a tone higher than normal. I checked the turntable of his phonograph with a stroboscope and found that it was indeed turning at the correct speed. I was quite mystified and still unwilling to agree with Ormandy until I suddenly remembered that the records of the Brahms against which I had checked Ormandy's had been made by the Boston Symphony Orchestra, which does indeed tune slightly higher than any other orchestra in America. Its "A" may go as high as 444 vibrations per second, whereas the Philadelphia Orchestra tunes absolutely to a 440 "A." I retired in confusion, admitting that I was wrong and that Mr. Ormandy's sense of pitch is indeed absolute.

He reads a score with quickness and facility, realizes its internal relations, proportions, and details with extraordinary accuracy; he memorizes scores photographically and easily, but I believe, temporarily and not with the elephantine permanence of Toscanini's mnemonic miracles. Ormandy gave me quite startling proof of the quickness, accuracy, and ease of his memorizing during our second sojourn in Minneapolis. At this time (1935) I was trying to get some good American music recorded, and because of the special circumstances surrounding our arrangements with Ormandy's orchestra a fortunate opportunity was presented here. Ormandy's quickness

and co-operativeness, and the fact that no talent cost was involved, suggested that music by an American, even though
commercially unsuccessful, would be effective "prestige" advertising. I persuaded Victor to commission a piece of eight
minutes' duration (two sides of a record) by Roy Harris, who
promptly produced his overture *When Johnny Comes March-
ing Home.*

Harris's music did not arrive in Minneapolis until the morning of the last day of recording; thus neither conductor nor
orchestra had time to give it much study. Ormandy was in a
rage—one of the few occasions when I have known him completely to give way to anger. However, even before he had finished breakfast he had his head in Harris's score, and an hour
later he had the score in his head. A perilous fifteen minutes
before recording time he declared he knew *Johnny,* then
ripped the score in half and threw it on the floor. We went
roaring to the Northrup Auditorium where the orchestra
waited, and twenty minutes later that overture was on wax.
Ormandy had rehearsed, corrected, conducted, and recorded
the piece after learning and memorizing it, in detail, in something less than two hours. He corrected mistakes in the orchestral parts—from memory!—and Harris, who was present with a
score in his hand, checked and found Gene correct. This was
the most startling stunt of musical assimilation and memory
I have ever known.

His memory is perhaps the most spectacular, but least important, of Mr. Ormandy's talents as a conductor. Considering other aspects of his musical equipment, I looked forward
with confident anticipation to his success in Philadelphia. A
quite large number of subscribers, and especially those who attended the orchestra's ten concerts annually in New York,
were not so confident, and at first the subscriptions fell off
considerably. I think this was in the end a wholesome and
beneficial thing. It changed somewhat the complexion of the
audience, the defection of so many Stokowski worshippers
making room for people who loved music but could not get in

to the sold-out Stokowski concerts. There were fewer of what we would now call the "bobby-sox brigade," and more people who were eager to listen to great music played well, no matter who played it. Of course it took some time to effect this adjustment, but Ormandy's performances attracted larger and larger audiences during succeeding seasons, and most of the Philadelphia Orchestra's concerts during the season 1944–5, at home and on the road, were sold out.

I was one of those who believed unwaveringly that Ormandy would succeed in Philadelphia. Sales of Philadelphia Orchestra recordings conducted by Ormandy clearly indicated that on a national scale the orchestra would not suffer in popularity; it seemed logical to conclude that locally it should do as well. There was no reason to expect the orchestra to suffer musically either, and indeed it has not. A man with Ormandy's tremendous talent, regardless of any question of profound interpretation, would certainly take nothing away from the orchestra, and could contribute to it. He inherited the orchestral talent and the orchestral tone that are the unique and peerless qualities of the Philadelphia Orchestra—qualities that Stokowski had created, developed, and preserved in miraculous degree. These could not disappear overnight even in the hands of a second-rate conductor, which Ormandy certainly is not.

How others fall heir to the fabulous tone of the Philadelphia ensemble recalls an amusing incident. Fabien Sevitzky, conductor of the Indianapolis Orchestra, founder and conductor of the Philadelphia Chamber String Sinfonietta, recently was rehearsing the latter for a concert. This group is made up entirely of Philadelphia Orchestra string players and includes most of the best of them. (Fabien himself is an ex-bass player of the orchestra.) In the middle of the rehearsal Sevitzky, who is somewhat given to overdramatizing himself, stopped the group and with an expression compounded of consternation, disappointment, and wounded feelings cried "Gentlemen! but gentlemen! Vare iss famous *Sinfonietta* tone?"

Even I, who rank myself an appreciable distance below Toscanini as a conductor, have been the beneficiary of the glowing warmth and richness of Philadelphia Orchestra tone. For irrefutable evidence, may I suggest you give yourself the pleasure of hearing Marian Anderson's records of "He Shall Feed His Flock" and "Es ist vollbracht" ("It Is Finished") with the Victor Symphony Orchestra in accompaniment. The first aria is done with muted strings only, the second with a full orchestra, all players in both records having been chosen from the Philadelphia Orchestra. Victor Symphony tone! [3]

Aside from musical reasons why Ormandy should have succeeded, and did succeed, with the Philadelphia Orchestra, there was a suspicion in many minds that a considerable number of the subscribers were tired of the excursions and alarums that, with increasing frequency, disturbed the always precarious relations between Stokowski and the board of directors of the orchestra. These usually involved threatened resignations, unkind comment on both sides, privately and publicly, and a general state of malaise that perturbed, irritated and, eventually antagonized some of Stokowski's most devoted admirers. This bickering also brought about a progressive reduction in the number of concerts conducted by Stokowski each season, until eventually an attitude developed which was expressed to me by a friend, also a friend of Stokowski: "What the hell," he asked, "is the use of having a conductor who won't conduct?" In Ormandy the orchestra association had a conductor who not only would but was very eager indeed to conduct; when he finished the season 1944-5 he had conducted 129 concerts in 33 weeks.

---

[3] Particularly worthy of note, in addition to Miss Anderson's magnificent performance, is the cello solo in "Es ist vollbracht," played with heartbreaking loveliness of tone and phrase by Samuel H. Mayes, first cello of the Philadelphia Orchestra. Incidentally, and apropos nothing, the stars of these recordings, Miss Anderson and Mr. Mayes, are both American-plus; each has Indian blood. Mr. Mayes is related to the late Will Rogers and is probably the only cellist in the world who is one eighth Cherokee.

ORMANDY IN AUSTRALIA

I think Mr. Ormandy's hold on the orchestra and its audiences was immensely strengthened by his Australian adventure in the summer of 1944 and by the enthusiastic press that reported it both in that far land and here at home. In the spring of that year the Australian Broadcasting Company decided to invite a conductor from the United States to give a series of concerts in the chief cities of that sub-continent. Of the five conductors whom the Australians considered, Ormandy was the only one who perceived the possibilities of this engagement, the others being unwilling to give up either summer holidays or more remunerative activities. As matters turned out, this opportunity was worth a good deal more than the fees it paid. The Australians were captivated by Ormandy, and the press at home, with the active encouragement of the Office of War Information, saw to it again and again that stories of his success were kept before American, and particularly Philadelphian, readers. Even the *Congressional Record*, most fascinating of journals, took note of Ormandy's activities, though with neither accuracy nor, apparently, approval. In the course of remarks delivered in the House of Representatives, Thursday, September 1, 1944, the Honorable Noble J. Johnson of Indiana had occasion to note "the enormous quantity of white diaper cloth sent to the Arabs, which was used by them to make head-dressings; that lend-lease money was used to send a symphony orchestra conductor, Eugene Ormandy, to Europe on a concert tour; the Detroit scandal where $1,721,000 worth of precious and scarce cutting tools were sold for $35,000. . . ." If Mr. Johnson's remarks on other subjects were as inaccurate as those on Ormandy's tour, his address must have been rather ineffective.

Such wrong impressions as the Congressman's were in fact

brought about by the misrepresentation of Ormandy's tour
in our own press. Representative Johnson was wrong in that
Ormandy didn't go to Europe and no lend-lease money was
used in any way in connection with his visit to Australia; but
our own press built up the story that Ormandy was a semi-
official ambassador; that in going to Australia he was making a
great patriotic gesture; that the OWI was sending him as part
of its propaganda for international good will; that Mr. Ormandy was making a great financial sacrifice and that only his
expenses were being paid, not through lend-lease but by OWI.
The truth of the matter is that his expenses were paid—not by
OWI or any agency of the United States Government, but
by the Australian Broadcasting Company. Mrs. Ormandy also
was taken along, expenses paid. Mr. Ormandy was paid his
fee—not his "regular" fee, no conductor ever gets that!—but a
good round sum that made a normally unremunerative and
expensive summer quite profitable indeed. I do not question
Mr. Ormandy's patriotic enthusiasm, nor do I doubt that he
would have undertaken anything asked of him by the government with no thought of profit. The necessity for representing
as a command performance and a profound gesture of international amity what actually was a very straightforward commercial enterprise does not seem apparent to me.[4]

Apparently Ormandy was confronted by some rather serious
musical problems in Australia; from all reports, including his
own, he solved them very brilliantly. Although there is no
full-scale symphony orchestra in Australia, the broadcasting
company assembled for Ormandy's visit a group made up of
players from five different organizations, none of them of great

---

[4] In justice to Mr. Ormandy it must be recorded that while in Australia,
whenever opportunity appeared, he gave of his services gratis at entertainments
for the troops. It is reported that he ingratiated himself very thoroughly with
General MacArthur, especially with the lament *Bataan*, excerpted from the
suite *My Country at War* by Harl McDonald. The conductor agreed, at the
general's suggestion, to return and conduct a victory concert in the Philippines
when MacArthur had liberated those islands, but has not had opportunity to
do so yet.

distinction. Somehow, he licked them into shape, and after his first concert I had a letter from him intimating that the resulting ensemble was remarkably like the Philadelphia Orchestra. An enthusiastic fellow! Discounting any slight exaggeration, Gene must have performed miracles. For his first concert he had six or eight rehearsals, which, however indifferent the talent, would in Ormandy's hands bring about very respectable results. Sir Thomas Beecham on his last Australian tour didn't do quite so well. When he arrived, the same group of players was assembled for him, and the special indulgence of six rehearsals was arranged. At the first, Sir Thomas went straight through the program once, and then with exaggerated courtesy excused the orchestra. Next day, the same thing happened. On the third, once through the program again without corrections, and Sir Thomas announced that there would be no further rehearsal before the concert, three days off. The manager of the orchestra, who had gone through hell and high water to get six rehearsals for the gay baronet (and who had to pay for them), incredulously asked if Sir Thomas wasn't going to use the remaining three rehearsals available to him. "Good God, no!" said Sir Thomas. The manager: "But, sir, these rehearsals are arranged and paid for; surely. . . ." "My dear fellow," interrupted the suave Sir Thomas, "this orchestra was lousy at the first rehearsal, lousier at the second, and incredibly lousy at the third. I can't let this go on; think what it would be like at the performance!"

The critics, especially those of the New York press and the reviewers of phonograph records, have constituted the last impediment to the complete secundation of Ormandy's career as a conductor. He has always been sensitive and often responsive to criticism, favorable or otherwise; one would not accuse him of pandering to it, but I do think he has always taken it too seriously whether it flagellated or flattered. When he was in Minneapolis it was usually highly complimentary, which was good for Gene's ego and a certain uncertainty of conviction, for the one really needed development and expansion, the other, reinforcement, corroboration, and support. When he took over at Philadelphia, however, this moral assistance was not forthcoming from the press either in that city or in New York, where the orchestra visits ten times a season. To make matters worse, the fashionable (and capacity) audiences in New York began, upon the defection of Stokowski, to withdraw their fickle support from the Philadelphia Orchestra, and to transfer it to Koussevitzky and the Boston Symphony. The press observed this and adopted an attitude that was at best patronizing; more often it seemed to regard Ormandy as a young upstart whose powers had already been demonstrated years before when he was conductor of the Capitol Theater orchestra. The reviewers of records, who had so warmly greeted Ormandy's Minneapolis Orchestra discs, followed the general line of the critical sorority when Eugene's Philadelphia recordings began to appear.

Now critics of music, not only in New York but in most large centers, are very strange creatures. As a public performer myself, with respect for my own musical convictions and, I think, a fair estimate of my own capability, I have often violently disagreed (but never argued) with the critics; nor was I willing to question their honesty, or at least their willingness to be fair, until comparatively recently. Now I have concluded, as one must who has the opportunity to observe closely the operations of some of them, that many critics are unfair, some of them venal, and most of them incompetent. Most critics of music are frustrated musicians, or even singers, with exhibitionist, sadist, and other tendencies even less frequently mentioned in gentle society. One or two eke out their meager salaries by blackmail. One offers—at a price—his services in preparing a debutant for a recital, and woe to the young artist who declines these services. Another suffers financial difficulties shortly before the appearances of certain artists, and often negotiates a loan from them at the critical moment—a loan that is of course liquidated by an enthusiastic review. A third admits that key signatures quite baffle him, and that he cannot read music. He boasts that he does not go to concerts; he prefers music by radio or record.

Critics will, if they can (and sometimes they can), slay a career with a sentence; conversely, once they have attached themselves to a star, as they often do with revolting tenacity, that star's light can never be obscured, never suffer the slightest aberration. Sir Thomas Beecham, for example, has been and is the darling of these creatures. Although many musicians recognize his gifts as conspicuous but distinctly limited, and though to many of them he is "a talented amateur," a certain critical sorosis finds equally palatable, but delicious, his capric capers, ponderous wit, frequent musical gaucherie, and occasional perfect performances. Incidentally, the playful knight rather inclines to agree with these gentry. I recall his indicating to me in quite definite terms that there wasn't in America a single orchestra worthy of his attention, at least for recording purposes, except the Boston Symphony. "And that band," he added with an exophthalmic leer, "I have NOT been invited to conduct!"

But, Ormandy and the critics: they had evidently set their faces against him in New York. One of them, first critic of a quite respected journal, might have indicated the general attitude when he said to a friend of mine who had protested his harshness with Ormandy: "Goddam it, I know the little by-blow is good, but I just don't like him." That was years ago; this critic, like most of them, has finally been worn down by the solid excellence of Ormandy's craftsmanship, his straightforward, unaffected, vigorous, and sometimes inspired readings, his careful preservation of the peerless qualities of the Philadelphia instrument, his obvious sincerity and devotion. Enthusiastically favorable reviews of Ormandy's New York concerts are lately the rule and not the exception; the same is true in Philadelphia, and the provinces rave. Even the feline Virgil Thomson of the *New York Herald Tribune* will forego his customary captiousness when Ormandy comes to town, and this critic is as cruel and as honest as he knows how to be. Mr. Ormandy had him as guest conductor of certain opuscules of Thomson's own contriving, not long ago. I hope that Gene did not intend this as a placating gesture, for much as Virgil Thomson must have enjoyed conducting his own music with one of the world's great orchestras, he is not a man to be suborned with bribery or a woman to be seduced with flattery. Indeed, did he suspect that his engagement was intended as a bribe instead of a conventional appearance by a composer-conductor, on his own merit and for a good fat fee, he would likely requite Mr. Ormandy's blandishments with more wasp-ish acerbity than ever.

Mr. Ormandy's assiduous cultivation of Toscanini and his circumjacent worshippers resulted quite happily for him temporarily and brought about his engagement during the 1944-5 season to conduct two concerts with the NBC Symphony. The fierce light that beats upon the Toscanini throne ultimately singed Eugene rather painfully, however. Virgil Thomson bestowed the kiss of death by praising Ormandy's performances and by not praising Toscanini's, and when Margherita De Vecchi intruded upon a touchingly friendly moment between Virgil and Gene she reported the incident to Maestro, whereupon Ormandy was promptly cast into exterior darkness, where he still languishes.

LAURITZ
MELCHIOR

⋙ Lauritz Melchior ⋘

The Great Dane

"*Sharlie, Sharlie, der Schwan ist todt!*" This startling announcement, delivered in a panting stage whisper, was successful in bringing about a momentary suspension in the waves of laughter and talk that filled my house one Sunday afternoon not so very long ago. Up to the point at which this dramatic line was delivered by Kleinchen (Mrs. Melchior), the noise of thirty or forty people talking at once and the pleasantly stimulated interest of my guests in each other had obscured another uproar on the third floor of our house, which is exclusively the children's territory, and had likewise caused the absence of the guest of honor, Lauritz himself, to be overlooked. I had for some time been conscious of a rather secondary but different kind of uproar, emanating from the third floor, and compounded of children's squeals, a baritone roaring of laughter, an occasional feeble quack, and sounds suggesting the ceaseless susurrus of the sea. I had not had time to investigate and hadn't the faintest idea what was going on until Kleinchen made her tragic announcement. Even then I was a bit mystified until I recalled that a few weeks before, on Easter Sunday, some misguided friends of ours had presented the children with a number of barnyard animals, including a duck. Fearing the worst, I headed for the children's part of the house and found it suddenly wrapped in a pregnant silence. I made my way to the bathroom, and there was a scene of real devastation. I don't know whether there was more water in the tub or on the floor or who was most bedraggled—Robin, David, or the room-filling figure of the gigantic *Heldentenor*. He stood in the middle of the room like a boy caught stealing jam, with the flaccid and dripping cadaver of a baby duck clutched to his massive bosom. "I didn't know he don't schwim! Nun—he iss todt," said Lauritz. It was indeed a dead duck, and Lauritz, David, and Robin were all heartbroken.

I am sure Lauritz got as much fun out of playing with that duck as the children did, and I am not at all surprised that he left our guests, preferring the congenial and natural society of children and the quacking of a duck to the more or less sincere adulation of friends and their endless twittering. In many ways Lauritz is simple and lovable as a child; even his features are amiable and rather infantile. Add to these his heroic dimensions and you have a unique and quite attractive personality.

I do not agree that the accumulation of flesh occasions a corresponding access of good humor. Queen Victoria was not easily amused; Roscoe Arbuckle gave evidence of a certain choler; William Howard Taft, according to the prematurely aged and whipped-down little private secretary whom I knew in Washington, was frightfully peevish; Schumann-Heink made a warmhearted, world-mothering sentimentality her trademark, but actually was no better-humored than the rest of us. On the other hand, G. K. Chesterton and Hilaire Belloc, of the fat men I have known, were certainly among the jolliest of human creatures; Paul Whiteman's merry disposition was changed by neither his gluteal accretions nor reductions; and Lauritz Melchior proves that if a fat man isn't necessarily always agreeable, he certainly can be on occasion. Left to himself, he has a kind of oafish good humor; when sufficiently prodded, he will often do things that are clumsy, boorish, or gauche, but there is no malice in him. Physically, Lauritz is a really remarkable specimen. He is several inches over six feet tall and admits to weighing 220 pounds. This seems to me a gross understatement. He is curiously constructed, with an enormous and corpulent torso set upon relatively slender, almost femininely rounded and distinctly handsome legs, so that he acquires a figure which, in combination with a tenor voice, is disturbingly reminiscent of those unhappy guardians of the harem. I do not mean to suggest any physiological similarity or any resemblance between Lauritz's trumpet-like tenor and what the London *Spectator* once referred to as "the shrill, celestial whine of eunuchs." Whatever his shortcomings may be, Lauritz is a male, a man, and a grandfather.

Not as proof, but as merely collateral evidence of this, I might cite his passion for hunting and the occasion when, before a crowd of witnesses, he startled the milling crowds in the concourse of Grand Central Terminal by appearing, just off a train from the north country, with a great shaggy bear, not long dead, nonchalantly draped over his shoulder. I recall too that when we were recording with Lauritz and Flagstad in our Hollywood studios he gave me a few uncomfortable moments. On the first day of recording we had completed the Immolation Scene. On the second day we were to do some retakes and also do the second-act duet from *Götterdämmerung* with Kirsten and Lauritz. I had, with some difficulty, persuaded Flagstad to undertake this recording on the day following the strenuous Immolation, and therefore was deeply disturbed when two minutes before the appointed hour Lauritz had not turned up. This gave Flagstad another opportunity to get balky, and between trying to keep her calm and in the back of my head figuring out what my superiors would say if I had to pay a large orchestra for a recording session without getting anything, I was in somewhat of a state. One second before the fatal hour Lauritz appeared, smoking an eight-inch cigar and apparently the worse for wear. I asked him, perhaps none too quietly, what in the world had happened to him, or less polite words to that effect. He calmly told me that he had been out shooting ducks since four o'clock that morning. It developed that he had not been home at all, had had nothing to eat, had smoked cigars interminably all day long, and was now ready to sing. I couldn't believe it, but Lauritz cleared his throat a couple of times, said "Let's go," and went. He never in his life sang better, and you may turn to the records for proof.

These records, by the way, were the root-cause of the only serious difficulty I ever had with Lauritz. They were released as part of an album of Wagnerian music in which Flagstad had the lion's share. This hurt Lauritz's not inconsiderable sense of his own importance, and the fact that Flagstad received eighty cents out of the selling price of each album, whereas Lauritz received only twenty, was utterly maddening to the financial brains of the Melchior family. Not many days after the publication of this album, I was informed by Constance Hope, who was a kind of personal representative as well as publicity agent for Lauritz, that the great man would like to see me at once, that he was in a state of considerable agitation, and that I had better go armed, if not with a lethal weapon, at least with a good set of answers. I presently presented myself at the Melchior suite in the Hotel Ansonia and found Lauritz in the closest thing to a rage that he can feel. Flanked by Kleinchen and Henry Jaffe, the shrewd lawyer for the American Guild of Musical Artists, and occasionally when his eloquence seemed to be flagging, egged on by these helpers, Lauritz developed a really impressive philippic directed at me, the company, Flagstad, and everybody concerned. I personally had nothing to do with the particular arrangement under which these records were released. That was a dictum of our whip-witted sales department. I knew it was hopeless to attempt to clarify this to Lauritz, so to put an end to the diatribe I accepted responsibility—which I shouldn't have done—and promised to make what repairs I could. I caused another album, specially designed to hold Lauritz's records only and with exactly the same quality of art work and other details used in the first edition, to be issued for Lauritz's particular benefit. I don't think he was mollified, nor do I think this accomplished much to increase his ratio of profit from the records with Flagstad. To give the devil his due, I must say that our people were right in releasing the records the way they did. It was perfectly in keeping with the whole combination career of Flagstad and Melchior, in every detail of which Flagstad was the main attraction and Melchior purely incidental. I think this was always the public attitude, and I think Lauritz and Kleinchen always knew it. Naturally, they could not afford to admit it. The arrogance and the bad taste of the Melchiors' insistence on his taking every bow, every recall at the opera house with Flagstad, and the absurd lengths to which they went to assure this, clearly indicate that they knew Lauritz was, as far as the public was concerned, the tail to Flagstad's kite.

Lauritz knows, if Kleinchen doesn't, how necessary to his career in Wagnerian opera a great soprano must be. That explains, I dare say, his eagerness to promote Astrid Varnay and to get me to engage her for Victor records as the successor to Flagstad. I think events have proved my judgment right in resisting this pressure. I had Traubel. Later, Lauritz turned from Varnay to Traubel and exercised what influence he had to bring about a joint relationship, so far, at least, as recording activities are concerned. He was not successful in this.

Lauritz's colleagues sometimes complain because he doesn't like to rehearse and will not do so if there is any conceivable means of avoiding it. Quite often he just doesn't show up. I was a little concerned about this a few seasons ago when I conducted a broadcast of the Philadelphia Orchestra, sponsored by the Chase National Bank, with Lauritz as soloist along with a big and nonprofessional chorus, the Choral Society of the University of Pennsylvania, numbering several hundred voices. I knew that rehearsal, and thorough rehearsal, was vital, if not for Lauritz, certainly for the chorus, the orchestra, and myself. To my pleasant surprise, Lauritz turned up and not only rehearsed with us tirelessly, patiently, and in full voice, but in other ways was distinctly helpful. Whether or not you like this high-pressured, constricted, brilliant, but rather erratic voice, it must be conceded that in the Wagnerian opera Lauritz is completely at home, as he demonstrated on this occasion; no singer knows better its demands, vocally and artistically; none knows better its traditional routine. Certainly no one should know better, for Lauritz has sung more than eleven hundred Wagnerian performances and over two hundred of *Tristan*.

Lauritz loves certain indoor sports as well as those of the great open spaces. Chief among them are cards and collecting decorations. I do not play cards and consequently cannot speak for Lauritz's prowess at bridge or poker, but judging from the character of his favorite partners—for instance, the late Artur Bodanzky, the most rapacious and merciless of poker players—I should say Lauritz must be an expert. He seldom has to be asked twice to join a table. Each year on his birthday he is host at a Gargantuan rout to which practically everyone he has ever spoken to is bidden. These parties usually begin about eight in the evening and end not before eight the next morning, and the collection of food and drink, at least in prewar days, was utterly incredible. The party would not go on very long, however, before Lauritz and his cronies would withdraw to an inner room where the most merciless of games, either poker or bridge, would get under way and continue without pause until the following forenoon. These parties became famous, and through them the canny Kleinchen not only gave Lauritz's publicity people something to write about, but paid off innumerable social obligations at a relatively reasonable cost per capita.

As for decorations, Lauritz has the most glittering collection in the world, I think, next to that of the late Hermann Göring. What's more, he wears them. He wears them—all of them—in scintillating miniature, and even against the vast acreage of his dress coat front their number makes a brave show. Not even Lily Pons can match Lauritz's collection, but Grace Moore came pretty close to it, for Grace was the most avid collector of honorary gadgets among the female species of the musical world. Which reminds me that there is one lovely jewel of a decoration that Grace could have had but, through one of her little idiosyncrasies, didn't get. A while ago Lauritz undertook to give a great benefit for some Danish project, and he thought, shrewdly enough, that he and Grace Moore would be attractive stars of such an occasion. He encountered Grace at a concert and mentioned that he had something he wished to discuss with her; she suggested that he phone the following day. Lauritz did so and was told that Miss Moore was not to be disturbed. The day after that, he phoned again with similar results, and this went on for I don't know how many days before Lauritz lost patience and engaged someone else. Some time later he met Miss Moore at a party and took the opportunity to remind her that she had asked him to call and that he had been unable to get in touch with her. When he told her what it was all about and that he could have gotten her the famous Diamond Cross, bestowed by Danish royalty to especially distinguished friends of Denmark, Grace was exceedingly unhappy and said that if Lauritz would only rearrange matters, she herself would pay the expense of Madison Square Garden or any other hall he would name if Lauritz could guarantee her that decoration. But it was too late.[1]

Lauritz and Kleinchen make a piquant combination since they are polar opposites in almost everything. She is excessively feminine, as he is masculine. She is tiny, pretty, and vivacious, where he is of cetacean bulk with no extraordinary physical attractiveness. He has a lumbering, honest, simple mind,

---

[1] I must explain that it was usually impossible to get Miss Moore on the telephone before 1:00 P.M., and very difficult after that. Grace, understandably enough, had the hotel switchboard shut off her phone until she told them it was all right to ring her apartment, but unfortunately, she usually forgot to instruct the hotel operators when she was available for calls. She also had a habit, which embarrassed her more than once, of answering the phone in a grotesque French accent and of describing herself as Miss Moore's maid until she could identify the caller. She wasn't always able to identify callers who sometimes turned out to be mighty important and mightily offended.

whereas Kleinchen's is quick, serpentine, and devious. Kleinchen has, however, a saving sense of humor, although it sometimes acquires that earthy quality which is, I think, peculiar to the Germanic peoples. She tells a story on herself that illustrates not so much her sense of humor as its sometimes indelicate references. The Melchiors were quite close friends of the late Sir Hugh Walpole and frequently have been guests at his country place. This literary gentleman was not only an artist but a practical fellow as well. His rate of peristalsis was such that he found it necessary to spend a great deal of time in his bathroom. To improve these shining hours, he had bookshelves installed in the bathroom within easy reach and while, of course, he did little serious reading there, he liked to browse through some of his priceless and beautifully bound first editions.

Kleinchen tells that on one weekend visit to Walpole's house she had occasion to use this bathroom and discovered, to her dismay, that while in truth there was an abundance of paper at hand, there was a sad lack of the particular kind of stationery in which she was most interested at the moment. Looking about in desperation, and perhaps hoping to find a first-edition Sears-Roebuck catalog, she finally selected the least impressive-looking volume and from it ravished those pages bearing the least amount of printer's ink. She later confessed her vandalism and pleaded *force majeure*, but both she and her host had difficulty in forgiving her when it was discovered that she had mutilated one of his rarest first editions. Kleinchen's Viennese accent and mixture of English and German in the telling of this story make it perhaps a great deal more entertaining than it seems in cold type. At least it indicates that Kleinchen at bottom has a sense of humor, and can stand for a joke on herself, at least as long as she tells it.

Recently it has been discovered that Lauritz has talents in what for him is quite a new direction. The radio audience, not very long ago, was treated to Lauritz's antics as guest artist of the Chamber Music Society of Lower Basin Street, and he was genuinely funny. Again, he appeared on the program called *Duffy's Tavern* and gave a very effective plug to the song *Leave Us Face It*. The result of these appearances was a motion-picture contract. I do not know whether or not this was based on Lauritz's ability as a crooner, which is not inconsiderable; he is actually a baritone rather than a tenor and often has the required huskiness. But he has been exploited as a clown, as I rather thought he would.

ARTURO
TOSCANINI

~§ Arturo Toscanini §~

A MINORITY REPORT

Not all of me shall die: my praise shall grow, and

never end . . .

Of me it shall be told

That, grown from small to great, I first

Of all men subtly wrought

Aeolian strains to unison

With our Italian thought.

HORACE: ODE XXX, BOOK 3
(Gladstone's Translation)

"O'Connell caro, non mi chiameranno mai vecchio. Non lassero dire la parola 'povero Toscanini.' Quando in mano mi trema la bacchetta, non faro più il direttore. Ma quel tempo non é ancora giunto."

We had been talking about Frederick Stock, for so many years conductor of the Chicago Symphony. Poor Stock had not been in the best of health, but had come through a serious operation successfully. However, he had for years looked older and feebler than he actually was, and someone in the group at Toscanini's dinner table had made a sympathetic comment. It was then that our host made the remark I have quoted above: "My dear O'Connell, they'll never call me old. I won't let anyone say: 'Poor Toscanini.' When my hand trembles holding the stick, I'll conduct no more. But that time is not yet."

I believe Toscanini meant what he said. He has never asked quarter, because of his age, from God or man or nature. To be sure, he has pleaded weariness or even age when it was a convenient way of extricating himself from an unwelcome situation, but no one who has worked with him or critically examined his work, has been able to detect the slightest diminuendo of the flaming energy, the merciless force with which he drives himself and everyone about him. Such dynamism in any man would be remarkable; in a man past seventy-five years it seems almost miraculous, but perhaps it is not the phenomenon it appears to be. I think the explanation lies largely in the fact that Toscanini's energy—mental, spiritual, and physical—is completely polarized, exclusively channeled in the direction of his work, rather than distributed over a variety of interests. The sturdy physique of an Italian peasant, the admirable diet of the simple people of Italy during childhood and adolescence, a life in which physical needs were never a problem—these certainly are factors conducive to longevity. Superimpose upon them a will of implacable determination, a power of concentration almost ferocious in its intensity, and obviously a decision to focus these and every other power in a single direction, and you have, I think, a formula for the conservation and preservation of energy.

I believe that Toscanini's obsession with energy, with force, his pride in possessing them in so full a measure, his idolatrous worship of these qualities, and his relentless application of them in his artistic and personal life, provide a possible key not only to the magical effect he has had upon his audiences and his consequent successes, but to the character of the maestro himself as man and musician. Energy, determination, concentration: these have made Toscanini what he is, and I think somewhat less of each would have made a greater artist and a nobler man. His energy causes him to drive rather than to lead; his determination, to dictate rather than to teach, and the fury of concentration he brings to bear upon the printed score leaves him little time, and apparently less inclination, for gentleness, for tolerance, patience, humility, humanity, or love. I have not known him, in years of acquaintance, countless conversations, and many hours of collaboration, to evidence interest in a book, a growing tree, a burgeoning talent, a picture that lived or a building that leaped to the sky, a work of drama other than that mongrel type, the opera. I do not believe (certain writers notwithstanding) that Toscanini is a student of Shakespeare; he could not be, and remain as simple, as selfish, and as savage as a child.

Sometimes people meeting Toscanini socially are quite astonished that his off-stage appearance differs from their concert-hall image of the man. His head and face have some of the same photogenic qualities that Hollywood exploits so skillfully, and similarly are less impressive under normal conditions than in the adroit lighting of the stage. The rapt and saintly and suffering face[1] actually has strong and rather heavy features, excepting the mouth, which, quite concealed beneath the exquisitely tended mustache, is rather small and petulant. Even in the reluctant smile, it relaxes and broadens but little. The eyes are large, and unnaturally "bright-dark," the pupils hugely expanded at most times in a faraway, *spirituel* gaze. Thus myopia serves mysticism. The face is rather swarthy and choleric, but below the collar-line Toscanini has the whitest and clearest skin I have ever seen. His ears are remarkably large.

---

[1] I like Walter Pater's gently ironic remark on such a face: "That sweet look of devotion which men have never been able altogether to love, and which still makes the born saint an object almost of suspicion to his earthly brethren."

Toscanini is not "lean," as he is so often described. True, when he conducts, his body becomes tense and he actually seems to grow taller. In fact, his finicky Italian tailoring conceals a rather dumpy little figure, impressively broad in the beam and of generous circumference at the equator. The hands that draw audible sculptures in the invisible air are indeed like a sculptor's—large, strong, and thick-fingered. His feet are the maestro's most aristocratic feature: small, shapely, and always exquisitely booted in the European style. He walks with a little, almost mincing swagger, turning his feet outward almost forty-five degrees. He is quick and agile as a cat, and if not restrained will run upstairs two at a time. I remember an amusing instance of this. We were talking—about music, of course—in the great hall of the rococo mansion Toscanini then occupied in Riverdale. Some question arose that he wished to settle by reference to a score (he undoubtedly knew it from memory, but I didn't), and he suddenly leaped to his feet, dashing up the enormous staircase to his study with the speed and agility of a cheetah. Margherita De Vecchi, a family friend through many years, happened to be present, and screamed: "Take it easy, you old fool!" to which the master paid not the slightest attention. He not only completed running up the stairs two at a time, but to show his defiance of Margherita (who can be terrifying) ran down again the same reckless way. He then calmly opened the score to precisely the questioned passage, and proceeded to discuss it without so much as a deep breath.

In all the reports I have read of Toscanini as musician, as man, or as both, I have not been able to find an objective or a factual account of him. It seems to me there are several kinds of people who have written about Toscanini. There are the sycophants and the flatterers, to whose influence he is by no means impervious, and who would use his name to elevate their own prestige and add to their own profit. There are those who write from a desire to agree with the majority and to advance the ignorant majority's opinion as their own in order to find a receptive audience. There are those too who, possessed of an enthusiasm for music, come to worship the evanescent shadow of a human being instead of the substance of the music itself; they respond to the protagonist rather than to the play, they adore the priest instead of the god. There are the snobs who feel that because Toscanini is the most difficult, inaccessible, and thoroughly exploited of conductors, he must therefore be the greatest of conductors and a person embodying all the noble qualities that we like to believe are possessed by great artists. I know of no one who has written about Toscanini from a basis of intimate acquaintance and professional collaboration, with the possible exception of the late Max Smith, and Smith laid at the feet of the master a devotion so fawning and canine as to disqualify him completely as an objective commentator. Certainly Lawrence Gilman, a critic of exquisite discrimination, a just, articulate, and sophisticated person, was completely bemused when he wrote his book *Toscanini and Great Music*.[2] I do not take too seriously the outpourings of Tobia Nicotra,[3] and find the book interesting only for chronological data. References to Toscanini in *Dictators of the Baton* by David Ewen,[4] the same author's *The Man With the Baton*,[5] and Howard Taubman's *Music on My Beat*[6] contain little but hearsay, backstage clichés, and insufferably tautological statements of all the worshipful nonsense that has grown up around this simple little Italian. The Toscanini I have known for ten or twelve years, with whom I have collaborated, whom I have entertained in my home and elsewhere, who has entertained me in his home and elsewhere,

---

[2] Farrar & Rinehart, 1938.

[3] *Arturo Toscanini*, by Tobia Nicotra, translated from the Italian by Irma Brandeis and H. D. Kahn. Knopf, 1929.

[4] Ziff-Davis Publishing Co., 1943.

[5] Thos. Y. Crowell Co., 1936.

[6] Simon & Schuster, 1943.

the Toscanini I have seen and heard and studied at close range in almost every social and professional relationship, is not the Toscanini who has been presented to the public.

Socially Toscanini can be, and usually is, charming and gracious either as host or as guest. His conversation concerns little but music, and tends to develop into a monologue, not so much because he insists upon having the floor as because others would as a rule prefer to listen to him than talk themselves. If he is in a pleasant mood he is very easy to entertain, and you'll usually find him before long in animated and perhaps exclusive conversation with the most attractive lady present. He can make a flattering gesture with lordly grace, and accept one in quite the same manner. He is completely conscious of his importance, and accepts tributes to it with the most disarming simplicity. Occasionally he asserts it. In one instance, related to me by Dr. Bergman, husband of Kerstin Thorborg, and himself an opera singer and manager, the maestro evidently wished to subdue a certain star tenor in a Swedish opera house, but was somewhat handicapped by language difficulties. He finally turned to Bergman and shouted, "Ask that man if he knows who I am, and tell him to get to hell off the stage." Bergman did as commanded, and the tenor drew himself up to his full height and shouted just as violently, "Tell him yes and no." Toscanini discharged Adriatic lightnings from his eyes, then suddenly laughed and proceeded with the rehearsal.

I was leaving Toscanini's Riverdale home [7] late one night after a long dinner and a longer conference. Usually the family Cadillac was generously assigned to take me back to town, but on this occasion the chauffeur had gone to bed. I asked permission to phone for a cab, and on being connected required

[7] For several seasons after returning to America to conduct the NBC Orchestra, Toscanini and his entourage occupied an old mansion in Riverdale. The monstrous ugliness of this edifice is compensated by the beauty of its location and landscaped grounds.

a car to be sent to the home of Mr. Toscanini. I felt a tap on the shoulder, "MAESTRO, not mister," said Maestro.

When you entertain him at dinner the menu may be quite simple. Toscanini always eats the same things; some unfriendly people add "wears the same clothes and plays the same music." There is enough truth in this remark to make it sting a little. Toscanini invariably wears gray striped trousers and semiformal short coat of black or oxford gray, starched white shirt and dark bow tie. As for food, he told me himself that he did not like to try new or strange things to eat or drink, and Walter, his son, warned me not to have anything unusual when the maestro came to us for dinner.

In the case of his music, even some of Toscanini's most vigorous champions admit that for the last twenty years his programs have been drawn from a rather limited repertoire—the Beethoven symphonies, those of Brahms and some of Mozart, Wagnerian excerpts, a little Debussy and Ravel, and a lot of inferior Italian operatic overtures. On the other hand, it must be recorded that in the past season or two with the NBC Symphony he has extended his programs to include a number of contemporary works, some of them American; and even the Sixth Symphony of Tchaikovsky, for which he has often expressed contempt.

When Toscanini dined with us we might have a thin hot soup, veal scaloppini Marsala, a salad of greens with olive oil and red wine vinegar, perhaps *zabaglione*, and *caffè* espresso, four times distilled. Perhaps dinner will be preceded (so far as our guest is concerned) by one ghastly Martini, which only Mrs. Toscanini can contrive. It will be warm and composed mostly of sweet Italian vermouth. Not to do the lady an injustice, I must add that this cocktail is special for the maestro; the *signora* can and does make an excellent Martini *secco* for others.

Champagne is welcome at almost any time. Toscanini uses it, as he does other creature comforts, in moderation. I once procured for him a really rare bottle of Marsala, which he appeared to appreciate, but I should hesitate to say that in general his tastes in such matters are particularly discriminating. He is interested in an old bottle if you tell him it is old, but I don't think the old and mellow Marsala impressed him any more than the "just fair" champagne. The signora—Carla—is more exacting, and has an acute and uncontrollable curiosity about everything. I remember the last time the Toscaninis came to our house for a late Sunday afternoon dinner. There was the usual entourage of relatives and refugees, a South American-European conductor, Harl McDonald, manager of the Philadelphia Orchestra, one or two of the orchestra "first" men, and the O'Connell quartet: as it happened, the party followed a recording session. All the musicians were delayed, and so the two mesdames Toscanini, the maestro's wife and daughter-in-law, arrived first and early. They were received by Miss Robin O'Connell, seated and put at their ease by that quite poised young lady, then aged eight. Presently my wife appeared, somewhat breathless, I suppose. She found the signora scrambling about on all fours, apparently looking for something along the edge of a small Chinese rug. Assuming that Mrs. Toscanini had lost an earring or something of the sort, my wife joined her in crawling about the floor, only to discover after a discourse in French, Italian, and English that the signora had not lost anything, but was merely investigating the texture and quality of the rug; and with quite charming naïveté, wanted to know what it had cost. I am sorry to report that she didn't find out; that rug has been a matter of contention in our household for some years, and I'd like to know myself just how much we were stuck for it.

After a while Mr. Toscanini and the rest of us arrived. I was promptly informed that the maestro was hungry. Food wasn't ready, as we had expected a few minutes grace after the arrival of our guests, and had so instructed the highly temperamental Italian cook we had hired for the occasion. I didn't dare go into the kitchen, and, as it turned out, my presence there was distinctly less than necessary. The cook deserted the place, and

with indignation sought me out and demanded to know who
was in charge in the kitchen—he or "that woman." Upon investigation I found "that woman" was *Signora* Toscanini,
busily engaged in an investigation, by hand, eyes, nose, and
possibly ears, of a huge pot of spaghetti steaming on the stove.
I explained to cook, and to my relief he felt proud and honored
rather than resentful. So dinner was good, even to the *zabaglione*. This last, by the way, is a delicate confection, a kind of
ethereal custard related to *sabayon* sauce; I can be quite greedy
about it. Toscanini once noted this, and ever after when I
dined at his home, there was *zabaglione*. Once it turned out to
be a rather durable, not to say refractory, custard. Then I saw
sheer murder in the maestro's eye. He snatched the dish from
under my nose, personally carried it to the kitchen; whereupon
there were lamentations, recriminations, curses, and terror
throughout the house, but in five minutes I had *zabaglione* to
dream about. Toscanini is indeed a "dictator of the baton"—
and of the *maison*, the *salon*, and the *cuisine* as well.

So far as I know he is always the genial host, but there has
been at least one occasion when as a guest he left something to
be desired. The party was a "surprise" for Toscanini. The
apartment where it was held was redecorated for the occasion
as a nightclub. The guests were commanded to appear in costume, some as waiters, doormen, and the like, some as entertainers. The powerful Sarnoff and the whip-cracking John
Royal outdid themselves in zany preparations and at length
the great man arrived. He was stopped at the entrance by John
Royal, disguised as a doorman, who demanded whether or not
the maestro had reservations. Toscanini, not quite understanding all these strange goings-on, was offended. He was
finally persuaded to come in, and for the rest of the evening
the company devoted itself to completely futile efforts to
amuse, to interest, even to attract the attention of the guest
of honor, exactly as doting parents would try to beguile a sulky
child. Dancers danced, singers sang, jugglers juggled, and
waiters waited in vain; Maestro Toscanini would not be

moved. Although family and friends pleaded, he would not eat, or drink, or speak; nor would he mercifully go home, but sat at a table in a familiar pose, chin in hand, his eyes gazing down the long vista of infinity, all through the endless evening. It was finally discovered that the maestro does not like to be surprised.

Toscanini's humors, and humor, are difficult to predict. In talking with him, "we must speak by the card, or equivocation will undo us." I do not know whether it is lack of familiarity with English (even after so many years in America) or sheer lack of humor and imagination that causes him so often to misunderstand and misinterpret. He is quick to suspect those most keenly and most honestly and most disinterestedly devoted to his undertakings; to imagine slights, to look for hidden meanings, to doubt friendship, to accuse of promises unkept when no promise, but only a hope, has been given. Samuel Chotzinoff, being a sensitive as well as a devoted soul, has suffered exquisite tortures on this account. I have seen his large and limpid eyes fill with tears at some brusquerie of Maestro. For a time he and I alternated in occupation of the doghouse. Even Walter Toscanini and David Sarnoff have, for varying periods, been cast into exterior darkness, and when Maestro was displeased, his mansion would be filled with the furtive weeping of souls in deadly pain, with cries as of the damned, or, as occasion required, with the silence of the tomb.

I was persona non grata for a considerable period as the result of a remark that in itself was at least harmless and intended to be complimentary. A group had gathered in the office suite of John Royal to listen to the first records made by Toscanini with the NBC Symphony. Mr. Royal was there, as were David Sarnoff, Samuel Chotzinoff, the Baron and Baroness (Jarmila Novotná) Daubek, various NBC functionaries, Toscanini and myself. The records were declared highly satisfactory by Mr. Toscanini, and Big John, anticipating the event, made the Royal gesture and had well-frappé champagne and canapés brought in. Everyone congratulated Mr. Toscanini on the outcome of his first recording session with the NBC Orchestra, and quite surprisingly to everyone, he congratulated me. Naturally and rightly I made little of my part in the work, and said that not I or my associates, but the maestro himself was responsible that the records were good. He appeared to pay little attention to my remark, but within twenty-four hours had sent word to my superiors to the effect that he would make no more records if I were to be present. The most delicate investigation finally revealed that, according to report, I had impudently told Toscanini that he, not the recording staff, was responsible whether records were good or bad.

I think it would be difficult reasonably to draw such a deduction from my innocent and rather too modest remark. Everyone present heard it, everyone understood it as I meant it excepting the maestro, but not one, from Sarnoff down, came to my defense. Not that I asked them to do so, especially after the then head of the Victor recording activities told me that if Toscanini would make no more records while I was present, then Toscanini would make no more records. At the same time he warned me, clearly if not in too much detail, of the forces associated with NBC and RCA that were deliberately coalescing for the purpose of discrediting me with Toscanini. The reasons for this appeared to be jealousy—my acquaintance with the maestro antedated the NBC people's by some years, and had been completely amicable; again, the fact that NBC looked upon Toscanini as its private, precious property, and upon me as an interloper, a possible kidnapper, and a dangerous enemy; and upon recording as a necessary evil that provoked Toscaninian outbursts that those surrounding him hadn't the wit to subdue. I was not impressed by this warning.

Toscanini loves no one. On his sleeve he wears not his heart, but his spleen. He is capable of jealousy; he is capable of resentment if one's admiration for him is less than idolatrous; but I think he is not capable of love. I am not speaking of the love for woman or for music; there is evidence enough that he has acquitted himself, perhaps nobly, doubtless notably, in both directions. I speak of love which is the union of two wills. Toscanini is not interested in a union of wills, but only in the imposition of his own. His will he imposes with implacable determination on family, on friends, composers, companions, and corporations; on Beethovens, Sarnoffs, and second violinists; on children, on cooks, on colleagues. I know but a handful who have resisted—his daughters and his grandchildren. All others must bow, and he brings to bear on all, whether cook or corporation president, the same degree of force. He may beguile a stranger with charm and graciousness until the stranger becomes a slave; he will bludgeon the intimate with threats of his displeasure and of dismissal from the charmed circle. Toscanini is an unhappy man not only because he cannot love, but because he burns his energy and torments his soul with little things and little people; with vindictiveness, with unreasonableness, with suspicion, and with hate. It is, to a certain degree, true that, as Lawrence Gilman remarked,[8] "Toscanini has a single track mind," but it is not true that that single track has no sidetracks or cindery bypaths shadowed by rank, coarse growths of pettiness, of meanness, and of a selfishness that is miraculously complete.

Not the power of the Radio Corporation of America, his greatest benefactor, not the commercial enterprises of Victor, which pays him scores of thousands of dollars annually, not the rights of his fellow artists, can stand in his way. The menace of his displeasure is always imminent, and it is a menace that no one, however great or small, should take lightly.

In recent seasons the old maestro, irked by the gadfly critics of his limited repertoire and with an acute if wrongly begotten interest in the profit aspect of recording, has chosen to enlarge his repertoire and his income by devoting himself to such important works as the overture to *Mignon*, *The Blue Danube* waltz, the *Nutcracker Suite*, the B-flat minor Concerto of

---

[8] *Toscanini and Great Music*, op. cit.

Tchaikovsky, and other works of similar genre. I, being responsible for Victor in such matters, was reluctant to undertake
them with Mr. Toscanini, first, because the more sophisticated
record public was clamoring for weightier things; second, because I felt that during the years remaining to Mr. Toscanini
he should devote himself, at least from the historical point of
view, to records of more significant works; and third, because
we had excellent, worthy, and highly profitable records of
these works by other artists in our active catalog. Again, to be
perfectly honest, I concur in the opinion of those critics who
have said that the maestro is incapable of the tenderness,
humor, and fantasy implicit in *The Nutcracker Suite* and has
no conception whatever of the rhythmic subtleties of the
Strauss waltz. Finally, the best-selling Red Seal record ever
made in all the history of recording was and is Stokowski's
condensed recording of *The Blue Danube*, and a close second
to it is the *Nutcracker Suite* in Stokowski's and other recordings. Neither artistically nor commercially were any new ver-
sions of these recordings needed or justified. Rubinstein's
Tchaikovsky concerto, though not up-to-date technically, is
musically far better than the performance of Horowitz, and
commercially satisfied the market quite well. Fiedler's *Mignon*
overture, issued not long before Toscanini's, enjoyed widespread success, as indeed it should have. The fact that these
recordings were made and issued, and constituted profitable
investments to the company, and were as well matters of pride
and profit to the artists making them, was not of the slightest
interest to Toscanini or his son, who had constituted himself
adviser and protector of his father, though being paid by Victor and later by NBC as a bona fide employee.

Mr. Toscanini was also considerably annoyed by the critics
who kept beating the drum for American music. The maestro
seemed quite unwilling to include any American music in his
programs broadcast by the National Broadcasting Company,
and only under the most sustained pressure did he finally and
grudgingly relent. In so doing, he nevertheless managed to

convey by implication his contempt for American music, choosing to program a dreary opus by a superannuated and expatriated fourth-rate American composer resident in Italy. Subsequently, of course, Mr. Toscanini did include some American works in his programs, and some of them, particularly the *Adagio for Strings* and the *Essay for Orchestra* of Samuel Barber, were beautiful performances of worthy music. Not as much can be said for his uncomprehending performance of Gershwin's *Rhapsody in Blue*, wherein his congenital literal-mindedness was his undoing.

I don't know whether one should consider *The Star Spangled Banner* as unequivocally national, since the tune is American only by adoption. The maestro did perforce play it, since that sterling American, James C. Petrillo, so decreed. Even here a version announced as an orchestration by Mr. Toscanini himself was used. My musical perceptions are not sufficiently acute to enable me to discover wherein this version is superior to various existing ones, or notably different from them. My estimate of the value of this work must be far wrong, however, for a wild-eyed enthusiast of the Middle West was so excited patriotically on hearing Mr. Toscanini's *Star Spangled Banner* that he rushed out and bought a million dollars' worth of war bonds in order to get possession of this precious manuscript. Others preferred a kiss from Betty Grable.

At the tail end of a recording session in New York one day, Mr. Toscanini asked me if he might make a recording of the national anthem. Of course we made it then and there, though we had no idea of using it commercially and no need of it, since we had recordings of the national anthem in every conceivable form, including several by symphony orchestras. Later it developed that Mr. Toscanini was incensed because we had not released his record of *The Star Spangled Banner*, although we never had any intention of doing so, never said we would, and never wanted to do so. It turned out that Maestro wanted this record released with Miss Dorothy Thompson reciting, on the reverse side, one of her more flaming diatribes, the record to be sold for the benefit of the Red Cross. I knew that the company would not countenance such a thing, as it has always studiously avoided aligning itself with any eleemosynary project. Furthermore, it could not discreetly endorse Dorothy Thompson or her opinions, directly or by implication. Finally, we had nothing conducted by Toscanini to put on the reverse side of *The Star Spangled Banner*. I explained these things to Mr. Toscanini and rather than confront him with an impasse, I made several suggestions, to wit: that we use his *Star Spangled Banner* on both sides of the record, but on the reverse side adjust its dynamics to the accompaniment level and superimpose the voice of a great American singer such as John Charles Thomas or Helen Traubel or anyone he might suggest; or that we apply to the reverse side of the label the Philadelphia Orchestra's recording of Sousa's *Stars and Stripes Forever*. The maestro flatly refused to consider the first suggestion, but in the course of a telephone conversation I had directly with him, agreed to the second. Two days later his son appeared in my office and told me that his father positively would not consider having his name appear on the same record with that of Ormandy.

I did not expect that a record of *The Star Spangled Banner*, even by Toscanini, would be very popular. No record of the national anthem, no, not even the one sung by Miss Lucy Monroe with myself conducting the National Symphony Orchestra, has ever enjoyed appreciable sales. If the "Star Spangled Soprano" can't sell *The Star Spangled Banner*, then certainly no one, not even Toscanini, can do it.

As I have said, the slightest objection to his will would cause Toscanini to threaten a severance of relations and a refusal to conduct at all. And yet, even in exercising and applying the sanctions at his disposal he would equivocate with the agile mind of a lawyer, the subtlety of a Jesuit, and the malice of a Florentine poisoner. After his quarrel with Gatti-Casazza he swore never again to enter the Metropolitan Opera House. That did not make it impossible for him to visit the offices of the Metropolitan as advocate for Jarmila Novotná for he brought her to Edward Johnson's office and pleaded with that worthy gentleman to do something for the lovely Czech baroness.[9] Toscanini had ventured into the Metropolitan to achieve something he desired, but technically hadn't gone into the opera house at all!

When, after certain difficulties with Sarnoff, he swore he would not conduct for NBC and for a season didn't—after Sarnoff called his bluff; nevertheless he did conduct that season the NBC Symphony Orchestra—not for NBC, but for the Red Cross. On leaving the Philharmonic he gave assurances that he would never return to compete with it—and the whole musical world knows what happened. But the NBC Orchestra was a radio orchestra, its performances designed not for the immediate audience, but for an invisible world of listeners; therefore, it did not compete with the Philharmonic! He sent explicit word to David Sarnoff on more than one occasion that he would not make records if I were present, though he did so. I was present, but carefully kept out of his way. He knew I was there, but as long as he did not see me I did not exist. I must say that he did, finally, give Sarnoff the choice of no O'Connell as musical director or no contract with Toscanini. Although Sarnoff, as far as I know, took no action on this, it was my resignation that ultimately relieved the situation.

My leaving the position of Victor's musical director, which I have reason to believe was quite gratifying to Toscanini and his camp-followers, was apparently not the answer to all Victor's problems with the maestro. On one occasion, in January 1945, when the NBC Symphony Orchestra had been assembled for the purpose of recording the Seventh Symphony of Beethoven under the maestro's direction, he appeared on the scene obviously in a fury, and after addressing to the orchestra a few exquisite insults such as: that their veins were full of ordure rather than of blood, Maestro kicked a few music stands

---

[9] Novotná was engaged by the Met.

out of his way and stumbled off the stage. Not even the blandishments of Chotzinoff could persuade him to return, and Victor was left holding the bag to the tune of four or five thousand dollars, with a very expensive orchestra engaged for recording but no Toscanini to conduct. Thank God this had never happened during my dealings with the man. However, the resourceful Mr. Macklin Marrow, Victor's musical director at the moment, was not to be baffled by the situation. He sent messengers scurrying to NBC's library for the music of some substitute masterpiece that could be recorded, and thus employ the costly orchestra that sat in the studio twiddling its fingers but not fingering its fiddles. A gem of an overture, exactly of the type that Toscanini himself loves to reveal with all subtlety and finesse, was chosen—the *Light Cavalry* overture of von Suppé. Though Mr. Marrow is a conductor of known ability and experience, the delicate nuances of this masterpiece somehow eluded him, and he turned the stick over to another conductor of possibly superior eminence, Mr. H. Leopold Spitalny, who conducted what I believe turned out to be a successful record of this notable work. This was a rather expensive record. No doubt Victor found it expensive in more than dollars, for Toscanini was shaken by new rages when he found that Spitalny had substituted for him.

I know only one person who has any real influence with Toscanini. That is Margherita De Vecchi. I think Margherita is charming—not with the graceful charms of femininity, but with uproarious honesty, candor, and fearlessness quite extraordinary in a woman. She comes from San Francisco and is the product of the vigorous Italian and Irish strains that have had so much to do with the development of that most beautiful and charming of all American cities. If there is one person in the world of whose devotion the maestro is assured, it is Margherita. There are few, if any, moments of tenderness between them. They argue with the vehemence and the vocabulary of cabdrivers, and their arguments usually end with

Toscanini making his submission. Margherita herself has told me how often her phone rings in the small hours, giving some color to Toscanini's assertion that he sleeps little or not at all.

Margherita is profane, forthright, and domineering. Perhaps it is these qualities that endear her to the master. In truth, he must weary of the concourse of satellites who so persistently "crook the pregnant hinges of the knee" before him: he must delight in a nature so like his own. If he loves anyone, it must be Margherita.

Toscanini is somewhat superstitious, not at all religious. While on occasion his language would suggest that he is on terms of extraordinary intimacy with the Creator and the Mother of Christ, he practices no formal religion. In conversations about Italian politics the references to the Pope made by both Walter Toscanini and his father were couched in such violent language that I have been quite embarrassed; and I am sure there would be sore hearts in the Vatican if it were known there that the maestro and his family censured the Pontiff, not for meddling in Italian politics, but for refusing to do so. One never sees on Toscanini's person or in his private living quarters any of the objects of devotion that good Catholics commonly venerate, though he invariably wears on the little finger of his left hand a ring set with diamonds and rubies in a cruciform design. His superstitions are trifling and harmless. Certain little formulas have to be executed before and after concerts, certain everyday objects have obscure mystical significance, and the maestro chose for each of his children a name beginning with the letter "W"—Wally, Wanda, and Walter. Walter has carried this into the next generation by naming his son Walfredo, but Wanda, in naming her child, interrupted the magic sequence.

TOSCANINI AND THE PHILHARMONIC

Toscanini made his debut in the United States on November 16, 1908, conducting the opera *Aïda* at the Metropolitan. He left the Metropolitan in 1915. He came back in the winter of 1920 for a concert tour with the horrible orchestra of La Scala and made his first appearance with the New York Philharmonic, now the Philharmonic Symphony Society of New York, in 1926. He resigned his directorship of that orchestra in 1936, when most musical organizations were in financial difficulties. I have often wondered about the real reasons that led him to leave the Philharmonic, and I have suspected more than once that the dwindling audiences and the precarious finances of the orchestra may have had something to do with his decision. It is startling to realize now that, at least in the last season of the maestro's tenure with the Philharmonic, it was no trouble at all to get a seat at his concerts, and particularly easy on Sunday afternoons. Those who really understood his unquestioned greatness were faithful to the end, but the first enthusiasms which had so wildly greeted him a few years before did not flame again until nearly the day of his departure.

For some time Victor had wanted technically modern records of Toscanini with the Philharmonic, and I had put a great deal of effort into an attempt at persuading him to make some records before he left, presumably forever. Thanks to the good offices of Arthur Judson and Bruno Zirato, we finally made an agreement and a group of recordings was made. They were completed only a few hours before Mr. Toscanini's departure for Italy, and therefore he had no opportunity to review them before publication. He delegated his right to approve or disapprove the records to a committee composed of Arthur Judson, bruno Zirato, Adolfo Betti (formerly of the Flonzaley Quartet), Maurice van Praag, personnel manager of the Philharmonic, and myself. The records were all passed and approved by this committee. Subsequently Toscanini disagreed violently in the case of one record, but otherwise concurred in our opinion and even ultimately tolerated the one record that was questionable.

When we recorded the Philharmonic in these sessions, and on prior occasions during performances, I had nothing but the happiest relations with Toscanini, and I can only believe that they were workable because they were direct, personal, and soon became intimate. No one came between Toscanini and myself during these proceedings. They were memorable, they were successful, and they were pleasant.

In passing, I should mention here that there has been a great deal of curiosity and impatience because Victor has not, since the first Toscanini-Philharmonic sessions, released a record of the Ninth Symphony of Beethoven conducted by Toscanini. The Victor Company has not been at fault in this, and, in fact, has several times recorded the Ninth under Mr. Toscanini's direction. It has been done on disc, it has been done on film, it has been done on film transferred to disc, at various notable performances. Mr. Toscanini has consistently and rightly rejected the records, usually because of the shortcomings of either chorus or soloists. I rather imagine that Mr. Toscanini would regard the satisfactory recording of the Ninth as his crowning achievement in the gramophonic field, but I mightily respect him for his impatience and dissatisfaction with anything less than a performance worthy of Beethoven and of himself. True enough, the performances we recorded were wildly acclaimed, as public performances. I should not like to embarrass the New York newspaper critics by letting them read their reviews and then having them hear the records. The truth is that there has not been a really great performance of the Ninth Beethoven in New York by Toscanini or anybody else within memory. The records prove it. Such is the Toscanini magic, such the musical myopia of the critics, that even bad performances seem beautiful and good when he conducts.

When Toscanini left the Philharmonic he gave assurances to the management that he would never return to compete with this orchestra, over which he had presided for so many years and with such distinguished success—the orchestra to which he owed his American fame and his American fortune. A little over a year later he was back in New York at the head of a directly competing orchestra. It will be of interest to look into the background of this situation for a moment.

First, consider that the Philharmonic had been for years the mainstay of the Columbia Broadcasting System as far as serious music was concerned. The Columbia Broadcasting System had likewise been the financial bread and butter of the Philharmonic. The National Broadcasting Company had no such attraction to offer, although indeed it had plenty of opportunity to make an arrangement similar to Columbia's with either the Philadelphia or Boston orchestra, either one of which was and is vastly superior to the Philharmonic. The logic of the situation would, I think, have dictated the engagement of an existing great orchestra by NBC, but logic sometimes loses force when personal elements enter. Mr. William S. Paley, head of the Columbia Broadcasting System, and Mr. David Sarnoff, head of the Radio Corporation of America, which controls NBC, are active competitors. Mr. Sarnoff saw an opportunity to achieve a coup for NBC. With this in mind, he dispatched Mr. Chotzinoff to Italy armed with plenipotentiary powers to inveigle Maestro Toscanini into returning to America as head of the NBC Symphony Orchestra. At that time, Mr. Toscanini was living in his island home, "Isola Mia." According to my friend Samuel Barber, at the time Toscanini's house guest, the old maestro had had enough of leisure. If the telephone rang or a cable arrived, he would complain pitifully to Barber that now that he had retired, the cruel world wouldn't leave him alone. But on such days as the little boat brought no mail, the telephone was silent, the cables uncommunicative, Toscanini would complain with equal bitterness that the world had quickly forgotten him. From this it might be deduced that the maestro was a little impatient for activity, energy being the touchstone of his whole nature. When Chotzinoff arrived, therefore, he had a remarkably simple and easy task before him, although he didn't know it.

The terms of the agreement, by the way, were rather interesting. They called for a net fee of four thousand dollars per concert and Mrs. Toscanini suggested that, in addition, the U. S. tax be paid by NBC. At the time, this would amount roughly to six thousand dollars per concert, four thousand dollars of which would be added to the Toscanini bankroll and two thousand dollars to the coffers of Uncle Sam. In addition, an orchestra was to be selected by a man agreeable to Toscanini (Artur Rodzinski), adequate rehearsal time was to be provided, and proper publicity, promotion, and exploitation were to be undertaken. It was distinctly understood that although the orchestra was to be organized by NBC and known as the NBC Symphony Orchestra, it was to be available commercially, along with the services of Toscanini, if NBC could find a customer rich enough to buy it.

In view of the latter provision of the contract, one cannot but be slightly amused at the tribute which Lawrence Gilman pays to Mr. Sarnoff in the opening paragraph of the author's note in his book, *Toscanini and Great Music*. He says: "It is a pleasure for me to avow, at the beginning of this book, an unpayable debt of gratitude to that valiant idealist, David Sarnoff, for having conceived and effected the restoration of Toscanini to the musical life of America—a debt which I share with millions of other music lovers on this continent. My colleague, Samuel Chotzinoff, whose co-operative tact, wisdom, and devotion equipped him as ambassador extraordinary in the successful accomplishment of a difficult task, has likewise earned my gratitude for his part in that formidable enterprise."

Mr. Sarnoff may be a valiant idealist, though in view of my acquaintance with him I might be tempted to enter a dissenting opinion on this point, but I know that he was not quite as idealistic as Mr. Gilman supposed. True, the NBC Orchestra was organized as an instrument for the uniquely gifted hand of Mr. Toscanini; but it was also intended to fill the orchestral needs of NBC, whatever their nature. In sections of various size the NBC Symphony has been and is now daily put at the disposal of any of the dozens of orchestra leaders who may want to use its members on NBC broadcasts of every type—from boogie woogie through soap-operas to "slumber music." This has led to a number of interesting developments, among them the resignation of various fantastically high-salaried players who couldn't stand being whipsawed between Toscanini and Stokowski on the one hand and a dozen obscure conductors and band leaders on the other; and who in some cases made the refusal of impossible financial demands the pretext for their departure.

TOSCANINI AND THE NBC ORCHESTRA[10]

Mr. Toscanini's first engagement with the NBC Symphony had not been in effect very long before the matter of recording developed. Victor had been given to understand, of course, that records would be made with Toscanini and the NBC Orchestra, and we had definitely planned them, though no final arrangements could be made without consulting the conductor about repertoire and other details. Meanwhile, Walter Toscanini came to me and, with a certain conspiratorial air, told me that he had, by the exercise of the most subtle and yet powerful means, persuaded his father to consider making records for Victor. This revelation was less impressive to me than it might have been had I not already known that Maestro Toscanini definitely wanted to make records, inasmuch as he had

[10] I want to relate in some detail the behavior of Mr. Toscanini and those associated with him in various capacities, inasmuch as the story reveals aspects of the maestro's character as man and musician, as well as significant incidents in the recent history of actual and recorded music.

planned to provide an estate for his children's children from
the royalties. However, I accepted Walter's help with what
good grace I could summon, and he was added to our little
Victor staff.

In discussing recordings of Toscanini and the NBC Orchestra, the first matter to come up was: "Where shall it be done?"
I did not ingratiate myself with the engineering department
of NBC, or with Mr. Sarnoff, or with Toscanini, when I went
emphatically on record as being opposed to doing any work in
NBC's large Studio 8H, from which Toscanini's broadcasts
originated. NBC had designed this studio, Toscanini had approved it, and Sarnoff had paid for it; but it was unquestionably one of the most unsatisfactory music rooms, from an
acoustic point of view, I have ever known. It was designed for
use in relation to microphones that were already obsolete, and
I knew that with the type of microphone we were using, any
recordings made in 8H would sound tight, dull, and lifeless.

My suggestions that we record in Carnegie Hall, home of
the Philharmonic, but one of the best music halls in the world,
were emphatically discarded, and it was decided that we
should record in 8H. We did so. The records made there at
that time were and are exactly as I said they would be, and
eventually Toscanini realized this and consented to make subsequent records in Carnegie Hall. Another and more remote
result was that Studio 8H was redesigned and considerably
improved, though even today it is far from an ideal room in
which to make music with large ensembles.

The next question concerned repertoire. Toscanini agreed
with me that he should and would plan his broadcast repertoire, as far as possible, to include works that for musical or
commercial reasons or both were in especial need of recording.
He did no such thing. Consequently, in the first season's programs there was little for us to record, and privately I was glad
of this because, and only because, I knew that we could not do
justice to Mr. Toscanini and his orchestra in Studio 8H.

However, it was during one of these recordings that in an effort to satisfy Toscanini I did something that probably had a bearing on my ultimate fall from his good graces. In a certain passage of the *"Eroica,"* the second oboe had one note and either failed to play it or played it so *piano* that on the record it was inaudible. This was the only defect of which Toscanini complained at the time the records were reviewed, though later on, after he had approved the records and thousands of sets had been sold, he discovered a great many more things he didn't like and was very resentful that nothing was done about them.

But to come back to the missing note. The passage in question was, happily, so exposed that I felt it was possible for us, by the exercise of certain technical means that I need not describe here, to insert the missing note on the master record. Recklessly enough, I told the maestro that we would try to do this. With the co-operation of Robert Bloom, then first oboe of the NBC Symphony, we were successful in doing this, and Mr. Toscanini approved the record. In accomplishing this little trick I had unwittingly opened a Pandora's box, because ever after Toscanini stubbornly maintained that if we could do what we did then, we could change the balance of the orchestra, fortify individual instrumental voices in a *tutti*, and do various other highly desirable but utterly impossible things. When we failed, he was furious. Many records subsequently made by Toscanini with the NBC and Philadelphia orchestras have been relegated to the limbo of forgotten things because the recording art is not sufficiently magical to revise his interpretations for him.

We had few opportunities to record with Toscanini and the NBC Orchestra the material we needed, and presently the Toscanini family became querulous because of the delay in issuing Toscanini-NBC records and the infrequency of such releases. I explained, with what delicacy I could accomplish, why we had not done more recording and why more records had not appeared. My explanation included references to the fact that the maestro's programs had either been so conventional and limited in scope that they provided little material that we had not already recorded by Toscanini or others; or at the other extreme, they had included a great deal of material of, at most, secondary importance, the recording of which would add little to the prestige and profit of either the conductor or ourselves. This explanation was unsatisfactory, and presently a ukase was handed down from on high, commanding us to record during broadcast performances *everything* that Toscanini played. This move seemed to mollify the conductor but resulted in very embarrassing complications for us. Naturally we asked Mr. Toscanini to listen to all the records we made, and though it had been explained to him that virtually all of these records were made for future reference and not for present publication, he did not or would not understand why they could not all be released. To tell him that nearly all this material was already in our catalog and available to the public, some of it on records conducted by himself, was not, to the maestro, a convincing argument; nor was he impressed by our recitation of the difficulties occasioned by wartime conditions.

When, however, Mr. Toscanini elected to conduct a few concerts, usually as public benefits outside of Studio 8H, and in programming them somewhat broadened his repertoire, I thought I saw a way of placating him. For example, he undertook to do an all-Wagner program—I believe as a Red Cross benefit—and I seized the opportunity to have him record Siegfried's Rhine Journey, the Death Music, and the Immolation Scene, as well as some excerpts from *Tristan, Lohengrin,* and other music dramas. These recordings were accomplished and not, thank God, during performances, but in private recording sessions where neither the difficulties superimposed by the presence of an audience nor the exigencies of broadcasting could interfere with us. Most of these records were successful, but the most important of all, the Immolation Scene, involved us in still further troubles with Toscanini.[11] The recordings made as a result of these special public performances had happy results—happy for the quality of the records, and too, for me, inasmuch as they justified my insistence upon recording in Carnegie rather than in NBC's studios. Toscanini admitted this, and seldom has made another record in Studio 8H since hearing the first ones made in Carnegie Hall.

Having won this point, I was emboldened to undertake another project that had long been gestating in my mind. I have referred to the resentment entertained by various American orchestras, their managers, and conductors toward RCA and NBC because of the competition of Toscanini and the NBC Orchestra. Also, it had become quite clear to Victor's court of last resort—the sales department—that an orchestra called the NBC Symphony was sadly lacking in prestige with the public. People who sold and bought records were impressed with Arturo Toscanini's prodigiously exploited name, but the NBC Symphony, as such, had little appeal. The consequence was that sales of Toscanini-NBC Symphony records were disappointing, being far below those of Koussevitzky and the Boston Symphony, or those of Stokowski and the Philadelphia Orchestra; [12] and they continued to be meager until the maestro's son-in-law was persuaded to help. (See page 240.)

A symphony orchestra usually has some local association, and benefits by local support and local pride. If you say Boston Symphony Orchestra or Philadelphia Orchestra or Bach Choir of Bethlehem, Pennsylvania, or even The Chamber Music Society of Lower Basin Street, people have a concept of a real entity actually in being, with flesh-and-blood members, supporters, followers, and enthusiasts. The NBC Orchestra has no reality, any more than the BBC Orchestra or the Victor Symphony Orchestra or the Columbia Broadcasting System

---

[11] For the details of the curious behavior of Toscanini in connection with these records, see page 195.

[12] These orchestras of course had much more extensive catalogs than Toscanini and the NBC.

Orchestra has any reality. I believed that I could kill a number of birds with one stone if I could persuade Toscanini to conduct various American symphony orchestras, and not necessarily the best ones. It seemed to me that this would take some of the sting out of the widely circulating accusation that he had returned here to compete with our people for his own profit, and at the same time his conducting and recording with various orchestras under contract to Victor would be profitable to those orchestras, many of them in serious financial difficulties; and Maestro would earn the gratitude rather than the resentment of their managers and supporters.

I should like to be able to report that Toscanini received this suggestion as a preposterous and impossible one and that I overcame his objections by my persuasiveness and tact, but this was not the case. He listened with interest to my proposal, saw the point, and in principle agreed to carry out the plan. To say that I was astonished at this is an egregious understatement. However, I set to work to make the necessary arrangements.

I turned first to the Philadelphia Orchestra, for a variety of reasons. In the first place, I wanted to help dismiss Toscanini's misgivings about my project by putting at his disposal an orchestra which, in certain respects, has no peer in this country or elsewhere. Secondly, Stokowski had not long before completely severed all connections with the Philadelphia Orchestra, and I wanted to find some means of maintaining its income (as well as the company's) from records, even without Stokowski. Again, its conductor, Eugene Ormandy, was and is a particular friend whose career is a matter of personal interest to me and whose tenure at Philadelphia was, at the time, by no means certain. No one could succeed Stokowski as Ormandy did and expect to start at the level of public interest and commercial success at which Stokowski stopped. It seemed to me that a series of records by Toscanini with the Philadelphia Orchestra would bolster up the orchestra's record income until Ormandy should have time and opportunity to build up a record repertoire sufficient to maintain the orchestra's income from royalties at its very high point.

In order to provide adequate rehearsal, it seemed advisable to persuade Mr. Toscanini to conduct some concerts with the Philadelphia Orchestra. The whole project was very carefully worked out, and upon Mr. Ormandy's invitation Toscanini undertook the concerts and subsequently the recordings.

TOSCANINI AND THE PHILADELPHIA ORCHESTRA

Toscanini entered into the Philadelphia engagement with a great deal of pleasant anticipation and in a highly co-operative mood. He was eager to discuss the programs he should play there, and permitted me to make suggestions with recording requirements in mind. I should point out here that recorders cannot go to any conductor or other artist and demand, off-hand, the performance of the works they want to record. In the case of symphony orchestras, this cannot be done because a great deal of preparation and rehearsal are necessary to recording, and rehearsals are expensive. Rehearsals specifically for recording are prohibitively costly. The logical thing to do, and the thing that all conductors with the exception of Toscanini have been willing to do, is to program the works intended for recording, thereby getting, without extra expense to anyone, two or three full rehearsals and at least two performances in advance of the recording session.

On the occasion of the Philadelphia engagement, however, Mr. Toscanini was exceedingly docile, and nearly every work he played during his visits there was included at my specific request. The conductor was amazed and delighted with the orchestra. Its quickness, agility, musicianship, glorious tone, and unique sonority were a revelation to him, as well they might be, for neither in Europe nor in America had he ever conducted an orchestra the equal of this one at the precise moment of which I speak.[13] At the first rehearsal he went completely through the program without once interrupting the orchestra. At the end he bowed, smiled, told the men that there was nothing he could suggest to improve the performance, and walked off the stage in high good humor. I must add, however, that the honeymoon was of short duration, and the usual tantrums were not long in developing during subsequent meetings of conductor and orchestra.

I spent tens of thousands of the company's money in recording the Philadelphia Orchestra under the direction of Mr. Toscanini. We accomplished, among other things, the recording of a performance of La Mer that is utterly incredible —a performance in which the very essence of ocean is miraculously distilled, under the burning gaze of this musician, into the encompassing circle of a thin black disc. We made a recording of the great C major Symphony of Schubert. The nobility of the performance would make you feel like a better man; its poignant beauty would perhaps invite your tears. We imprisoned in plastic wax and gross metal the ephemeral magic of A Midsummer Night's Dream. The morbid introspections and the unreasoning tears of the "Pathétique," somehow made healthy, rational, and masculine, are inscribed by Toscanini's hand on enduring and infinitely fecund matrices —but I think you will never hear any of this music. I think you will never know the hypnotic loveliness, the rhythms caught in mid-air, the translucent colors of Ibéria as Toscanini gave them to us to set down on wax, or know the grisly terrors or the sweetness and exaltation of death that Toscanini adumbrates from the dark score of Tod und Verklärung. No, not even the raucous vulgarity or the raw earth pigments of his Feste Romane will be vouchsafed to you. Maestro says no.

Dollars were by no means our only expenditure in connection with Toscanini's Philadelphia recordings. We have never

---

13 He had conducted the Philadelphia Orchestra some years prior to this engagement.

approached any recordings with such careful, such painstaking, and such exhaustive preparations of men, machines, and material. The ablest and most experienced recording men were assigned to these sessions. The best recording apparatus, in quadruplicate, was set up in the Academy of Music, hundreds of specially cast wax plates were provided, and for safety's sake, duplicate masters of acetate were made simultaneously with the wax masters. All equipment was tested meticulously just prior to the recording sessions. Only the most advanced recording techniques that we knew were employed. The orchestra was "on its toes," ready and eager to give its very best. The conductor was neither harried nor hurried, and presented himself at the recording sessions apparently in a happy mood. He was to play music that he loved with an orchestra he admired under conditions approaching closely as possible to the ideal. What went wrong? Why must these masterpieces of performance and masterpieces of recording be denied those who love music?

The answer contains three elements: the captious, petulant, and unreasonable criticism by Toscanini of himself, of the orchestra, but mainly of myself and the recording men; the manner in which, under the difficulties of wartime labor conditions, the matrices of Toscanini's Philadelphia recordings were handled in the processing plant; and the activities of Walter Toscanini. To state these reasons so briefly is to oversimplify them. I think fuller explanation, which will never be forthcoming from any source other than this book, is due you.

Toscanini has the right, under his contract, to pass judgment on his own records, and without his approval the company has no right to publish the records. As everyone knows, Toscanini is a demanding person, but more demanding of himself than of anyone else. Paradoxically, I had never, up to the time of the Philadelphia recordings, had any serious difficulty in getting him to approve his records. He would make a recording over and over until it appeared to be satisfactory, but once having put it finally on the wax, he would, as a rule,

approve it. Notable exceptions to this were the previous recordings of the Ninth Symphony, and as I have mentioned,
I could not quarrel with his disapproval of these. Yet he would
not approve a single complete work he recorded with the
Philadelphia Orchestra. Special factors, however, entered into the Philadelphia Orchestra recordings. The Philadelphia
Orchestra was, in Toscanini's mind, Stokowski's orchestra,
and I wonder if he was determined to show the world in general and Stokowski in particular that he could make this
orchestra sound better than Stokowski could. He couldn't,
didn't, and can't, for a variety of reasons, only one of which I
need cite. Toscanini is utterly impatient with, does not understand, and stubbornly refuses to understand, the possibilities
or the limitations of recording and reproduction. He will not
adjust himself to the exigencies of recording. He performs for
recordings exactly as he does for a concert. He will not, by so
much as one decibel, modify his dynamics to either the upper
or lower limitations of recording, nor will he redress orchestral
balance in relation to the conditions under which recorded
music is normally reproduced. All these requirements can be
fulfilled by the recording engineer guided by a musician, but
the Italian conductor forbids any attempt at such adjustment.[14] He lays the performance in your lap, so to speak, and
lets you make the best of it, but woe betide you if it isn't the
best when he hears it reproduced. The maestro does not know,
does not care to know, and refuses to learn, how to operate
a phonograph, but he will fling one of his records on the
turntable, frantically twist a few knobs, and smash his glasses
on the floor when the results don't please him.

Stokowski, on the other hand, thoroughly understands recording from every point of view, including the commercial.
I think he feels that conducting for records is fully as subtle,
worthy, and rewarding an art as conducting in the concert
hall for a present audience, and like the rational and intel-

---

14 I have violated this prohibition a hundred times, and successfully too. If I
had not, there would be no Toscanini records.

ligent man that he is, he has taken the time and given the effort to learn the special requirements of recorded and reproduced music. That is the reason why Philadelphia Orchestra records conducted by Stokowski are utterly unique in the textures and colors of tone, in breadth of dynamic range, and freedom from mechanical or electronic interference and, in general, for sheer beauty of sound. I do not mean to imply that Mr. Stokowski takes an active hand in recording, as has so often been reported. In my dozen years of work with him, he has never entered the recording room. His part is done strictly as conductor, and that is enough. He knows the effect he wants to produce on the record and he knows how to get it by conducting, not by badgering the recording engineers.

Toscanini's excessively severe criticism of his Philadelphia records, then, arose, I think, mainly because in certain respects they did not compare with the best of Stokowski's recordings, or, in fact, with the best of Ormandy's. From a purely performance point of view there was little that any reasonable person could adversely criticize except, perhaps, a few seconds of uncertain ensemble in *Ibéria*, some bad intonation in the vocal parts of the *Midsummer Night's Dream* music, and certain other and inconsequential details.

I do remember suggesting to the maestro during a recording session that the oboe, where it first pronounces the principal theme of the first movement in the Schubert C major, was not sufficiently prominent. Marcel Tabuteau's tone and ultrasubtle nuances are notoriously difficult to record. Sometimes they cannot be apprehended even in concert performance, but conductors, as a rule, are so beguiled by the beauty and finesse of this great artist's work that they leave him severely alone. Ormandy always allows Marcel to play in his own way; perhaps Toscanini felt that he should do likewise. At any rate, he impatiently brushed aside my suggestion. When he heard the proof record, however, he complained of the very thing that we had asked him to correct.

Walter Toscanini helped us a great deal by pointing out

to his father that there is a larger sonority in Ormandy's "Pathétique" than in Toscanini's, and chiefly for that reason the maestro rejected this recording. What Walter pointed out is true. What Walter knew but neglected to point out is that subsequent to the recording by Ormandy of the "Pathétique" we were compelled by our musically very sophisticated engineering and sales brains to limit the dynamic range of all records, and that long before Toscanini recorded with Philadelphia we had been required to make, and had made, all records at a lower level of volume than formerly. This was because of complaints from owners of obsolete phonographs, on which the modern recording with its extended dynamics would not play satisfactorily. For twenty years I have been vociferous in my demands of the company that we record for the best and not for the worst phonographs. I have accomplished exactly nothing in this direction.

Toscanini's criticism of himself and of us was not, however, as serious as the treatment given the wonderful and costly master records in the processing laboratories. Wax and acetate master records went flawless into these laboratories. They emerged pitted, pocked, and perverted. I say perverted because in some instances, in an effort to reduce the scratch that inexpert handling had brought to the records, a polishing stone was run through the grooves, eliminating some of the scratch and all of the high frequencies that give music color and brilliance. Where this was not done, the records sounded like a concerto for fried egg, popcorn, and symphony orchestra. Nevertheless, a substantial number of these records was put into acceptable mechanical condition.

When Toscanini listens to a record he is not particularly conscious of mechanical defects such as crackling and popping sounds, ticks, and scratches. He concentrates on the music. I have the feeling that he actually did approve a good many of the Philadelphia recordings without reference to such mechanical defects. Some of his approvals were transmitted to us through Walter, with the reservation added by Walter that mechanical defects would have to be corrected before the records could be released. The Victor Company accepted Walter's verdicts as his father's, and consequently the release of whatever records may have been approved was delayed while Victor tried to extirpate the mechanical defects in them. The maestro didn't know what was going on, and little by little approached his rather low boiling point because the records hadn't been released. When, after weeks and months of delay, no records appeared, he suspected, I think, some kind of sabotage, probably accomplished by me; and I think his suspicions arose out of the fact that I am a friend and admirer of Stokowski. I have never made a secret of the fact that I am; neither has my relation to Stokowski ever influenced me in the slightest degree in any matter of company business. I have worked with every notable conductor and orchestra in the United States and Canada, and no one connected with these conductors or orchestras has ever complained of any unfairness on my part. Toscanini has a suspicious mind. The thing he suspected could have happened in an opera house, or perhaps in any of the circles where Toscanini feels at home —but not in America; not, certainly, in a commercial organization like Victor. I think he came to suspect that my whole Philadelphia project was engineered as a plot to undo him. The entire Toscanini retinue "whose own hard dealings teaches them suspect the thoughts of others" always seemed to have a psychopathic fear of intrigue and plottings.

I put this aspect of the situation quite definitely aside and reported in meticulous detail not once but several times to all the Victor head men, including my immediate superiors, research and engineering forces, the sales people, Walter, and even to his father. I analyzed each record in detail, mechanically and musically, pointing out that while nearly all had serious *mechanical* defects, few if any had serious *musical* or *recording* defects, and that a great many of the faults brought about in processing or pressing test records could be, with care and time and labor, eliminated or greatly modified. I made it clear that out of all the Philadelphia records we did have a number of sets of extraordinary musical, historical, and commercial value. I added my opinion that in the matter of superficial defects we should make compromises with our standards and ask the Toscaninis to do likewise, since an opportunity to get such records would not likely appear again.

Little or nothing was done, however, to correct the corrigible flaws in the records; time went on, no records appeared, and nobody seemed to be able to give Maestro a satisfactory explanation of the situation. Indeed, nobody could approach him except Walter, and there were times when *he* couldn't. When he did, his story must have been less than convincing because the whole problem finally was brought to the direct and personal attention of the head of the Radio Corporation of America. Representatives of various departments at Victor were asked to meet with Mr. Sarnoff at his house one afternoon and clear the whole matter up. We met on the day appointed.

My contacts with Mr. Sarnoff during my Victor connection were rather infrequent, never intimate, and always friendly. My opportunities to observe him and the conclusions I drew from my observation do not and cannot produce a three-dimensional picture of this very remarkable man. Of his brilliance, imagination, and daring as an organizer, there can be no question, and he has conceived and realized a number of projects that influenced for the better the course of music in America. Regardless of the accuracy of Lawrence Gilman's estimate of Mr. Sarnoff as an idealist, the fact is that a great symphony orchestra under a great conductor came into being because David Sarnoff thought of it and provided the means for its existence. The help which ten years of broadcasting of the Metropolitan Opera by NBC accomplished for the opera organization would really be difficult to measure. As for the union of the phonograph with the radio industry, I have always felt that this was a kind of shotgun wedding and that the young and vigorous radio industry never entered into it with much enthusiasm. I am informed by Mr. Sarnoff personally that this is not and never has been the case; that it was he who conceived and accomplished the unification of Victor and RCA because he firmly believed in the logic and effectiveness of such a union. I am happy, after twenty years of misapprehension, to stand corrected.

Mr. Sarnoff is always an interesting person. His rather Oriental countenance can assume the inscrutable aspect of Buddha, the ingratiating smile of Billiken, or the hard-eyed, implacable severity of the great business executive. But he is really at his best when the Napoleonic afflatus is upon him, as it was on this occasion. Gone was the persuasive eloquence that has so often beguiled conventions of tube buyers into larger and larger orders; gone the eloquence with which he had so often charmed the genial gatherings of Victor distributors; gone the urbane assurances that boards of directors have heard, spellbound; gone the suave confidence that had reduced to pliable and willing servants the supercautious bankers J. and W. Seligman, the steel-hard and chromium-smooth lawyers Sullivan and Cromwell. In short, here was no beating about the bush. "D. S." strode furiously up and down the room, discharging vast clouds of cigar smoke along with commands, threats, exhortations, and injunctions upon all present. *"The words of a wise man's mouth are gracious. . . ."* Ostensibly this meeting was called to enable Mr. Sarnoff to find out why the Toscanini records had not been issued and who was at fault. As it turned out, the boss couldn't wait to hear anybody's explanation, but contented himself with a two-pronged *Diktat* imposed as of that moment on his quailing guests: first, *all Toscanini records, regardless of any commitment to any other artist or any consideration of the necessities imposed by announcement, advertising, distribution, and the like, must be put on the market within thirty days.* Second, if he could find out that any person in the organization was delaying the execution of this command— well, "that person wouldn't remain in the company for five minutes"; and if the guilty person turned out to be Arturo Toscanini, well, the maestro would be fired likewise.

Parenthetically it must be said, in explanation of Mr. Sarnoff's imperious attitude and impossible demands, that he did not and could not know all the details, mechanical and otherwise, of a business so vast and complicated as RCA; that he did not really intend to interfere with our commitments to other artists, but only, in all probability, to enforce his own commitments to Toscanini. He was doubtless under considerable pressure from that quarter; he was ill, feverish, and therefore pardonably short-tempered at the time of this interview, and one may suspect that the inability or unwillingness of his subordinates to give him satisfactory answers to problems that should have been theirs but had been thrust upon him, quite infuriated him. Under happier conditions, a complete and straightforward story from those concerned would have brought positive action from the General; but it would have been helpful as well as positive, constructive even if violent.

Marveling, perhaps, at the absurdity of Mr. Sarnoff's ultimatum, aghast at the threatened terrors of separation from the payroll, and recoiling in horror at the chief's final *lèse-majesté*, the group took refuge in awed silence—all except two—Walter and myself. Neither of us had much to say, but at this point I protested to Mr. Sarnoff that what he demanded was a physical impossibility. Mr. Sarnoff wanted to know why and then, with characteristic impatience, didn't wait to discover the reasons but modified his demand and made it three months instead of thirty days. In spite of his decision and the sanctions with which it was fortified, nothing resulted but more confusion; nobody, not even Arturo Toscanini, was fired; and not one of the Toscanini-Philadelphia records has yet [15] been made available to the public. "*And the end of his talk is mischievous madness.*"

---

[15] May 1947.

Maestro has scarcely spoken to me since, but he has spoken of me in some detail and, I must add, with something less than the most scrupulous regard for charity or accuracy.

I recite the particulars of this whole story because, first of all, it can hardly be without interest to the many thousands who have anticipated with such interest records by the Philadelphia Orchestra under Toscanini's direction. Again, it illustrates how the maestro's musical judgment, so widely regarded as being of practically papal infallibility, can be vitiated and perverted by his own jealousies, suspicions, and susceptibility to the sly intrigues of those who surround him.

When I resigned as musical director of Victor at the end of March 1944, one of my very few regrets was that the Philadelphia project seemed to have ended in a complete debacle. My own conscience was clear. I knew that we had taken every ordinary and some extraordinary measures to assure a series of recordings that would give the world of music a living memory of a great musician at the zenith of his powers. I know that my colleagues, the recording engineers, gave their ultimate effort and made no error. I know that our investment of our most devoted effort, thought, care, equipment, material, and money has been desperately jeopardized or irrevocably lost, partly because of the maestro's own personal and musical faults; partly because of the unwanted, unwarranted, unintelligent, and utterly unnecessary intrusion of others; and mostly because of the unfortunate wartime manufacturing conditions that allowed so many of these precious records to be debased and defiled beyond redemption.

TOSCANINI IN GENERAL

In this country there is a multitude of people who regard Toscanini as "the greatest conductor in the world." A considerable number of musicians, including even some conductors, entertain this opinion, and among the musically

unwashed it is a belief as respectable as that which holds
motherhood sacred. The ever-active Toscanini promotion and
publicity, and the ubiquitous voice of the radio, have often
given forth this dictum; therefore, it must be so. There have
been occasions when I could myself entertain the rather reckless suggestion—but what is Mr. Toscanini's opinion?

I am sure that Mr. Toscanini does not consider himself the
greatest conductor in the world. I am sure that he regards
himself as the *only good conductor* in the world. "*Natura il
fece, e poi ruppe la stampa.*" [16]

This is by no means the arrogant assumption that it may
seem superficially. As a matter of fact, every conductor at one
time or another considers himself the best of all conductors.
If a man is not convinced that he brings to the music he plays
something superior, something individual, something a little
beyond what anyone else has perceived in the music, he
shouldn't dare to be a conductor and probably wouldn't. I
think that Mr. Toscanini, according to his principles and
perceptions—and these are always firm, fundamental, uncom-
promised, and clear—is the world's greatest conductor and *is
the world's only good conductor.* He is simply, completely,
sincerely, and irrevocably convinced that there is only one
way to play a musical work, and that way is *his* way. I should
amend that and say that he believes his way is the composer's
way, and he arrives at this decision by reading every musical
work in the most rigidly and meticulously literal fashion. If
you can believe that a printed score, with its relatively few
marks of expression, with its almost total lack of the power
to suggest the suppleness of a phrase, the quality or color of
a musical texture, or the psychological compulsions that have
no expression but in musical sound itself, can delineate the
spiritual essence of a musical work, then you can reasonably
believe that Mr. Toscanini has no peer among living conductors.

---

[16] Nature made him, then broke the mold. Ariosto: *Orlando Furioso.*

But I think a literal reading of almost any score can lead one rather far astray. The style, the rhythmic subtleties, and the whole spirit of Gershwin's *Rhapsody in Blue* completely eluded the maestro, because he insisted upon playing this not too important piece of music precisely as it was written. The waltzes of Strauss in his hands certainly lose all traces of the Viennese *Schlamperei* with which some conductors endow them in nauseating degree; but on the other hand, this light-hearted music comes forth under Mr. Toscanini's direction with no more lightness or suppleness than one hears when it is played by a little man with a monkey and a hurdy-gurdy. In music wherein the parts are so written that if played precisely and with proper attention to indicated dynamics they sound with pellucid clarity, and where the form is so rigidly established that any deviation from it becomes an intolerable gaucherie, Toscanini is indeed supreme. Maestro's Mozart, Haydn, and Beethoven come into this area of his musical operations, but even here he has sometimes been led astray by the verbatim quality of his readings. He worships a Beethoven score as if it had come with the ink still wet from the hand of that great man: ignoring the fact that there probably is no Beethoven score published that hasn't been tampered with, in which dynamic and metronomic marks haven't been inserted by some obscure hack in the employ of Breitkopf and Härtel or other publishers. He is deeply and properly concerned with dynamics, and dynamic contrasts rather than shadings; with utter precision as to attack and release and absolute justice as to the duration of a note; with vitality and definition of rhythms and with *tempi* so just as always to be critical—that is to say, balanced on the razor-edge that lies between "too fast" and "too slow." His dynamics, though, are absolute and untempered, I think. A *fortissimo* is always "all out" and a *pianissimo* is always just at the threshold of hearing. He himself has said that one should play an "ff" so strongly that he can't hear his partner and a "pp" so softly that his partner can't hear him. Here is a masterpiece of clear

and practical definition. It is likewise wrong. Must "ff" always
and inevitably signify the limit of one's capacity to generate
tone, or "pp" the limit of one's ability to suppress it? I do not
think so, and I do think that it is this concept of dynamic contrast which makes Toscanini's music so sharply black and
white, which makes, for instance, his Mozart so often seem
granitic, driven, steel-skeletoned, merciless, and cold. Even
this kind of playing has its uses, and if I were in a position to
do so I should recommend to all conductors that they study
Toscanini's records as virtually perfect representations of
music that sounds precisely as written, and I should further
recommend that they should go on from there and interject
some element of humanity and warmth.

Another aspect of Toscanini's music that is disappointing
to me, is a certain grayness so far as orchestral color is concerned. In countless hours I have spent at Toscanini rehearsals and recordings, I have never once heard him make a
suggestion or a criticism to any player respecting the quality
of his tone. I can readily believe that this indifference to the
emotional values of tone color springs from the sources I have
indicated above—from the conviction, perhaps, that the music,
if played precisely as written, will speak for itself. If you think
that it will, then I suggest that you compare the performance
of, let us say, the Tchaikovsky "Pathétique" by Koussevitzky
and Toscanini; or the performance of the Tristan prelude
and Liebestod by Toscanini and Stokowski; or the performance of La Mer by Koussevitzky and Toscanini; or the performance of the Brahms Second by Ormandy and Toscanini.
I will confess that I, probably like you, have at times been so
beguiled, even in the performances I have named, by the
maestro's ageless vigor, the beauty of his stage presence, and
the knowledge of his sincerity that I have momentarily agreed
with him in his own estimate of his standing among conductors. But the modern phonograph record is a merciless critic,
and having had opportunities to study recorded music such
as few people have had, I must finally dissent.

Winthrop Sargeant, in a sympathetic essay published in the magazine *Life*,[17] has some very interesting things to say about Toscanini, his talents, and methods. Unfortunately, a fair proportion of these things are, conservatively speaking, inaccurate. The statement that "the Toscanini beat is . . . the most expressive, accurate, and lucid vehicle for conveying musical thought that could be imagined" is flatly contradicted by many players, some of them great players, whom I have questioned. If this statement were true it would not be necessary for Toscanini to rehearse a single phrase for an hour before getting it the way he wants it—and this has happened, to my personal knowledge. Toscanini's downbeat, that is to say, the first beat in a measure, is decisive and clear, as a rule, but from then on it is often difficult to locate. An orchestra thoroughly accustomed to him has little difficulty, but even the most alert, responsive, and sympathetic orchestra in the world—the Philadelphia—has great difficulty, and that is true of even those players in it who have often played under Toscanini.

Toscanini talks very little at rehearsal. He seems to prefer to play a passage over and over again without explanation until he gets it the way he wants it. This is often baffling to the players and infuriating to the maestro. Yet what talking he does usually consists of the eloquent maledictions, picturesquely sacrilegious oaths, and plain coarseness to which modern Italian—"that soft bastard Latin"—so effectively lends itself. In recording sessions, however, Mr. Toscanini is a little more explicit. We play through a section of the work to be recorded, and usually all goes well. Nevertheless, at the stopping point Maestro will pick up the score, then with an amiable if rhonchisonus *dunque!* (now!) and a crepitant *critica!* (for the criticism!), he will point out in rather elliptical English that he wants a little more second trumpet here, better ensemble there, more power in the *fortissimo*, and so on.

---

[17] January 17, 1944, p. 76.

He may even rehearse a bar or two but usually will go ahead
and make the record. In the course of time Maestro came to
take my word for it that a record did or did not have to be
repeated and, as a matter of fact, we did not have to repeat
records very often.

Mr. Sargeant, in his article, makes a statement I consider
utterly preposterous. He says: "The 'old man' can pick out
and correct an individual fiddler's intonation in the midst of
a heavily orchestrated score, or detect instantly the absence
of a minute shading in the third-clarinet part while the rest
of the orchestra is playing full blast." Under some circumstances, any moderately musical person could do the same
thing with respect to the fiddles, but under the circumstances
of an orchestra concert or an opera performance, Toscanini
can't do it, and neither can anyone else. Line up forty fiddlers
so that they are each equally distant from the conductor and
have thirty-nine of them play in unison and one play a dissonance and any musical half-wit can put his finger on the
culprit. Seat the same number in the grouping customary for
the orchestra, add the varying distance to the varying phase
of the sound waves that reach the conductor, plus the varying
intensity of tone from each instrument, plus the varying
quality of tone from each instrument, and plus several other
variants, and nobody can identify, except by sheer guessing
or through details other than aural, the atonic bum.

Toscanini's ears, however acute they may be, are subject to
the same laws of physics that govern those of ordinary human
beings, a fact that seems difficult for his worshippers to
apprehend. It may be conceded that in a great orchestral *tutti*
he or any other musician, from the vantage point of the
podium, could hear an incorrect or dissonant note from the
third clarinet (though Toscanini's own records prove that he
has been ignorant of or has disregarded many such lapses),
but even from the advantageous location of the conductor the
composite sound wave produced by a hundred instruments
playing "full blast" is of a form and intensity that defy analysis

by ear. This is ten times more certain when the matter in question is "a *minute shading*" in the third-clarinet part or any other part; and what would the third clarinet be doing with "minute shadings" when the orchestra is playing "full blast"? Who would know, or care, or hear?

Most conductors observe a certain punctilio in referring to their colleagues. It is a convention of their craft that if they comment at all on other conductors they speak with what meager generosity they can summon; though at the same moment they may be assiduously plotting to get the other fellow's job. Toscanini is guilty of no such hypocrisy. I have heard him excoriate conductors from Abendroth to Zimbalist without reserve, without charity, without compromise, and without malice. For this I find no fault in the man. I have indicated elsewhere that he quite candidly believes that he is not merely the greatest conductor in the world, but the only good one. It would therefore be just as illogical for Toscanini to admit good in another conductor's interpretations as it would be for the Pope to concede virtue to Shintoism. The nearest thing to praise of another conductor I have ever known the maestro to utter was, oddly enough, directed to my insignificant self after I had conducted, in his absence, two weeks of the NBC Symphony. The maestro heard the broadcasts and sent word, as usual by Walter: "Not so bad." I considered this absolutely fulsome. I recall too that when I next talked with him, weeks later at his home, he thoroughly, exquisitely, and not unkindly dissected my playing of each and every work. I could not accept all of his opinions, but discreetly kept my ears open and mouth shut. I was and am grateful for his interest and admonition.

When I was engaged for these concerts, by the way, I was simply terrified lest Mr. Toscanini himself should come to my rehearsals. Fortunately, he was out of the country at the time, which spared me the ordeal which might have developed from the distressing habit—attending other conductors' rehearsals —which maestro had acquired. It must be very disconcerting.

Various conductors have "sweated it out" in the presence. As for his own rehearsals in America, admittance—except for a favored few of the critics, two or three friends of the moment, the signora, and perhaps a score of music-hungry and lean-pursed refugees—is difficult. In Europe, however, you can buy your way in for a few American pennies.

I think that Mr. Toscanini has had a baneful effect on musical beliefs and standards in America. He is not always right. Unfortunately, the exploitation of his name by NBC and Victor has convinced a myriad audience that he is always right. The innocent, unthinking, and musically underprivileged who crowd Studio 8H when Toscanini conducts and the millions more who listen to their radios go into ecstasies no matter what the maestro does. To a judicious musician this is ordinarily painful and pitiful. On occasion it is infuriating, especially when Toscanini essays music to which there is no guide but his own taste and his own inner spirit. The quality of these were revealed, embarrassingly, I think, on Easter Sunday of 1945, when with a soulless choir and a misguided orchestra he directed a performance of the final chorus of the *St. Matthew Passion* of Bach. The essential quality of this music, with its singular combination of tenderness, pity, and triumph, music in which Bach, as it were, holds in his arms the bleeding body of the Saviour and comforts Him as a father would a pain-tormented child—the essence of this music, I say, completely eluded Toscanini. His conception of it revealed him as a man of exquisite, ineffable, and almost infallible vulgarity—a peculiarly Italianate and melodramatic and theatrical vulgarity, exposed in a variety of musical horrors from the "wah-wah" effect in the chorus to the labored and obvious expansion and contraction of orchestral phrasing and the incredibly cheap overemphasis on the self-significant dissonance near the end. No human heart that is reached and humbled and sobered by Bach's piteous peroration can respond with the crass exuberance of shouts and handclapping, yet this tortured performance, a cross between two theatrical misconceptions—the Met at its worst and MGM at its best —drew salvos of applause and hysterical bravoes which in themselves damned it. *"Forgive them, for they know not what they do."*

KIRSTEN
FLAGSTAD

⊷§ Kirsten Flagstad §⊷

IN THIS BOOK I have written about certain people because they are famous, eccentric, notorious, contemptible, or otherwise interesting, either as artists or *in propriae personae*. Kirsten Flagstad is an exception. Hers is not precisely a glittering personality, though an amiable one; and with respect to her singing I find it possible to control my enthusiasm. I introduce her briefly here because perhaps the most interesting thing you have heard about her is untrue: the Nazi sympathies that have been imputed to her, both directly and through implication, by some of her colleagues and many of the public.

Elsewhere I have mentioned the ineptitude of musicians as politicians. I add here that in their political activities musicians are generally amoral, erratic, inconsistent, and often actuated by greed, selfishness, and even baser motives. I should hesitate to assert that ordinary politicians are notably innocent of these defects, but among musical politicians these qualities are more evident, for all musicians are congenital exhibitionists; therefore their defects are more obvious. They are vicious politicians, however, for two other reasons. American orchestral musicians are preponderantly of European birth or European immediate ancestry. Many of them do not comprehend the abstract ideas of fair play, free speech, free conscience, because they have been exposed to such concepts for a rather brief time. They are quick enough to sense the advantages to themselves that accrue from these principles, but they are not so quick to concede the same rights to the other fellow. Musicians are all either dictators at heart, or they yearn for a dictator. A musician is either a tyrant, or he must have a tyrant to curse; otherwise he is not happy. This is understandable, I think, because musicians, like other artists, are under an irresistible compulsion to express *themselves,* and are therefore logically intolerant of anyone else's expression. This is an admirable, desirable, and necessary attitude in art, for an artist must be invincibly convinced that *he* is right; but when it extends to other human activities it can be dangerous and troublesome.

Another influence that makes musicians bad politicians is the fact that so many of them have been closely touched by the spread of the Nazi blight. No one will quarrel with a musician who has been driven from his home or whose blood relatives have been abused by the perverted powers of Germany and Italy. To be intolerant of Nazism is normal and respectable. To extend this intolerance to innocent or helpless individuals is neither. As a musician, I am ashamed to confess that some of my colleagues have used our American loathing of Nazism and Fascism to bring about the embarrassment of a rival, the extirpation of a personal enemy, or even for objects as mean and contemptible as personal gain or social advancement. A whispered "He's a Nazi" or "He's a Fascist" can do and, in cases that I know, has done serious injustice and damage. Ezio Pinza, on flimsy evidence, was pilloried as a Fascist, and was long detained on Ellis Island though no crime or misdemeanor was ever proved against him. Testimony that he was sympathetic with the Fascists eventually was assayed as the merely malicious talk of a peevish woman, to which one of Pinza's colleagues at the Metropolitan generously contributed.

The case of Wilhelm Furtwängler too is interesting. His engagement was suggested by Charles Triller, a director of the Philharmonic; and by unanimous vote of the board this man, who is unquestionably one of the three or four greatest living conductors, was chosen to succeed Toscanini. Furtwängler, though holding a post [1] under the Nazi regime, which had taken control of music as of everything else in Germany, was neither a member of the National Socialist Party nor in sympathy with it. These facts were known to the directors of the Philharmonic and to most people in informed musical circles. Nevertheless, after having been officially invited, Furtwängler was denied the conductorship of the Philharmonic because of agitation organized against him on the ground that he was a Nazi.

Furtwängler had accepted the invitation in good faith. No one had inquired concerning his political beliefs; nor, in my opinion, had anyone a need or a right to do so. Nevertheless, I do not think that Furtwängler would ever actually have come to New York, for his position was, and no doubt is, exceedingly difficult. He confided somewhat later to a musician friend of mine, a renowned singer, that he never had been a member of the Nazi Party and had no sympathy with it; that he envied her the freedom (she was a Swedish subject) that permitted her boldly to refuse engagements in Germany; that he wished he could do likewise; that he would love to accept the New York appointment and get out of Germany forever, but was certain that if he did so, the Nazis would hold his aged father as hostage; and he could not bear to be the instrument of his father's torture and probable death. Furtwängler knew that if he did come to New York he would be questioned pretty closely about politics. If he could be quoted as less than forthright in his condemnation of the Nazi regime, he would be in trouble with us. If he did adversely criticize it, he could consider himself the mediate cause of his father's death. His behavior, then, did not conform with the ideal of heroism, but it was human, weak, understandable, and therefore, I think, forgivable.

The musicians, and the people who for ulterior reasons in-

---

[1] To which he was appointed without his knowledge or consent, while absent on tour in the Near East.

terest themselves in music, can hardly congratulate themselves on behaving more nobly than Furtwängler. They were willing and eager to damn a man, and almost mortally injure the Philharmonic Symphony, without convincing evidence, or any evidence at all—and this to serve no democratic or American ideal but merely to promote their own selfish purposes. If I must concede honesty of purpose to some of them, I must at once accuse them of ignorance and stupidity; for in their hatred of Fascism they employed the characteristic methods of Fascism. These very people are those who subscribe to the most resounding euphuisms on our tolerance of race, creed, and color. They will agitate laws compelling fair employment practices. They will enthusiastically swear allegiance to our government that guarantees any accused man the right of a fair trial, but individuals they happen to resent are damned, untried and unheard; discarded, despised, and rejected.

The Nazis more than decimated their best orchestras when they eliminated Jewish musicians, and the musicians' protests on both sides of the Atlantic were loud, long, and piteous. Rightly so; but it is difficult to account for the inconsistency that raised the hue and cry after Furtwängler because he conducted Nazi-controlled orchestras in Germany, and at the same time elicited lamentations for those musicians who, for racial reasons, were not permitted to play for their Nazi masters, though they were eager to do so. These Jewish musicians were compelled to leave their orchestras and we protested; Furtwängler was morally compelled to conduct, and we cursed him for it. Was conducting for the Nazis a vice, and fiddling for them a virtue?

We complacently congratulated ourselves on our tolerance when we continued to play in our concert halls and opera houses the music of the great poet of Nazi ideology and Hitler's favorite composer, Richard Wagner. This must have been on the theory that the only good Nazi is a dead Nazi. I subscribe to this theory, and to the theory that hell will yawn as hungrily for us as for Hitler if we imitate his methods and retaliate in kind. If Furtwängler was artistically qualified—and he was—he should have been brought here to head the Philharmonic regardless of his politics. Personally, had I had the power I should have brought him here even if he were known to be a Nazi. I should have done so if only to indicate to the Germans and to the world that America has no fear, and that Americans do not descend to that attitude which exiled Mann and Einstein and thousands of others to our country and kept Furtwängler miserably in his own.

It is difficult to track down the origin of the malicious talk concerning Mme Flagstad and her political beliefs. There is some indirect evidence that her husband, Henry Johansen, was at least acceptable to Vidkun Quisling and his German overlords, and when I talked with him years ago he was outspoken in his admiration of the Germans. Yet even he may not have been a thoroughly convinced Nazi, for early in 1945 he himself was imprisoned by the Germans. After the Germans were thrown out of Norway, Johansen was imprisoned by his own countrymen and, I believe, died in jail. The story that Mme Flagstad departed America because of her Nazi sympathies is absolutely false, and this I know from my own conversations with the singer. The truth is that she wanted to go home to her husband long before there was any apparent danger of war, or very serious concern about Nazism in this country. She was tired of singing, tired of Wagner, tired of the Metropolitan, and she longed to settle down quietly with her husband in her own land. She did postpone her departure, partly at the importunities of the Metropolitan management, partly because she wanted to see her daughter, who loved the United States, married and securely established in this country.[2]

My relations with Mme Flagstad were always friendly and

---

[2] Flagstad's daughter is now married to an American businessman and lives in Bozeman, Montana.

cordial, though not intimate. I knew her well enough, however, to deduce that temperamentally and spiritually she would be incapable of entertaining in her clean and simple mind a thought that smacked of Nazism. Mme Flagstad is neither brilliant nor profound, but she is invincibly honest and decent. When she gave her word [3] via transatlantic telephone to her friend and accompanist, Edwin McArthur, that she had no Nazi sympathies, had not sung for the Germans, and had not been in Germany except in transit from Switzerland to her Norwegian home, I believed her. Perhaps it is of no practical importance to Mme Flagstad whether or not we think she is a Nazi, but I should like, as far as I can, to help keep her memory clear, clean, and happy.

Mme Flagstad contributed more, I think, than any other individual to the resuscitation of the Metropolitan Opera. Whether or not this was a desirable objective is beside the point. The Met was well on the way to a condition of desuetude. Even the most die-hard stockholders seized an opportunity to unload their financial obligations, while cannily preserving (just in case!) those seating privileges and similar matters to which these obligations were supposed to entitle them; but cobwebs hung in the boxes. David Sarnoff gave the Met some NBC time, and after several solicitations from the Metropolitan became a member of the board, but even his unquestioned sagacity didn't help. The Wagnerian opera particularly had long been deteriorating; nor could the overstuffed Melchior and lesser heavyweights accomplish much to decelerate the process of decay. Flagstad did. The sudden incidence of this cold, rather inflexible, brilliant voice, powerful and broad-ranged, well routined in the Wagnerian music drama, upon the bored or outraged ears of those who persisted in attendance at the Met, was as refreshing as a bottle of sparkling, ice-cold Evian to a man with a *Katzenjammer*.

---

[3] Reported to me in detail.

Through Mme Flagstad's success interest in opera generally was stimulated. The Met was saved.

Mme Flagstad contributed more than a little to the revival of interest in recorded music; she did not initiate it, for recording had for some time been in a healthier state than it had known for many years previously. Yet Victor itself had not regained confidence in recorded music, and got little encouragement from the masterminds of RCA. Not even the NBC Artists Bureau, then Flagstad's managers, had the enterprise to approach Victor in the matter of recording, notwithstanding the fact that the country from coast to coast was ringing with Flagstad's voice and Flagstad's triumphs. It was necessary to exert considerable pressure in persuading Victor to offer a recording contract to Mme Flagstad; but eventually I accomplished this, and her managers finally signed a contract with Victor for her as casually as if she were the veriest tyro.

Mme Flagstad's first recordings were disappointing to me, because at the time we could not afford the use of an adequate orchestra or the rental of a suitable room in which to record. Regardless of these handicaps, at her first session Mme Flagstad made four double-faced records. She worked steadily, stubbornly, soberly, ably, until she felt satisfied with her performance. She completed the records in three hours, and I assure you they represented a tremendous amount of hard and conscientious effort. Afterward I had every reason to believe that she might feel exhausted, and so I suggested that since it was late in the afternoon and she was starving, at least a cup of tea might be in order. Mme Flagstad firmly vetoed tea, but indicated a certain interest in cocktails, so we adjourned to the Sert Room of the Waldorf. There was a susurrus of feminine excitement as we entered the room: "Flagstad, that's Flagstad," and Mme Flagstad was quite the center of attention. When we were seated I asked if she wasn't tired. She said: "No, not at all if you mean vocally; but you know, I do feel dreadfully tired right here." "Right here" was a point located about five-sixths of the distance between Mme Flagstad's very sturdy knee and her even more impressive hip. "Oh," I said, "I know conductors' feet get tired but I didn't suppose that using your voice would fatigue your leg muscles." "Yes," she said, "right here—feel! The muscle is all stiffened up." I gingerly poked a finger in the general direction of the lady's lap, but not satisfied with this tentative exploration, she very innocently, before the eyes of two hundred curious women, took my hand and clapped it hard against the inside of her thigh, saying: "No, *there* is the place! Can't you feel that muscle?" I could, did, and damned near died under the lubric stares of two hundred Park Avenue felines—but no one was embarrassed except myself.

This incident was rather typical of Mme Flagstad's behavior generally. She is completely honest, direct and innocent to the point of naïveté. She took the most ingenuous delight in her prodigious success in America, particularly because, I suppose, European opera houses, whose audiences had been quite familiar with her for years, had never regarded her as exactly a star. She knew that there were singers at the Met certainly her equal and probably her superior, as artists; and she never quite understood why, as an imported artist, she should be regarded as a goddess. This could have been accounted for, perhaps, had she been a discovery of the Metropolitan Opera management, as those precious gentlemen would have you believe she was. As a matter of fact, her voice was no stranger to those acquainted with recorded music, for it was available on records under the name of Kirsten Flagstad Hall years before Madame ever set foot in America. These records were not impressive; there was nothing in them to indicate that the singer's smooth, bright voice would ever awaken the enthusiasm of the American public. Had I been more enterprising or had Mme Flagstad Hall's records been mechanically better, Victor might have anticipated the Metropolitan's "discovery" by several years.

It has been noted that Mme Flagstad's first records for

Victor did not fairly represent her. The brilliance and amplitude of her voice were certainly not of such a mean degree as to be captured in an oppressively small studio or clearly outlined against the kind of *schrammel* orchestra the Victor Company grudgingly provided. The public, while it welcomed records—any records—by Flagstad, was quite conscious of the musical and technical shortcomings of her first efforts under the Victor label. Madame herself was pleased with them, and I was ashamed. For this reason I badgered Victor with such persistence that I was finally able to provide for Mme Flagstad the personnel of the Philadelphia Orchestra and Mr. Eugene Ormandy as accompanist and the acoustically beautiful Academy of Music as a recording chamber. I wanted to record Flagstad in a way that would do her justice musically and technically; I put at her disposal the world's best conductor-accompanist and one of the world's greatest orchestras; I provided every detail of facility and background that could contribute to the making of really distinguished recordings, and I had high hopes.

At the time I was not conscious of the strong friendship that had sprung up between Mme Flagstad and her accompanist, Edwin McArthur. McArthur was one of the ablest accompanists in the profession. He is a pianist of conspicuous ability in a technical sense, and a mentor and coach whose advice in matters of musical taste, interpretation, tradition, and kindred matters could profitably be noted by any singer. Flagstad conceived a warm and friendly affection for Edwin. At the same time there grew within her a powerful feeling of gratitude and affection for America and Americans because of the warmth of her welcome here and the fortune our country poured into her hands. When, therefore, McArthur made known to Mme Flagstad his ambition in the direction of conducting she saw an opportunity to repay in some measure the generosity exhibited toward her by our country and our countrymen. She determined to use her own suddenly acquired and powerful prestige to promote the career of a young and talented American musician, and naturally the musician she selected was McArthur. For the generosity of her impulse and the purity of her motive I salute Mme Flagstad, but I cannot congratulate either Flagstad or McArthur for wisdom or discretion. Having conceived this idea, Flagstad pursued it with invincible persistence and bovine stubbornness, while McArthur exploited the situation with understandable and, I suppose, pardonable eagerness. The singer carried her enthusiasm to the point where she would refuse an engagement with orchestra unless McArthur was engaged to conduct for her. Her power at the box office was reflected in managers' offices, and she was able to impose her will with regard to McArthur not only upon various symphony orchestras with which she— and he—appeared, but even upon the august Metropolitan Opera Association as well. If I were to name the orchestra conductors who were distressed and humiliated by Flagstad's generous but ill-advised behavior, I would have to include almost every one in America, with the notable exception of Arturo Toscanini, whose opinion of Flagstad could charitably be represented by the symbol zero.

I do remember that one orchestra manager, whose integrity is unquestioned even by those who most bitterly envy him, held out against the power of the Flagstad name. This was George E. Judd, who guides the destinies of the Boston Symphony Orchestra and the Boston "Pops." A certain organization wished to subscribe, that is, to buy out completely, a Boston "Pops" concert—a situation which is very agreeable to any orchestra's manager. This organization wanted not only the "Pops" but wanted Flagstad as soloist. Though outside soloists are rare at the "Pops" because their intrusion is not consistent with the "Pops" tradition, type of program or the spirit of the concerts, nevertheless, Mr. Judd agreed to have Flagstad. The organization subscribing the concert, having won this point, went a little further and, at the instance of Mme Flagstad, required of Mr. Judd that Mr. McArthur be engaged to conduct for the soloist. Judd properly consulted

Arthur Fiedler, the conductor of the "Pops," and Mr. Fiedler kindly agreed to have McArthur as conductor for Mme Flagstad. The subscribing organization thereupon, unquestionably at the instance of Mme Flagstad, demanded that Mr. McArthur be permitted to conduct not only for the soloist but the entire "Pops" concert. Then Mr. Judd did not consult Mr. Fiedler at all, but simply informed the subscribers that the "Pops" had a conductor—namely, Arthur Fiedler—and that nobody under any circumstances could displace him. To have Edwin McArthur conduct as accompanist for Mme Flagstad was one thing; to have him imposed upon the orchestra as guest conductor was quite another, and Mr. Judd would not agree to any such arrangement. The subscribers thereupon threatened to withdraw Mme Flagstad as soloist and were promptly informed that while Symphony Hall would be honored and happy to entertain Mme Flagstad as soloist, the success of the "Pops" season or any part of it did not depend upon any soloist, and if Mme Flagstad chose not to appear the "Pops" season would undoubtedly proceed as usual. Mme Flagstad did not appear; Mr. McArthur did not conduct; the Boston "Pops" are doing very well.

Eventually I was required to record the Immolation Scene with Mr. McArthur conducting. This was done in Victor's Hollywood studios with an orchestra drawn from the San Francisco Symphony. Without reference to anyone or anything except recording conditions, I cannot but assert that these records were pitifully inferior to those made by Flagstad and Ormandy. Victor paid an unnecessarily and unreasonably extravagant price for this recording, and the public, excited by increasingly extravagant advertising, was disappointed, and to this day is still disappointed, in the Flagstad Immolation Scene. This matter is doubtless of only academic interest to anyone concerned with recorded music, for the Traubel-Toscanini Immolation has been available for some time, has superseded the Flagstad performance, and is infinitely superior to it. I mention the incident merely as an example of Mme Flagstad's persistent, sometimes perverse, but always honest and generous determination to further the interests of a young American conductor whose artistic devotion and wholesome friendship had contributed to her success in our country.

I have noted that Mme Flagstad is not a glittering personality, but she is a warm and amiable one. Her charm is a function of her simplicity, honesty, and candor. She is vital and vigorous, but hardly vivacious; she has much of the solidity and some of the contours of a granite hill, and I dare say, vocally speaking, a comparable durability. These qualities are most useful in a Wagnerian singer, but their utility is, I think, inversely proportionate to a more expansive field of musical endeavor. To leave the opera house after a *Götterdämmerung* vocally unwearied and fresh is indeed remarkable and admirable. This Mme Flagstad has always done and no doubt still can do. Unfortunately, she can leave a concert platform after an evening of lieder in exactly the same condition. The truth is that she has the vocal stamina to deal with the exigencies of any Wagnerian opera where she is properly a part of the orchestra, responsible for little more than the production and articulation of a certain amount of tone. Because she is physically robust, this responsibility is no great drain upon her energy. Unfortunately, in the field of song she contributes exactly the same thing, and little more; which is not what the field of song requires for its cultivation. It is rather sad that the same voice that can soar so magnificently above Wagner's orchestral tempests is used with such childish inadequacy and ineffectiveness in the subtle intimacies of lieder.

A physiognomist might find in Mme Flagstad's face clue to certain inadequacies in her work. In the junction of her nose and brow and in the cold opaqueness of her ice-blue eyes, one might detect a sculptured symmetry so perfect as to be devoid of interest. Such proportions often indicate emotional placidity and flaccidity; and they certainly do in this case. I have been in the company of Mme Flagstad under a great variety of circumstances, and I have yet to see her disturbed, excited, moved, relaxed, or interested in or by anything. Neither the customary quart of champagne which she enjoys *solo* after each performance, nor the rather formidable procession of Martinis that moves in her direction on occasion, seems to affect her one way or another. In this, I suppose, her Nordic hardheadedness is an advantage, but her imperturbability can often be quite baffling. The very wholesomeness and emotional stability of this woman, however, are disarming and even amiable qualities. Beyond doubt she is capable of warm feeling, for she is adored by her daughter and by her friends. I think she is not capable of *expressing* warm feeling, and that is fatal to an artist.

SERGEI
RACHMANINOFF

Sergei Rachmaninoff

[1873-1943]

"Sorrow is better than laughter: for by the sadness of the countenance the heart is made better."

ECCLESIASTES vii: 3

MOST PIANO BUILDERS, most practitioners of piano playing, most composers for the piano, and most of the pianists' public are indifferent to, ignorant of, or unconcerned with the highest and most beautiful function of the instrument. This function is emotional expressiveness, generated and communicated primarily through the quality of tone. Piano tone is susceptible of countless variations, and its expressive possibilities are proportionately varied. Tone "color"—the combination of intensity and essential character in tone—is more directly and powerfully expressive and impressive to a sensitive listener than any other factor in music because its appeal and its impact are simple, sensuous, and nonintellectual, uncomplicated by philosophical concept, kinæsthesia, or visual apprehensions. Tone is to the piano what modulation and intonation (in the nonmusical sense) are to the speaking voice: the device by which myriad shades of meaning can be expressed, by which significance above and beyond the mere sound of words can be communicated. Tone need not be black and white because piano keys are; rather, piano tone is a full palette of musical colors, infinitely if subtly varied. How does it happen, then, that anyone can be indifferent to it? For the answer, look to the piano builders, the practitioners of piano playing, the composers for the piano, and the pianists' public.

Piano makers have not in a generation contributed a single basic or significant improvement in piano tone. Aside from certain tentative and philosophically erroneous attempts through electronics and electrical amplification,[1] they have totally ignored the most obvious fault in the piano—the absurd inequality of power between the upper and lower ends of the keyboard. They have similarly neglected the inequality of tone that is almost chromatically progressive throughout the piano scale. Instead, they have concentrated upon the development of a lighter and faster action (Steinway), which in itself results in some sacrifice of tone, and in this development they have succeeded. In doing so they have put into the hands of the contemporary composer a medium for the easy exploitation of the piano's most obvious and most vulgar qualities—its powers of rhythm, velocity, and dynamics. The piano builder and the piano composer have then both played into the hands of the mere virtuoso, who in turn plays to the most primitive musical instincts of the public, and only to these instincts. Listen to almost any of the present-day pianists, or the music of present-day composers, and whether you hear the most uninspired boogie woogie or the most pretentious of long-haired products, you will inevitably and invariably find that nothing in the art of playing the piano appeals to them except the rhythmic impulse and the brittle and startling dynamic contrasts which the instrument can provide. At the worst, the composers treat the piano today as a mere tool of their trade; at best, as a blatant percussion machine, a vehicle for the exploitation of the (to me) insufferable brilliance of Horowitz,

---

[1] I refer to certain experiments of Josef Hofmann and RCA Victor, in collaboration.

the desiccated didacticism of Schnabel, the preciosity of Hofmann, the archness of Iturbi.

These stars and others shine not in the full glory of the piano, which is in partial, almost total, eclipse; but rather have their orbits in a dreary if incandescent penumbra—an atmosphere filled not with the warmth and tonal effulgence of the instrument, but one made up of merely brilliant particles. Mr. Horowitz seems interested in the fact that he can play faster and louder than anybody else; to me his playing is "faultily faultless, icily regular, splendidly null." The Herr Professor Schnabel is convinced that only he can deliver an *appoggiatura* as Beethoven intended—though he does not obey his own dicta. Hofmann is absorbed in the mechanism of the piano, to which he has made important contribution; Iturbi turns to boogie woogie, which any Harlem hack does better: not one of these artists concerns himself to any appreciable degree with the articulate, expressive, lyrical tonal voice of the piano. There are players who do, but the public, which has been persistently seduced from the tonalist by the technician, pays most attention and money to those I have just mentioned. Of course, there is Walter Gieseking, who may be considered out of this world since he appears to have ingratiated himself with the Nazi Germans. There is George Copeland, surely a great master of piano tone, but he will not work at his profession and has no audience. There is E. Robert Schmitz, who really understands the tonal functions of the piano, but who, fortunately or not, prefers, apparently, to impart his knowledge to students rather than to the dubious understanding and taste of audiences. Alfred Cortot exploited very considerably the tonal resources of the piano, but technically has never been startling. Robert Casadesus is a French logician whose logic and playing are both somewhat rigorous. Rudolf Serkin is a scholar, a philosopher, a poet, and a pedagogue—but not yet a tonalist. Among the younger men, a Russian-American named Istomin shows signs of employing more than vigor and velocity in piano playing; there is Jesús María Sanromá, who won his first triumphs more on virtuosity than anything else, but who in his maturity appears to be rediscovering his instrument. Eugene List has intelligence and sincerity and an impressive but not electrifying technique, and will doubtless discover that the piano is not a musical machine gun. Rudolf Firkusny, when he gets away from the classical repertoire and plays what he really loves, begins to project the glowing tonal essence of piano music. Jeanne Behrend, a brilliant and thoughtful pianist, seems more interested in composition, I think, than in playing. Hilda Somer is a delight to the eye. William Kapell is too immature physically and spiritually; his extraordinary facility does not compensate for his frailty or conceal a certain superficial attitude. Time should cure him.

There is, thank God, Artur Rubinstein.

Excepting Rubinstein, there is no one presently before the public who knows or can make us know the piano as Gabrilowitsch and Paderewski and Szumowska and Pachmann knew it and made us know it—now that Rachmaninoff is dead.

If pianists themselves do not recognize the tonal resources of their instrument, it cannot be expected that many in their audience will come to demand, recognize, and appreciate tonal beauty. Tone, like every living and active [2] thing, must be conceived before it can be born. The birth canal of the tone-wave courses through the channels of the ear, and tone does not exist until it is heard. Ears sensitive to it and capable not only of receiving it but of discriminating among its subtleties are as much a part of tone as the vibrating body that generates it. The physicists may not agree; indeed, many of them will argue that the character of piano tone cannot be influenced by the player except with respect to its intensity. Rachmaninoff knew that they were wrong, and proved it. He

---

[2] I use the word "active" in its Platonic sense; that is to say, capable of producing an effect on something else, as distinguished from "passive," or capable of being affected by something else.

demonstrated every time he played that variations of tone quality can be accomplished by pressure, weight, force, pedaling, and by the laxity or rigidity of the fingers, wrists, elbows, and shoulders. If you have ever heard him play his Second Concerto, you could have observed a beautiful illustration of this. The eight solemn chords at the beginning, each individually shaded and colored, yet progressing as a unified phrase and with growing power toward an inevitable climax—these darkly glowing chords, sheerly because of their tonal differences, constitute one of the great exordia in music.

I think it was this tonal luster, overlaying all of Mr. Rachmaninoff's playing, that gave him his greatest distinction as a pianist. Perhaps, too, he concentrated upon tone for this very reason, for he was shrewdly aware that technical prodigies are eventually unsatisfying, aware too that a half-dozen pianists were his equal and one or two his superior, in a purely technical sense. In his later years he concentrated almost entirely upon his own music, which was cannily devised to accommodate both the strong and the weak points in his own technical equipment, thus leaving him free to focus his thought and effort upon the musical and emotional values of his music without apparent concern for its technical demands. This may be why his piano music often seems lacking in depth and significance in other hands than his. I think, for example, that the Rhapsody on a Theme of Paganini is a brilliant, sometimes impudent, some times acrid satire and a mockery of life's impermanence and triviality. I have heard several eminent pianists play this music, and all of them except the composer himself played it as a merely virtuoso piece. It is, to be sure, full of cruel difficulties, but these are not the reason for its being; and even the difficulties themselves have never been satisfactorily surmounted by any pianist other than Rachmaninoff for the reason that they were plotted by him, for him, and by the magic of tone made into an implement of emotional expression and not primarily for audience impression.

Rachmaninoff was always amused by the fact that while he had given more effort to the composition and performance of his Rhapsody than to any other of his concerted works, it was the only one in which he ever faltered. This happened at Minneapolis a few years ago when Eugene Ormandy was conductor there. At a certain point Ormandy noticed that the pianist had departed far from the score and was wandering from one modulation to another in a very curious way. This happened during the solo passage and Ormandy, in alarm, stole a look at Rachmaninoff's face. The pianist was obviously in great distress and his expression said to Mr. Ormandy, as it would to any conductor, "For God's sake, go on." Ormandy consequently quickly indicated the next *tutti* to the orchestra, and with the first note, of course, Rachmaninoff's memory functioned again. He afterward said that he nearly always got in trouble at that particular point in the Rhapsody because the first time he heard Moiseiwitsch play the piece he too went astray at that particular point. Rachmaninoff claimed that ever afterward he had great difficulty getting past the measure in which Moiseiwitsch had made his error without doing the same thing himself. This little aberration of Rachmaninoff always seemed to me very strange indeed in a man with such powers of concentration and of such fierce egocentricity.[3]

This man knew that the world of music is a jungle inhabited almost exclusively by a few lions, a multitude of tigers, a numberless pack of jackals, and not a few snakes, all of them venomous. He could not be numbered among these fauna; or if he could, certainly he was one of the small pride of lions who, fiercely determined upon their own purposes, are aware of but indifferent to the prowlings of lesser beasts. He knew the power of money and was acutely conscious of a dollar's value,

---

[3] Curiously, the same mishap befell Artur Rubinstein not once but twice during the 1944–5 season, at performances with the Philadelphia Orchestra in Baltimore and Washington.

yet I think that he required money more as a tribute to his eminence as a pianist and composer than because of any acquisitiveness for money per se. Furthermore, his personal representative, Charles Foley, is that rare person, an Irishman with both acquisitiveness and acumen highly developed; no Jew, no Greek, no Scot, nor even an Armenian is a match for such a man. Mr. Rachmaninoff's business affairs were invariably handled by the lovable Charlie, who drove a hard bargain; the artist himself never, ostensibly at least, entered into such matters. I came to know Mr. Rachmaninoff too well, however, not to understand that his was the will which dictated his affairs in the minutest detail. It must be added that hard though his dealings in financial matters may have seemed to me and to my employers, they were invariably fair, reasoned and based on a very objective consideration of the facts. I recall that when his Second Concerto was first recorded it was not protected by copyright, and no copyright royalty was paid on it so far as I can remember. Mr. Rachmaninoff simply accepted his royalty as a performer. When subsequent works were recorded, however, they were protected by copyright. The company legitimately and with acumen tried to persuade Mr. Rachmaninoff that he should not exact a royalty in addition to his due as a performing artist, since he was playing his own music and therefore promoting its popularity. Mr. Rachmaninoff very reasonably differed from this viewpoint and held that he should be paid both as composer and performer. Once having arrived at this conclusion, nothing could make him retreat from it, and he was paid accordingly. The same sort of case developed when he conducted some of his music with the Philadelphia Orchestra. Here the company wanted to pay him merely as conductor, but having by copyright protected the music in question, he correctly and justly asserted his right in royalties both from his performance and from the provisions of the copyright law. I have a feeling that Mr. Rachmaninoff's persistence along these lines was not entirely selfish, since Charlie Foley, for whom he had the warmest affection, had and has an interest in the publishing of Rachmaninoff's works.

My first meeting with Rachmaninoff was at Victor's New York studios. Everyone there was considerably in awe of him, as indeed I was, and though he had been in the studios for half an hour, no one had dared approach him. He sat at one end of the room "like Patience on a monument," his hands hidden in a specially designed muff that was connected to a nearby electric light circuit. He neither spoke nor put forth his hand when I came up to him, but turned on me a smile which, though faint, was of such gentleness and warmth and understanding that I have never forgotten it. I was there to make things easier and pleasanter for him; actually it was he who made them easy and pleasant for me. Subsequently I learned that he did not like to talk before he played, and I discovered too that his hands were always remarkably cool and as smooth as a girl's. They were also extraordinarily powerful, and Rachmaninoff, almost alone among the great pianists, had what romantic people like to describe as the "artistic" hand—long, slender, and tapering.[4]

Everyone is familiar with his economical and unromantic haircut, which, together with certain other features, brought a suggestion of a newly released convict or even of the hangman himself. His eyes were almost Mongolian in their obliquity and generally inscrutable expression, yet they could light up with the most engaging warmth and friendliness. The lips, full, sensitive, pendulous, and somewhat equine, were, oddly enough, the least expressive feature of his face. I often wondered how he managed, without painful accidents, to insert between his lips the cigarette butts he smoked continuously.

---

[4] Most of the great pianists have rather short, thick, and somewhat ugly hands. Notable exceptions were Paderewski, whose hands were rather small and delicately made, and Gabrilowitsch, whose hands were beautiful in the romantic sense. Josef Hofmann's are so small that he must use a special piano with keys narrower than those of the standard instrument.

He used a curious kind of cigarette, which I believe he made himself, and would invariably break it in half before smoking; the half couldn't have been more than three-quarters of an inch long. Continuous practice perhaps accounted for his digital and labial dexterity. He liked a sturdy highball or two or a bottle of red wine, particularly after settling a matter of business, and he could be a charming and genial host.

He was not easy to know, and had few friends. Those he cared to win, he won; and they adored him. Once given, his friendship was steadfast and confiding, but terminated instantly if he detected the slightest, the best-intentioned, or harmless deceit. For a long time I flattered myself that I had his confidence in musical matters until eventually I realized that he was not in the least concerned with the technicalities of recording and would take my word that a given record was a good record only because he was quite indifferent to its quality as a recording. He was concerned solely with his own performance and rarely would permit the publication of any record in which his own playing was not flawless.

Mr. Rachmaninoff was one of the most completely individual personalities I have encountered among musicians. Almost his every thought and action were dedicated not merely to music but to *his* music. Although his life span encompassed several musical periods, he was not substantially affected by any of them. He knew and profoundly admired Tchaikovsky and others among the Russian romantics, but apart from a certain racial flavor in his music he had nothing in common with them, nor with Brahms or Debussy or Strauss. He was a contemporary but not a modern. His estimate of his own worth and the worth of his music was an exceedingly generous one and made with complete candor and conviction. I think it was likewise correct, in most instances. I would except the Fourth Concerto and the Symphonic Dances.

My only disagreement with Mr. Rachmaninoff came about because of the Symphonic Dances. I have never felt that this music added a great degree of luster to the composer's name, but what was more important, it was not notably a success with the public. The work was dedicated to the Philadelphia Orchestra, which Rachmaninoff admired more than any other. He wished to record the Dances with the Philadelphia Orchestra and to conduct the work himself. For various reasons irrelevant here, this was not practicable, and I discreetly postponed the matter until it was not only impracticable but impossible. A little later we engaged the Chicago Symphony to make Red Seal records and one of the first things on their program that season was Rachmaninoff's Symphonic Dances, whereupon, conditions being quite different from those existing in Philadelphia, I proposed that the Chicago Orchestra record the Symphonic Dances. Rachmaninoff was not at all enthusiastic, and when it developed that Dr. Stock and not Rachmaninoff would conduct, the composer became actively resentful and things were rather uncomfortable between us for a time. When I was in a position to tell him the whole story, however, I was restored to his good graces.

The pianist was very exacting of the conductors with whom he played and would never submit his own will or his own concept of a work to the man with the stick. He was invincibly convinced of the rectitude of his musical ideas and with the most implacable determination would enforce them upon his colleagues. Where he could not do this with reasonable amiability on both sides, he simply wouldn't play. This, as he told me himself, was why he would not play with Toscanini, and I think it is fair to infer that the same reason accounted for the extreme rarity of his appearances with Koussevitzky. He preferred Ormandy to anyone, though he collaborated successfully and in the most friendly fashion with Stokowski. Ormandy has always been the delight and Stokowski the terror of soloists, but Rachmaninoff was not one to be terrified. I remember once when he had been called for rehearsal at eleven in the morning, he appeared with his customary punctuality and found Mr. Stokowski in the midst of rehearsing a Tchaikovsky symphony. Rachmaninoff, who in spite of his apparent *sang-froid* had a very sensitive nervous system, paced up and down off stage for perhaps three minutes while Stokowski continued to rehearse; then, as if suddenly coming to a conclusion, he ambled out on the stage, sat down at the piano and banged out a few thunderous chords in the middle of Stokowski's Tchaikovsky. The conductor, of course, stopped the orchestra immediately. Rachmaninoff, looking up at him with a face of stone, rumbled in his basso-profundo, "The piano is here; I am here; it is eleven o'clock. Let us rehearse." The maestro meekly obeyed.

I do not know that Rachmaninoff literally believed "sorrow is better than laughter," though, to be sure, he was often engaged upon somber reflections, but his melancholy was of a philosophical, not a morbid kind. He never felt sorry for himself. He had not, at least prior to the invasion of France, where a daughter was sequestered in occupied territory, any personal tragedies to mourn. He was grave but not grieving, and often disclosed a healthy cynicism and a rather twisted but not unkind humor that were evidence of a vital and eupeptic personality. The serious, even the saddest, aspects of life engaged his interest. Death itself was a fascinating subject for speculation, but his consideration of such matters was quite detached and impersonal. In years of acquaintance I never heard him laugh, but his smile reverberated. The sadness of his countenance made many a heart glad, for to those who viewed him from the remoteness of the audience it was almost the *insigne* of a master whose coming was always welcome. To those who knew him more intimately that grim countenance was the disguise for a warm and human personality. With his friend Kreisler, and their friend and manager, Charles Foley, I have spent many an hour over spaghetti and red wine in some obscure Italian restaurant, and at such times it seemed to me Rachmaninoff would lose his customary appearance of a deflated Buddha. He was quite uninhibited and entertaining as a raconteur, and his stories were invariably, curiously, and refreshingly brief. He was completely indifferent to his surroundings and quite unpretentious. He could be entertained easily and seemed to feel equally comfortable in the East Room of the White House or in a one-arm restaurant. Material things aside from money and creature comforts interested him very little. He must have been the despair of tailors, for his clothes fit him as if they had been carefully made for someone else. His collars were almost always several sizes too large, and with them he would wear rather discouraged neckties knotted in such a way as to show a big gold collarbutton in front. He had one overcoat, I remember, that might have been handed down from a hansom cab driver of Victorian London. However ill adjusted such details might be, Rachmaninoff was nevertheless always a figure of power and dignity and magnetism. He was bored with applause, but did, I think, require and indeed enforce honest respect for his playing, his music, and himself. Exaggerated or insincere courtesy or fulsome praise disgusted him. It was such unwelcome deference that elicited from him the only vulgar word I ever heard him utter. He had just completed the first performance of one of his concertos with the Philadelphia Orchestra and repeatedly was recalled to accept thunderous ovations. Each time as he would leave the stage one of the first violinists who was sitting near the door would leap up, bow profoundly, and in a stage whisper unctuously voice his unwelcome praise. The first time this happened Rachmaninoff nodded curtly; the second time he glowered; the third time he spat out (in English) what the French delicately call *le mot de Cambronne.*[5]

Rachmaninoff felt that fortune had been wonderfully kind to him in that he was the only great composer who could leave behind him the best of his music in definitive performances and audible form. His four concertos, all played by him as soloist; his *Isle of the Dead* and Third Symphony conducted by himself; the Second Symphony conducted by Eugene Or-

[5] *Merde.*

mandy; his Rhapsody on a Theme of Paganini played by himself and conducted by Stokowski; and many of his smaller works were recorded when, as pianist and conductor, Rachmaninoff was at the height of his powers. There seems no doubt that in the future all great musicians, creative, executant, or both, will have this experience which was uniquely Rachmaninoff's. I am happy to have had a small part in bringing it about.

ARTHUR
FIEDLER

✑ Arthur Fiedler ℘

"A monument more durable than bronze"

HORACE: ODE

BOSTON does not ordinarily rear monuments to living citizens, however eminent; but there stands on the Charles River Esplanade a magnificent pile of granite that is a monument to Arthur Fiedler, though strangely enough his name does not appear on it. This is the Edwin Hatch Memorial, the most beautiful and effectively designed outdoor orchestra shell in America. It was erected with funds provided by the will of Edwin M. Hatch as an expression of his wish to provide the citizens of Boston with something that would accomplish the greatest amount of good for the greatest number of people. It is improbable that Mr. Hatch ever envisioned the form his gift would take. The form it did take is a result of the efforts of Arthur Fiedler, who not only provided the *raison d'être* of the shell but virtually singlehanded persuaded the city fathers of Boston that the funds so generously bequeathed by the estate of Mr. Hatch should be used for this purpose. Within the entrance of the Hatch Memorial is a magnificent bronze tablet, very properly bearing the name of the donor of the building, with less propriety inscribed with the names of various politicians, contractors, and other such gentry, but curiously—and I think scandalously—omitting the name of Arthur Fiedler.

More than ten years ago Fiedler conceived the idea of the Esplanade Concerts. Moved perhaps by consideration of the limited capacity of Symphony Hall and the unlimited appetite of people for good music, he proposed to bring the music of the Boston Symphony Orchestra, or as much of it as possible, to great masses of people, and to do this at the minimum of expense. There was a rickety though acoustically good band shell on the Charles River Esplanade, facing a superb level stretch of greensward running along the Embankment. There were forty or fifty members of the Boston Symphony Orchestra willing to risk a few weeks of their time and all their artistic efforts. There were a few wealthy friends who might possibly be willing to contribute at least enough to assure the musicians a minimum compensation for their work, and there were tens of thousands of Bostonians who never had opportunity to hear either the Boston Symphony Orchestra or the gayer but equally well-presented Boston "Pops." Adding up these factors, Fiedler came to the conclusion that an annual series of concerts on the Charles River Esplanade was feasible, and the history of these concerts through the past ten years and more has proved that he was correct.

The early years were not easy, for to finance such an undertaking requires a very considerable sum. Year after year with unflagging confidence and courage Fiedler went to his friends and to his own resources in order to present the Esplanade Concerts; year after year the attendance grew until at present it is by no means uncommon to look out from the Hatch Memorial at an Esplanade concert and see thirty thousand people eagerly awaiting the first note of the orchestra. Not one of these people is required to pay for admission. For ten cents one may rent a chair, and a tiny fraction of this dime goes to the Esplanade Concerts. Here and there are posted little containers like mailboxes, into which you may, if you wish (though nobody asks you), deposit a dime, a dollar, or any other coin you feel like giving.

When Arthur Fiedler learned of the terms of the Hatch

will, he saw an opportunity to replace his decrepit old band-
stand with a modern, beautiful structure that could be designed to accomplish many services to great masses of the
people, but which primarily could be an adequate setting for
the Esplanade Orchestra. His own powers of persuasion and
his natural acumen were effective, and the beautiful Hatch
Memorial with its skillfully engineered acoustics, its adequate
dressing rooms, its air conditioning, its modern system of
sound reinforcement, and its monumental dignity are in the
truest sense Arthur Fiedler's monument in Boston. Whether
or not it bears his name, the association of the building with
Fiedler can hardly be forgotten because it was the superb
gesture of democracy in music that brought the Esplanade
Concerts into being that also made possible, practical, and a
final reality the Edwin M. Hatch Memorial.

The Boston "Pops" concerts are nearly contemporary with
those of the Boston Symphony Orchestra, though they have
not always been as successful. There have been times when
there were nearly as many people in the orchestra as there
were in the audience. In spite of this, the "Pops" were continued, partly as an evangelistic gesture on behalf of the Boston
Symphony and partly as an economic aid to the musicians of
the orchestra. The "Pops" extends the playing season of the
Boston musicians by as much as ten weeks, and though in
pre-union days the "Pops" Orchestra was paid less than the
Symphony, the Boston job was a desirable one because of
the longer season and greater stability of tenure.

The "Pops" Orchestra has had a long line of conductors,
from Adolf Neuendorff and John C. Mullaly to Alfredo Casella
and Agide Jacchia, but the orchestra never was a consistent
success, nor did it ever artistically or otherwise reach its highest
point of development until the conductorship of Fiedler.
Arthur's musical ability, his acute intuitions with respect to
public taste, his employment of good showmanship without
sensationalism, his shrewd estimate of the Bostonian audience,

have resulted in a situation wherein it is virtually impossible
to buy a single seat for a Boston "Pops" concert, and any seat
or seats must be purchased weeks in advance. This is not a
wartime development; indeed it antedates the war by some
years. It is the result of Arthur Fiedler's skill, imagination,
and leadership and George E. Judd's canny management—
plus, I suppose, the genial atmosphere of the "Pops" themselves, where a glass of wine, a cup of "Pops" punch, or a
cigarette are not considered incompatible with the dignity of
Symphony Hall. Yet, prior to the first recording contract between the Boston "Pops" and Victor the institution was so
little known outside of Boston that the company was quite
reluctant to undertake recordings and even wanted to change
the name of the sixty-odd-year old organization because of its
unfamiliarity to the country at large. Indeed, the records sold
in England do bear the label "Boston Promenade Orchestra,
Arthur Fiedler, Conductor." Mr. Judd firmly refused to have
the name changed as far as American record sales were concerned, and his faith in the ultimate success of the orchestra
on records under Fiedler's direction has been justified. The
Boston "Pops" became an important attraction on the
radio under the sponsorship of Allis-Chalmers, and Fiedler's
records sometimes have earned more in royalties in the course
of a year than those of Koussevitzky.

I have often been irritated or amused by record reviewers
and music critics who, in spite of the evidence, prefer to assume that every Boston "Pops" Orchestra performance is a
rowdy and somewhat careless thing, in some way inferior to
the performances of the Boston Symphony Orchestra. The
fact is that Boston "Pops" concerts are prepared with as much
seriousness and devotion, with the same meticulous care that
precede those of Dr. Koussevitzky. It is true that the "Pops"
Orchestra has not so many rehearsals, but this is in a measure
balanced by the fact that Mr. Fiedler works so rapidly, so
surely, and so knowingly. Fiedler is one of the most thoroughly

cultivated musicians I have ever met. He has the incomparably thorough training of the old German school. In his methods and his work there is no particle of fake or pretension; he does not need these common ingredients of the conductor's art. His beat is clear, incisive, unspectacular; his spoken directions to the orchestra expert, concise, and completely assured with respect to each note and each instrument. His manner in dealing with the orchestra has a certain abruptness but no lack of courtesy; he is friendly but not intimate or particularly companionable with his men. There is a certain relaxation of discipline but not of attention during rehearsals, and discipline at "Pops" concerts manages to be rigid without intruding itself upon the light-hearted atmosphere and without disturbing the good will or the good humor of the players.

Apart from his job Arthur is one of the gayest and most interesting of companions, and in the course of a long and intimate friendship I have had many an occasion to observe this. He is equally at home in a Beacon Street drawing room in the company of the elect of Boston and in the back seat of a Police Department prowl car with a riot gun across his knees, a taciturn cop for chauffeur, and perhaps a gin-sodden derelict or a dangerous thug sitting beside him. Arthur and I have more than once, in company with a certain delightful police captain of the Joy Street station, spent the night scouting the less polite byways of Boston, in which Arthur has an extraordinary and intelligent interest. He has an insatiable appetite for life in all its manifestations. He can be scholar or playboy, ascetic or *bon vivant* with equal zest. A certain hard cynicism has not modified his capacity for friendship, though I did entertain the idea for some years that it had incapacitated him for profounder sentiments. I was happily disabused of this idea when comparatively recently Arthur, somewhat surprisingly to his friends, deserted the ranks of Boston's eligible bachelors.

During most of my acquaintance with him Arthur occupied a princely apartment in Commonwealth Avenue. This establishment was presided over by a charming soul, Mrs. Louise Smith, who in her ample person combined the capacities of a whole staff of household assistants, not to mention a certain fiercely maternal quality that Arthur ostensibly resented and implicitly demanded. When in Boston I was always a guest at Arthur's hospitable quarters, and after serving a certain novitiate was finally accepted by Louise and taken into her heart, which I am sure is big enough to accommodate quite a few people, including Arthur's wife and little Johanna.

It was from this apartment of Arthur's that we once sallied forth upon an escapade that developed into one of the maddest and pleasantest and most harmless week ends we ever had together. During a period of sixty hours we managed to take in a cocktail party at Stockbridge, Massachusetts, a concert of the Boston Symphony Orchestra at the Music Shed at Tanglewood, a light supper at the home of Mr. and Mrs. Hollis M. Carlisle in Springfield, breakfast at the Copley-Plaza in Boston, audition and approval of fifty new Boston "Pops" records, a champagne party in Lexington, a bite to eat in the New Haven railroad station, and, in New York, the final installation of Arthur aboard a banana boat for Puerto Rico.

Eheu fugaces! Arthur the benedick has necessarily abandoned such hijinks. Even his precious tropical fish, upon which unresponsive creatures he lavished the care and devotion of a proud father, now languish in their air-conditioned aquarium. There is a baby in the house; and he who was once Boston's number one bachelor, he who "would never allow a wife or a child to interfere with his ordered and satisfactory life," he who would squirm with irritation at an "A" that vibrated one cycle sharp or flat, now has attuned his ears and his life to a baby's cry. The "Pops" go better than ever, and perhaps there is a connection.

HELEN
TRAUBEL

◂§ Helen Traubel §▸

"A voice that in the distance far away
Wakens the slumbering ages."

SIR HENRY TAYLOR : *Philip Van Artevelde,*
Pt. 1, Act 1, Scene 5.

FAILURE. A curious word to associate, even remotely, with Helen Traubel: musically, artistically, the most important member of the Metropolitan Opera Company, the joy of the song-loving public in eighty or ninety American cities each season, the darling of the local concert manager, the most sought-after singer for the least undignified, least vulgar, and probably most remunerative of broadcasts; rewarded by the ecstatic acclaim of two continents and the handsomest income of any singer in the concert field today; and what is really important, gifted with a voice of opulent beauty, challenging power, grateful warmth, and humanity, a voice that serves an unerring, a convincing musicianship. Failure? Helen couldn't fail. I did.

I failed because it was my job to discover treasures such as Traubel, to get control of their services for recording purposes, to see that records worthy of them were made—*and made accessible to the public*; and in Traubel's case I was not successful in doing all this. True, I did get her name on a contract at a time when, though she was in every respect the great artist she is now, comparatively few were familiar with that fact. I did get some adequate records of her voice. I did get her name into a few advertisements. I did get her recorded (badly) with orchestra in our studios—records which in no way represented Traubel's voice or musical personality. I did have her record, with the Victor Symphony Orchestra, in the Academy of Music in Philadelphia and in New York's Town Hall—records entirely worthy from the artistic viewpoint, and commercially the most successful of any Traubel record released up to that time. I did arrange and supervise her truly wonderful recordings of *Im Treibhaus*, *Schmerzen*, and *Träume* with Stokowski and the Philadelphia Orchestra—miracles of singing, of conducting, of accompaniment, every one. I did solely and personally arrange her engagement with Toscanini and the NBC Symphony for a concert in Carnegie Hall, and there recorded, the following day, the utterly miraculous, the electrifying Traubel realization of the Immolation Scene from *Götterdämmerung*. Yet, notwithstanding sustained effort applied through every device and at every point I could imagine, I failed with Traubel; failed to overcome the ignorance, the stupidity, the dull lack of imagination, the indifference and inertia, the wicked malice, envy, and jealousy that have until recently impeded Traubel's efforts in recording.

I don't think that the field of recording was the only territory in which these rank and noxious growths appeared. There is a curious similarity between her recording career and her concert career while it was managed by another RCA agency, the NBC Artists Bureau. George Engles was titular managing director there; the work was actually done by Marks Levine. During her relationship with this bureau, I understand, Helen was guaranteed ten thousand dollars annually; and having grown a bit cynical after so many years in the music racket, I have often wondered if this was what in other and equally murderous rackets is called "hush money." Helen didn't get, through the NBC Artists Bureau, anywhere near enough engagements to justify such a payment, though she did sing on a few "sustaining" broadcasts. The bureau had at the same time a great singer named Flagstad under its management. Logic, if not ethics, would have suggested the suppression of competition. Flagstad was having an unprecedented success; why introduce a competitive factor? Besides, Kirsten was European, she was enormously popular, no suspicions of Nazi sympathies had been suggested; whereas Traubel wasn't born in Norway or Denmark or Poland—hadn't ever been in Europe!—but came from St. Louis, Missouri, U. S. A. At any rate, the name of Traubel, as a candidate for Red Seal records, was never presented to me. I have no means of knowing how often it was proposed to local concert managers, but Helen sang few concerts indeed.

Let me digress a moment to emphasize the fact that Traubel at no time has considered herself a rival or competitor of Flagstad or anyone else. Helen is so honest, and musically so shrewd, that she does unquestionably admire what is good in any and every artist; and she is not niggardly with her praise. She turns upon herself the same powers of discrimination, and rightly believes that her own gifts and accomplishments entitle her to a certain place in the musical world without reference to or comparison with any other singer.

It was never my practice to wait for an artist's name to be brought to my attention by a manager. Without prompting from anyone or influence by anything but my own judgment, I engaged such artists as Rose Bampton, Claudio Arrau, Leonard Warren, Dorothy Maynor, Eleanor Steber, Patrice Munsel, Arthur Fiedler and the Boston "Pops," Pierre Monteux, Vladimir Golschmann, Norman Cordon, Emanuel Feuermann, Eugene Ormandy (Minneapolis Symphony), and many others—not one of whom had achieved, at the time, any notable eminence in the estimation of the general public. The person most responsible for the storming of the ultimate barriers that lay between Traubel and triumph was, I think, John Barbirolli. Barbirolli brought about Helen's engagement for some Wagnerian programs with the New York Philharmonic-Symphony and also conducted for her on the Ford broadcasts. The first got her the ear of the critics; the second, attention from several million people. It was one of these broadcasts that fired my enthusiasm for Helen Traubel's singing, and the next morning I had arranged by telephone an interview with her and her then manager.

The first startling thing about Traubel was, to me, her laugh. The second was her size. I heard the laugh, even before I observed the size, from a hallway adjoining her manager's living-room in his New York apartment; and it is a laugh one can never forget. It is loud, warm, musical, uninhibited, and contagious. I have only to tell a certain Irish story to get it going. One doesn't need to know what she is laughing at in order to join in—even if the subject of her risibilities happens to be one's self. (It often has been, in my case!) Helen has been identified in a ball-park, a movie theater, an opera house by the *fortissimo* outgiving that comes when her sense of humor is touched; comparatively few have heard another laugh, low, rich, and intimate, and reserved, I think, for family and certain close friends. It's a pity that the awful pretentiousness and implausibility of the Wagnerian music-drama don't allow for a few guffaws from the goddess here and there; Traubel would certainly "lay 'em in the aisles" with a laugh and nothing else. As for her size: Traubel's person, like her voice, her heart, and her mind, is beautiful and big. Nature has apparently decreed an appropriate and proportionate frame for her. She is six feet tall, possibly taller; and I insist that she is built *proportionately*. Her bone structure approaches more closely the inverted pyramid of the male than the characteristic rhomboid form of the female; she is broad in the shoulders, extraordinarily deep-chested (and I refer to the thoracic cavity precisely—not to mammary equipment), relatively and quite noticeably slim in the hips. She has delicately boned, but not small, feet and hands, disproportionately slender legs. Helen's remote German origins have left her the peach-blow complexion and the red-blond hair that are probably typical; but her eyes, instead of being corn-flower blue as one might expect, are a curious color—somewhere between gold and hazel, and nearly the color of her hair.

Traubel is beautiful in the best sense of the word. The obvious and theatrical details are there of course—the extraordinary eyes, the lovely color and texture of skin, a certain majesty as she sweeps into your vision mantled in God knows how many skins of the mink. There is in the contours of her face and head something that quite transcends these details. There is the immeasurable joy of an artist who lives wholly, honestly, and intensely for her art, and the immeasurable pride of one who is acutely and yet humbly conscious of her own achievement in the art that has its genesis, its being, and its instrument in her own body. There is the serenity of a great spirit that has designed its own life and undeviatingly follows that design as life unfolds. There are kindness, and compassion, and sympathy—a quick but not superficial sympathy; rather, one directed by both intuition and intelligence. There is a radiance that can shine only in the face of a woman loving and beloved; there is a tolerance of human frailty and aberration; and there is, finally, the complacence of one who has borne without flinching and who knows, understands and forgives "the slings and arrows of outrageous fortune." Traubel is not only beautiful; she is happy.

I do not mean to give you the impression that this remarkable woman lives at all remotely from the world, absorbed in the mysteries of lieder, the cultivation of the "hylo-glossus," the technique of tone-production, and the proper sound of the German ü, ö and ä, or similar austere pursuits. Contrariwise, she lives a rich, full, and vigorous life. She loves human and earthy things, and she loves people. The exactions of a professional life leave comparatively little time for social contacts, but, though Traubel infrequently accepts invitations during the season, she has a small circle of intimates with whom there are sometimes gay dinners and relaxed evenings.

Often she cooks dinner herself, and does it well. She likes also to dine out, and orders like a little girl with a whole dollar to spend in the five-and-ten. I mean that Helen knows and likes good food and does justice to it—but always orders much more than she can eat. Perhaps that accounts for the contours of Mr. William Bass, her husband, which suggest the spherical; I start to gain weight myself after a few dinners of the Traubel variety.

Luchow's on Fourteenth Street in New York has been one of Helen's favorite dining places—probably because her husband likes it. I shall never forget a certain bird we had there —an enormous pheasant, roasted, and served with tail feathers temporarily restored, with glossy neck rising a good twelve inches above a silver salver large enough for a skating rink. With this was purple sauerkraut, a glorious wine, and various less important incidentals—and afterward, *Apfelpfannkuchen* of incredible circumference and memorable flavor. This Gargantuan repast, however, could have served as mere hors d'oeuvres to certain lobster dinners at the old Bookbinder's down on Philadelphia's Walnut Street. Here there is a genial colored man in charge of the lobsters, and he has learned that when Traubel appears the largest crustacean in the place is doomed. Have you ever seen a four- or five-pound lobster? I have—two of them at once on the table, one for Helen and one for Bill. The assault upon these monsters of the deep would be preceded, perhaps, by a number of steamed clams, a pint or so of snapper (turtle) soup, and followed by a good solid dessert and coffee. The odd part of all this is, however, that Helen would continually and slyly slip a good half of her lobster onto my plate or Bill's. She took delight in ordering these submarine terrors, but we did most of the eating of them. However, on the way to the Ritz after dinner, a double-dip chocolate ice cream soda wouldn't be improbable—improbable as it may seem.

The rumor that Traubel is a baseball fan sounds like part of the build-up as a really "American" artist; nevertheless, it is true. I did look upon this story as one of those "phonies" like Melchior's prize chickens (reared in the Ansonia Hotel, perhaps), but I can personally vouch for its verity. On one of the occasions when I was engaged to conduct the National Symphony at the Watergate Concerts in Washington, Helen was soloist. After rehearsal and lunch, we went to see a ball-game. Helen's presence became known, and no less a personage than Clark Griffith sought her out in the stands and wished to meet her. He did, and in ten seconds they were involved in a profound discussion of the game, the prospects of the Cards, and the frail physical appearance of one of the DiMaggios. Griffith really talked to Traubel as one authority to another, and wound up by asking for her autograph on a baseball. Helen really enjoyed that game, and while she is too discreet to attract attention to herself, she did let go a few Wagnerian yells about the eighth inning. Little did the startled fans know they were getting a Metropolitan voice and grand-stand seat for the one price.

Two other delights of Traubel's life are riding in trolley cars and shopping. Philadelphia is generously equipped with both trolleys and department stores; these, together with Bookbinder's and the Philadelphia Orchestra, constitute a private kind of heaven for Mme Traubel. She doesn't appear to get so much fun out of the new, slick, almost silent, and very swift kind of trolley that runs from Bookbinder's to the Ritz; I think she prefers the older, more classical flat-wheeled variety they now keep somewhat to the back streets. But the Philadelphia Wanamaker's, with its acres of opportunities for "shopping" and even for buying things, makes up for everything.

ADRIAN AND ISOLDE

One shopping and buying expedition with Traubel I shall not forget. It resulted in the costumes designed by Adrian for Isolde, Brünnhilde, and other roles, which startled the

Metropolitan two seasons ago. Adrian is probably the most inspired and intelligent designer of stage costumes for women known to the American scene. He is the husband of Janet Gaynor, and formerly did all costume design for one of the most important motion picture producing companies. A few years ago he decided to work independently of the pictures, and his success has been emphatic. I went with Helen and Mr. Bass several times to Adrian's sumptuous atelier in Beverly Hills when he was developing the costumes. I went the first time to see the costumes and the other times to see the models. I was fascinated by everything I saw.

The costumes probably were a great success with the public. They were shrewdly designed for the regal Traubel figure, and the rather static Traubel stage deportment. Their lines and colors were superbly adapted to the visual requirements of the huge Metropolitan; they were marvelously plastic and beautiful in line, incandescent in color, in every way becoming to the diva, the theater, the opera, and the situations for which they were made. They had no resemblance to the badly laundered nightgowns, frayed burlap sacking, and moth-eaten carriage robes that pass for Wagnerian costumes at the Metropolitan. Because they didn't, because they were different, because they weren't traditional, they found no favor with most of the critics. They couldn't find anything in Traubel's singing to be catty about, but they had a picnic with Adrian and the Isolde costume. I don't know what the management thought, but doubtless the idea occurred to them that the critics don't pay for their seats, and the public buys all the seats and standing room too when Traubel's name is on the billboards.

The result of my first interview with Helen and her manager was, within a few days, a signed contract for her to make Red Seal records. Later, I dealt with that fine, loyal, wise man, Lawrence Evans, whose guidance has been enormously helpful to Traubel. I was very proud that Victor had engaged

Helen; she herself told me a little later that she was proud
too, and that ever since childhood, she had wanted more
keenly to be a Red Seal artist than anything else—even a
Metropolitan prima donna. I had great hopes for her records,
even though at the time the renaissance of the record business was not quite complete. I encountered difficulties from
the start. At first I was not permitted the expense of an orchestra for her and had perforce to be content with a few records
of lieder. No one living can sing them more beautifully, but
lieder are not the ideal thing with which to startle a mass
market such as I felt Helen could and should reach. When
at length I did get the money for an orchestra, it had to be a
small and inadequate one. Helen Traubel appreciated my difficulties, and was incredibly patient. I hadn't her forbearance,
however, and determined to take matters into my own hands
and spend a little money without authority.

My opportunity to do this came in connection with a Philadelphia Orchestra recording session. I made certain arrangements for keeping a part of the orchestra—about fifty-five
out of a hundred and eight—after the regular session; Helen
agreed to be there, and we chose to do the scena "Dich teure
Halle," together with its brilliant orchestral prelude (never
before recorded in its entirety) and the noble aria "Divinités
du Styx" from Gluck's Alceste. I rehearsed the orchestra for
about five minutes in each aria, having previously worked them
out with Helen and the piano, of course; and in a total time
of twenty minutes [1] we recorded both numbers. In truth it
took no longer to make the records than it takes to play them;
Helen sang them once, and that was that. The Wagner turned
out magnificently; the Gluck was not satisfactory. We made
it again later, in Town Hall, with a different orchestra, and we
are proud of it. I am not proud of the fact, however, that the
puissant and wealthy RCA so dealt with one of the greatest
of living singers that I had to resort to petty subterfuge in order

---

[1] This constituted a union half-hour, and cost Victor the sum of $392.

to provide her with an adequate orchestral accompaniment.

I give you some detail of this recording because it was to
have a bearing on subsequent events of more importance. The
record itself was mentioned in some quarters as "the record
of the year," which I do believe it was—notwithstanding the
subsequent pronouncement of a self-appointed record critic,
now one of Mr. Toscanini's worshippers, that the Gluck aria
was marred by "wildly wayward conducting." This comment
struck me as being rather odd, since it happened that Toscanini's own, unsolicited opinion was that on this record he
had heard for the first time the *"Divinités"* aria correctly done;
and that my tempi and phrasing were absolutely correct. "Believe a woman or an epitaph, or any other thing that's false,
before you trust in critics."

Not long after the release of this record Mr. Toscanini decided to give a benefit concert with the NBC Orchestra in
Carnegie Hall—I think it was for the Red Cross. He elected to
make it an all-Wagner program, and proposed to do certain
sequences from the *Ring* with the solo voices. He was not interested in any Wagnerian soprano that he knew, and no one
in his immediate retinue seemed able to suggest a satisfactory
one. He mentioned the matter to me, and I immediately
proposed Traubel. The maestro said that he did not know her
or her work, whereupon I was reckless enough to guarantee
him that he would engage Traubel sight unseen if he would
hear a record she had made. He agreed to listen, I sent him
the Wagner-Gluck record, and Traubel was engaged. Mme
Flagstad was available, if I remember correctly, but Toscanini
definitely and explicitly did not want her. I had a double
purpose in plotting this engagement of Traubel. I wanted an
occasion that would bring her most powerfully to public attention; I wanted to follow it up with some really sensational
records. Therefore, while Toscanini was still afire with enthusiasm for Traubel, I proposed that he should not only do the
Immolation Scene with her on his program, but also should

record it with her. He liked this project and agreed to undertake it. We had in our catalog two recordings of the Immolation Scene; a third had been made but never issued, but none, I supposed, could possibly equal a new one, done with the most modern techniques by a singer such as Traubel and with Toscanini as conductor. So, we did the *Götterdämmerung* scene on records the day after the public performance.

There has been more than a little controversy concerning these records. Already they have been a major factor in Victor's loss of Traubel's services as an artist; disputes about them have contributed to the estrangement of Toscanini from Victor and from me; mechanical manipulations of them in an effort to satisfy what seemed to me the conductor's petty, captious, and unreasonable criticisms have robbed them of some of their pristine bloom and brilliance; and I question that they will ever be released to the public in their original form or with their original quality. Here is exactly what happened:

As always, when we were recording a work that extended over more than one record surface, I prepared the score for Toscanini, indicating where necessary interruptions between record sides were to occur. This is a matter of timing, of finding a satisfactory point of suspension or resolution to coincide with the end of the record and within the playing time of the record, of utilizing a reasonable proportion of possible playing time, of so arranging matters that we shall have an even number of record sides, and of doing the least possible violence to the music. But the playing time of a record is variable, being a function of the width of the "lands" between the grooves, and the width of the lands is determined by the dynamics of the music. The more powerful the sound wave, the wider and stronger the land must be, in order to confine the oscillation of the cutting needle. But the wider the lands, the fewer you can cut in a given area; and the fewer you cut, the shorter the playing time of the record. Clear?

At any rate, taking all these factors into consideration, I

submitted to Toscanini my suggestions for dividing the twenty-odd minutes of the scene. I made five divisions, six sides. Maestro approved all division points but one, and he chose to leave a chord hanging in the air, whereas if he had played but one additional chord, as I suggested, the record would have come to a tonic close, logical and ear-satisfying. However, there was no dispute then, and just to make certain that everyone understood and approved the divisions, Toscanini, Traubel, and I went through the score with the piano just prior to the recording.

We made the records with much less distress than I had expected; and when I heard the proof records I was really wild with happiness. Things *had* gone smoothly. Not once did any utterance of Traubel evoke a Toscanini criticism; what few difficulties there were developed in the orchestra, and these were little things easily and quickly corrected. For the most part the work was rehearsed once, then done quickly for the record. Everyone was enthusiastic, everyone did his best, and the final records showed it.

I brought a set of the records to Traubel and she was delighted. Indeed, she might well be, for never had the real Traubel voice, with all its power, its divine tenderness, its human warmth, its lustrous color, been imprisoned on a record. The orchestra flashed and thundered and whispered and sang and breathed with the voice; those records were, I firmly believe, the closest to perfection we shall ever know. Toscanini was profoundly impressed, but did not give unqualified approval, though I could not at the time worm out of him nor out of his son and agent Walter any reason for withholding it. Ultimately it developed that the cause of his unwillingness to give approval was not musical, but commercial—not, actually, *intelligently* commercial: simply stupid.

It happens that the Victor catalog lists a recording of this music, done by Flagstad and the orchestra of the San Francisco Opera (San Francisco Symphony men) under the direction of Edwin McArthur. This recording is contained on four sides, the Traubel-Toscanini on six. This happened because, first of all, Victor's Hollywood studios, where Flagstad recorded, have equipment that can cut at rather high volume levels a standard twelve-inch record that will run well over five minutes; the portable equipment used in Carnegie Hall is limited to four minutes, eight seconds, with high volume level. Secondly, the Flagstad recording is done safely and conservatively, and the limit of time duration is employed, whereas with Toscanini I did not wish nor dare to modify his dynamics, as would have been absolutely necessary if we had adjusted our recorders to finer groove-and-land, and consequent longer playing time.

Walter Toscanini, after months of prodding, finally divulged the information that his father was not satisfied with the records or with the divisions in them, that they would be more expensive than the Flagstad Immolation, being extended over six sides as against her four, and that therefore people would not buy them. I was honestly surprised to discover that Toscanini would permit such considerations to enter into his attitude toward his own recordings; but taking my cue from him, I pointed out that people *would* buy his record, and *would* pay more, and indeed *should*, because a Toscanini-Traubel record is worth more than a Flagstad-McArthur record. Meanwhile, Toscanini displayed to various friends, privately, the keenest enthusiasm for the records as music, even taking the discs to dinner-parties to gloat over them in company with his hosts.

Meanwhile, Traubel was getting rather impatient for the records to appear. At that time they could have accelerated the career that she has since accomplished singlehanded; and they would, I am sure, have overcome the inertia of Victor and stimulated interest in other records of Traubel. So I agreed to reduce the six sides to five, by re-recording; not an easy thing to do in this case, but possible. It was done successfully, and Toscanini approved the re-recording—according to Walter. BUT—before the record could be released, certain brass parts would have to be reinforced! In other words, I would have to manage, somehow, to fortify, at certain moments, a single line in the complex Wagnerian score. If this could be done at all, it would need the services of the NBC Orchestra's first trumpet, but he was not available, because Mr. Petrillo had forbidden union members to record for Victor. Here was a situation!

Theoretically, what Mr. Toscanini wanted could be done, but only with a certain loss of quality, of brilliance, and sonority, as well as gain in background noise in the records. I was unwilling to undertake it, and from a musical point of view I didn't agree that any further prominence of the trumpet leit-motiv was required. I even arranged to have Frank Black and Samuel Chotzinoff come to Camden, listen to the records, and say whether, in their opinion, what Maestro wanted was really necessary. Neither of them could find a flaw of any sort in the records.

At this point Walter performed a miracle. Despite the union ban on recording, the Toscanini name was so potent with President James C. Petrillo, of the American Federation of Musicians, that permission was given for the employment in recording of Mr. Harry Glanz, first trumpet of the NBC Symphony. By a process too technical for description here, we carefully overlaid the original first and second trumpet parts (in certain phrases) with a new layer of sound, so that they appeared much more prominent. You will remember that, by somewhat the same process, we had already reduced the records from six sides to five, and that Toscanini had approved the re-recorded fifth side. In reinforcing the trumpet part, we did not touch the fifth record side again as the maestro had already approved it. Now he withdrew his approval of the fifth side, and demanded that the trumpet be reinforced here also. In other words, if by chance the records ever reached the market, you would be sold a record of a record of a record—a thing far removed from the glorious revelation of Wagner's music, Traubel's voice, and Toscanini's orchestra that we first heard from the disc.

Just about here I quit. By a coincidence, so did Traubel.

I understand that since then, the entire *Götterdämmerung* set has been again re-recorded, and what I have heard of it is not what I should like to hear, though still rather magnificent.

On the whole, the association of two of the artists I have most admired turned out, in spite of its auspicious beginnings, rather disastrously. It did, however, produce an incident that demonstrated Traubel's musical integrity and her loyalty, for which I must ever be grateful. There arose a question of how we should fill out the *Götterdämmerung* set to six sides, since to release an odd-sided set is uneconomical, and unsatisfactory to people who buy records. Toscanini suggested, indeed urged Traubel to record with him the *"Dich teure Halle"* which, you may recall, she had already done with me. Traubel stoutly refused, and said plainly that she had made the record with me, that she could find in it no flaw important enough to justify remaking it, that it came as near to satisfying her as she could possibly expect, that, much as she would and did enjoy singing with Toscanini, she did not think it would be fair to Victor or to me to do this record over again without some very compelling reason. In a word, she said no.

I have always had a certain respect—indeed, a profound admiration—for Mme Traubel's vocabulary of vituperation and profanity. I have prayed nightly that it might never be turned on me, at least in my presence, for I'm sure I should wilt under it. Never, in my acquaintance with her, has Helen so exhaustively explored her *Schimpflexikon* as in connection with the *Götterdämmerung* episode in particular and her recording situation in general. I am afraid that finally she lost interest in the records, perhaps in all records. Or, possibly her new connection will be sufficiently agreeable to obliterate the remembrance of things past. At least it is bringing her voice into the lives of many new thousands who will treasure it.

In the course of some random reading, I encountered recently the following lines, written about Traubel:

"Here is a voice cast in an Olympian mold, a personality warmly and nobly human. No name among the immortals of music is more proudly set down in these pages. Here is a native American, born in the American city of St. Louis, of native American parents—who is already of the elect in the world of song. Helen Traubel's voice, in sheer musical quality, in heroic amplitude, in range and expressiveness, in warmth and communicative power, is the peer of any; even more important is the fact that it is directed, supported and used by a musical intelligence, a fastidious taste and a glowing personality of the most exceptional rarity and charm.

"This artist, who looks like a goddess and sings like a goddess should, did not reach fame overnight. Perhaps she could have, perhaps she should have; but she preferred the long and difficult way of steady, persistent study; of contempt for easy success and easy rewards; of slow, sure development; of broad and profound, rather than specialized and superficial musical culture."

It occurred to me that the writer of those words made a fair estimate of Traubel, and really, even if he was a little extravagant, meant what he said.

I know he did. I wrote those words seven years ago.

I meant them then.

I mean them now.

JASCHA
HEIFETZ

⊷ Jascha Heifetz ⊶

"To thine own self be true. . . ."

"AND WHO, Mr. O'Connell, will pay the hotel and 'raveling expenses of myself and my representative, from New York to Philadelphia, Camden and return?"

"You will, sir."

The question was asked with the iciest hauteur, which is perhaps why my answer to Jascha was rather "curt, clear, concise." The occasion was the first recording I had undertaken with Heifetz, more than ten years ago; it was also one of the first I had ever been responsible for, and I felt a certain strain. I had been warned that Heifetz was aloof, difficult, and overbearing; and that if he felt he could successfully impose this attitude once, I'd never thereafter be able to cope with him. All this was untrue, and though Jascha accepted my statement calmly and without question, I have to this day regretted its uncompromising and abrupt quality. I have come to understand him rather well, and from that understanding has developed a warm and durable friendship, highly prized indeed. One of the things I began to understand on that very first occasion of our working together was that Jascha not only likes, but insists upon having, everything strictly *en règle*, and strictly in accordance with his understanding of the *règles*. In the instance I cite, Jascha wasn't interested in the few dollars involved in a two-day sojourn in Philadelphia or Camden, where our studios were located at the time. He was very much interested in seeing to it, personally, that the company would fulfill all its obligations, and pay his expenses, if it were "so nominated in the bond." For my part, I was very much interested in seeing to it that expenses were kept at the minimum, because at that stage of the renaissance of recorded music, any disbursement for which I was responsible would be gone over with a rather jaundiced eye, and I had obtained authority to proceed with recording under our contracts only on my representation that it would cost nothing except our materials and labor. I was happy, therefore, that Jascha so meekly accepted my verdict, and I began at once to regard him with a much more friendly eye. The truth was that his contract required him to present himself, at a mutually convenient time, at our studios in Camden or elsewhere, to complete the requirements of our recording agreement. There was no stipulation respecting the expenses of his traveling, and I was determined that we would not be responsible for them. The records we made—the Richard Strauss sonata,[1] a lovely little piece called An Einsamer Quelle, and one or two other morçeaux—wouldn't have justified much financial investment anyway. Wonderful they were, but the Strauss sonata, difficult, ungrateful, and appealing mostly to the connoisseur, never sold very well. Anyone who ever thought Heifetz "cold," however, should listen to his tone in An Einsamer Quelle! Not many did.

At this same recording session I had a rather startling experience of the fiendish accuracy of Jascha's sense of pitch. Naturally, I had had our piano, a fine Steinway concert grand that had been used for a season by Rachmaninoff and then bought by Victor, tuned for the occasion, and the tuner had finished not five minutes before Jascha arrived. I asked him to stay

---

[1] I am reliably informed that the first performance of the Richard Strauss violin sonata, in this country, was accomplished by Arthur Judson—yes, the Arthur Judson, concert manager of Heifetz and many other great artists, and guiding hand of almost all symphony conductors in America.

around a few minutes until we could get started, and it was rather fortunate that I did so. Jascha came in, laid down his violin case, walked over to the piano, touched a note and said, "This piano is out of tune." I indignantly disagreed, and Jascha just as vigorously insisted he was right. He touched another note and I said, "If that 'A' isn't absolute 440 I'd give a ten-dollar bill to anybody who would prove it." [2] Jascha said, "You are right, it is a 440 'A,' but I tune to 444." Whereupon I recalled the tuner, Jascha gave the tuner his "A," and we sat there and waited while the piano was pulled up to 444 "A" from top to bottom. I may be wrong about the exact frequency of Jascha's "A," but at least it was not more than three or four cycles different from the standard 440.

Curiously, Heifetz and I had another disagreement over expenses, and this time in connection with one of the last of his recordings, the Walton concerto, which he recorded with the Cincinnati Symphony under Eugene Goossens' direction. I had been at some difficulty and very substantial expense in arranging this recording. Jascha and Gene were quite leisurely in making the records—which is as it should be, but Victor, footing the bills, doesn't see it that way—and when after considerable unexpected cost and other irritations I was confronted with a bill for about sixty dollars for traveling expenses, from Jascha, it was too much; not too much money, but too much irritation. Sixty dollars isn't a great sum in comparison with the several thousands I had spent for the orchestra musicians' services, but out of sheer mulishness I wouldn't pay it. There was considerable acidulous correspondence between J. H. and myself, both of us being pretty stubborn. I had a feeling that I'd have to capitulate eventually, so I cast about for some kind of face-saving device and thought I had found one. I agreed to pay Jascha not his traveling expenses, but rather the recording fee of a union musician, which in fact

---

[2] Pianos are tuned to 440 "A"; that is, the "A" above middle "C" vibrates at the rate of 440 cycles per second, and all other notes on the piano are brought into a modified mathematical relationship with this "A."

we were required, by our arrangement with the American Federation of Musicians, to pay any player who recorded for us, be he Heifetz, Rachmaninoff, or some obscure fiddler. This would have amounted to eighty-four dollars, as against the sixty-odd dollars Jascha demanded for expenses. Jascha very calmly, firmly and good-naturedly refused the eighty-four dollars and reiterated his demand for sixty. He got it. Ever since we have regarded each other as poor businessmen. He says I am because he thinks I wanted to pay more than he asked; I think he is because he took less than he should have been paid.

Once convinced he is right, Heifetz is the most stonily stubborn individual I have ever met. He has a set of principles devised by himself, and as far as I know wholly admirable. No power this side of paradise can force or persuade him to deviate from them by one-tenth of one degree. In the instance I have just cited, he felt that, regardless of what his contract might say, the company had asked him to change his plans and the course of his tour in order to make a record, and therefore should in equity be responsible for the personal expenses he incurred. That the making of the record was to his advantage, that the company spent some thousands of dollars in making it, had no bearing on the case. His expenses should be paid— by the company. Why didn't he take the larger sum offered him and call it expenses? For three reasons: his very sensitive conscience would be troubled, his meticulous accounts would have to include something equivocal, and he would be tacitly accepting working conditions imposed by the musicians' union, which at the time he was vigorously opposing. This last seemed especially entertaining to me later when I found that for many years Jascha has been an honorary member of the union—the Los Angeles local, I think. In return for his services, gratis, at a benefit sponsored by the local years ago, the privileges of a union worker—but not the responsibilities— were bestowed on him. I wonder if Mr. Petrillo knew this when Jascha was so vigorously having at him.

Certain aspects of his playing really represent corresponding qualities of the man himself. Of his personal and artistic integrity, almost unique in the whole world of musicians, I need not speak. But he is also careful, meticulous, precise, scrupulous, and ethical in everything he does. He is reluctant to make a promise, or any kind of commitment whatever; but once made, agreements and promises are kept to the letter. This has been embarrassing to him at times, I am sure. I could almost see his mental distress on one occasion when, I suppose, he must have come as close as ever he could to breaking his word. Some very nasty reports about me had been brought to him, very likely in confidence, and he actually writhed in indecision as to whether he should tell me of them to protect me against those who were circulating them, and in doing so violate his *parole* to people much closer to him than I was—or, knowing these stories to be untrue, let me go on in ignorance of them until the inevitable damage resulted. Jascha never explicitly quoted these stories to me or mentioned anyone's name as author of them (I got the facts from other and less scrupulous sources), but in retrospect I can see that he gave me more than one subtle warning, and many an oblique suggestion, which I was too naïve at the time to appreciate.

Heifetz is so direct and honest himself that he often doesn't see, or at least doesn't want to see, dissimilar qualities in others. We had been for some time agreed on the validity of a project that had become a "pet" of mine and of which J. H. was to be an important part. I have long believed that all the truly great masterpieces of music should be recorded by *all* the ablest interpreters. There are conductors other than Beecham who have something to say in Mozart, others than Koussevitzky can set forth the music of Tchaikovsky. Stokowski is not the only exciting conductor of Wagner. Every great interpreter projects every great work with authority and intelligence, if not necessarily definitively; and each first-rank interpreter has an audience that thinks *he* is number one man, and that is entitled to satisfaction on records. It was part of my plan that each of the most distinguished violinists under contract to us should, as circumstances made it practicable, record all the unequivocal masterpieces of violin literature. I wanted first of all Heifetz, whom I consider absolutely *hors de concours* of living instrumentalists, to undertake all the five or six really master concertos. The project had progressed. He had recorded the Sibelius with Stokowski (and discarded it, I thought unreasonably); he made it again in England, satisfactorily; he had done the Brahms with Koussevitzky; his Tchaikovsky was in our catalog; the Walton, which he considers as ranking with the others I have mentioned, was in prospect; so were the Mendelssohn, the Chausson *Poème*, and the Elgar. The presence of Toscanini, and the excellence of the NBC Symphony, suggested the possibility of a glorious Beethoven concerto, and I agreed with Jascha that if arrangements with Mr. Toscanini could be made, we would undertake the work at the first opportunity.

I was unable, for more than a year I think, to penetrate to Toscanini with this idea. It was necessary at the time, for reasons I don't recall, to approach the maestro through Samuel Chotzinoff. I didn't anticipate any difficulty here, since Chotzinoff is Jascha's brother-in-law, and might be presumed favorable to Jascha's project. Month after month went by; Jascha needled me, I needled Chotzinoff, and nothing happened. Finally I decided that a violation of NBC-Toscanini protocol was less important than a rift between Jascha and myself: I went directly to Toscanini (who possibly had been prepared by J. H.). I found him instantly responsive, and we recorded the concerto in one of the most strenuous and rewarding working days I can recall.

This recording brought about one of those occasions when Toscanini must have thought I was insane. I had, after some prolonged and serious efforts, convinced him that NBC's Studio 8H was not a satisfactory place for making records, and we had definitely decided to do them elsewhere. Now, however, I insisted on making the Beethoven concerto in that studio. I had good reasons, I think. Toscanini and Heifetz are both precisionists. With them, a sixteenth note is exactly so long and no longer. If, upon the note that is played, you superimpose the resonant period of a concert hall, you either to some extent soften and blur the musical line, or if the effect is exaggerated, actually distort time values, and in any case rob the music of a certain intimacy and clarity of detail. Carnegie Hall, where if my own taste were to decide, we would have made this recording, has a resonant period (when no audience is present) of approximately one second. You may call it "echo," if you wish. NBC's Studio 8H, to which Toscanini had accommodated the balance of his orchestra, has a resonant period of about six-tenths of a second. If you don't believe four-tenths of a second make a world of difference, listen to two records made respectively in these halls; or recall, if you can, the quality of the broadcasts of the Philharmonic-Symphony and those of the NBC Orchestra when Toscanini first came. Records show a proportionate difference.

It is difficult to record with enough clarity and detail and precision to please Toscanini; when at the same time Heifetz is involved, the difficulties are multiplied not by two but ten times over. Heifetz may not be more the perfectionist, but he has better natural equipment for being one. It is pleasant to report that my judgment was accepted by both artists, that the recording session was without untoward incident though it exhausted, through its length and tension, everyone concerned, that the records were approved by Heifetz and Toscanini, and indeed are of jewellike perfection. It was rather entertaining to observe these two men, so alike in some ways, yet so disparate in age, disposition, and musical outlook, working together during this recording. Outwardly they observed the most rigid punctilio; actually they were as wary as two strange cats, each determined to give the other no opening for criticism, each fiercely resolved upon perfection in every mood and tempo. I must say in candor that this did result, I think, in rushing of tempo here and there, but perhaps this is merely my perverted and malicious imagination. At any rate, the records were issued. Not inappropriately, the album in which they were presented to the public bore on its cover a huge multicolored jewel—an attempt on my part at flattering Heifetz, which he completely ignored. "Heifetz" (and Jascha didn't know it) means "jewel."

HEIFETZ COLD?

If you mean, "Is he cold in human relationships?" I answer with an emphatic negative. If you mean "cold" musically, my answer is precisely the same. If you mean that his playing is preternaturally perfect technically, if you mean that every move of bow and arm and wrist and finger is absolutely controlled, exquisitely calculated, if you mean that he never abandons himself to emotion or tears a passion to tatters, if you mean that his approach to music is objective, that he scrutinizes it as a lapidary examines a gem stone, weighing, assaying, evaluating the spiritual and intellectual qualities, if you mean that he brings to bear upon music intelligence and intuition of singular power and penetration—if by "coldness" you can mean these things, I'll agree that Heifetz in his music is cold. I have never been convinced of the soundness of the Horatian advice *"Si vis me flere dolendum est primum ipsi tibi"*—"If you wish me to weep, you must first weep yourself." I know no artist, musician or other, who can afford to abandon himself to emotion; I know no musician who ever does. Such abandon is a luxury the audience pays to enjoy; the performer has other things on his mind, and must have. Emotion is certainly the motive power of art, but emotion *isn't* art, it's nature; music and painting and acting are devices, essentially unnatural, for sublimating, transmitting, and regenerating emotion, and are not designed, primarily at least, for the emotional debauchery of the interpreter.

When Heifetz appears on the stage there is no posturing. "What went ye out to see? A reed shaken by the wind?" You often do—but not at a Heifetz recital. You do perhaps observe a face of Oriental impassiveness, but I think that this expression, or absence of it, comes about because Heifetz pours into his playing every last iota of concentration, of nervous and muscular strength, of a co-ordination of mind, heart, and hand so exquisitely adjusted and so precise that even a smile or a frown would disturb it. If you consider too that despite a certain arrogance of manner Heifetz is actually diffident and really modest you will understand, I think, how it happens that he can give an impression of remoteness and frigidity.

I will not forget an incident, one not without certain humorous aspects, that came about in connection with Jascha's recording of the Brahms concerto. It illustrates not only his artistic integrity, but at the same time a degree of human warmth I found quite touching. We had as usual spent a great deal of recording time and money on this work, as indeed the importance of the music and of the artists would dictate. Ten days later I took the records to Koussevitzky, who had conducted, and to my secret surprise, he approved them without reservation. I was surprised because I had noticed certain details that I thought the fastidious conductor of the Boston Symphony would not overlook. Frankly, I was gratified too, because authority—and money—to make this recording had not been easy to get; having obtained them, I was eager and anxious about making the investment a profitable one.

A few days later, in the backwash of a February snowstorm, I drove from Camden, New Jersey, to Heifetz's place in Connecticut, and my troubles began. I skidded from ditch to ditch on those country roads, fearing not so much for my pretty Zephyr, or even for my own bones, as for those precious records. I became lost, and to be late for an appointment with Jascha is unforgivable. In attempting to make up lost time I was arrested and further delayed. Finally, when embarrassed, panting but triumphant I produced the records in Heifetz's house, the final appalling blow fell. They wouldn't fit his phonograph.

Let me explain that at the time—I assure you not since this

experience!—test records, that is, the "proofs" submitted to
the artist for his approval, were rather roughly made. Their
playing surface was good enough, but they varied in diameter
quite considerably, and were always more than twelve inches
in this dimension. Heifetz had a Capehart automatic instrument, so designed that a record even a little in excess of twelve
inches in diameter would not fit on the turntable. If you think
Jascha's face is cold you should have seen it when this situation developed! I had to think fast, and I did get an idea. "You
call this a farm, don't you, Jascha?" A tight-lipped affirmative.
"Well then, a farm must have tools; tools must be sharpened;
you must have a grindstone; where is it?" It was Jascha's turn
to think fast, and he did. Grinning like a little boy, he led me
to the tool house where we found a grindstone, one that was
operated by pedals like a bicycle. For more than two hours we
slaved there, alternating in pumping the wheel and pressing
the records edgewise against it. I dare say you have often
noticed that records break or chip easily around the edge—but
don't ever think the material isn't hard!

Finally we had the records roughed down so that they would
fit on the turntable. Really they were marvelous. The same
little troubles I had noted at the audition with Koussevitzky
were there; no matter how tightly I'd close my ears they
wouldn't go away, and at the appearance of each one Jascha
would look at me with the eye of a basilisk. I knew I was lost
before we had finished, but determined to bluff it out to the
bitter end. Jascha knew perfectly well how much the company
had at stake; he knew Koussevitzky had already approved the
records; and he knew how desperately I wanted the records
approved, how much this approval would mean to me personally and professionally. We discussed them rather vaguely,
Jascha knowing that he couldn't approve them, and knowing
that I knew he couldn't, knowing too that I hoped he would.

Canny Jascha! Kindly Jascha! Somewhat cruel Jascha! He
couldn't honestly approve those records; he had reason to believe that his non-approval would not encourage the possibility

of doing them over again in Boston; he knew that I knew every musical reason why he couldn't give his approval. So he didn't give it. He said, in effect, that he would neither approve nor disapprove the records; that I might take them back to Camden without his veto, and he implied that we might issue them. "But," he said (and he was taking a hell of a gamble), "you are a musician, Charlie. I know exactly how you feel, and you know exactly how I feel about these records. You are also a friend. Consider everything involved, and use your own judgment." It is impossible for me to convey to you the importance of this remark by Heifetz. He wasn't trying to evade responsibility; that would be impossible for him. He didn't and doesn't care about the opinion of anyone but himself in musical matters. He was, however, giving me a bolt-hole, to use or not use as seemed wiser to me. At the same time he knew, the fox, which side would win when my musical and personal feelings came into conflict with more material considerations. The records went back to Camden as "not approved"; the sky did not collapse, Koussevitzky was easily persuaded to do them again, and the result is a truly beautiful recording of the Brahms.

I did not have so much luck with Jascha in the case of another and more recent recording. Arthur Benjamin has written a quite fascinating work for violin, viola, and orchestra, and Heifetz wanted to record it as his annual concerto. Circumstances made it necessary to do the recording in California. The only orchestra and conductor available were the Janssen Symphony of Los Angeles and its founder-conductor, Werner Janssen. William Primrose played the solo viola part. After a bitter struggle, we finished the recording, but I fear you will never hear it. It was a trying experience for Werner, unaccustomed to our kind of recording, with a new orchestra, and everyone ill at ease and somewhat in awe of the great Heifetz. The whole atmosphere was charged with animosities. The record is a good one, a satisfying one, as perfect technically as records ever are. Perhaps Werner should have made some places a little smoother; perhaps if he had exhibited more poise and less fever, Jascha would not have been so antagonized. At any rate, approval of the records has been long withheld by Heifetz—Primrose and Janssen dissenting; and I think, and I have told Jascha that I think, his approval is petulantly, capriciously, and unfairly withheld.

That amazing series of chamber-music works [3] issued by Victor during the last several years represents the beginning of another long-range project in which Heifetz was a most interested, helpful, and enthusiastic collaborator—indeed, the mainspring. I think it is extraordinary that a group of virtuosos, men of such extraordinary individuality, force, and diverse temperaments could come together, even in music, and so completely submit themselves to ensemble. This is the final proof not only of great musicianship but of greatness of spirit —and these qualities I would never deny to Heifetz, to Rubinstein, to Primrose, and certainly not to my beloved friend, the late Emanuel Feuermann. Making these records, though it represented extremely taxing labors on the part of the artists, was really a joy. There were difficulties, to be sure, but somehow the spirit of this ensemble made itself felt so strongly that all difficulties, personal and other, were resolved quickly and amicably. There was no haste, there was no compulsion, there was no thought of anything but making music, making it beautiful, and making it permanent. I think everyone sensed that an extraordinary achievement was being accomplished, though, like big-league ball players when a pitcher is trying for a no-hit game, we kept our mouths shut and our fingers crossed until it was all over. The issue of these records put Victor definitely, if perhaps only temporarily, in the lead-

---

[3] Beethoven—Trio No. 7 in B-flat ("Archduke")
Dohnanyi—Serenade for Violin, Viola, and Cello in C major
Brahms—Trio for Piano, Violin, and Cello in B major
Schubert—Trio for Piano, Violin, and Cello in B-flat major
Mozart—Divertimento for Violin, Viola, and Cello in E flat
Beethoven—Duet in E flat for Viola and Cello
Chausson—Concerto for Violin, Piano, and String Quartet

ing position so far as recorded chamber music is concerned, which is exactly what I wanted to accomplish. However, I have no means of knowing whether the success of these works will be followed up by others of equal worth. I do know that the same ensemble cannot be gathered together again, for the untimely death of Feuermann completely destroyed the enthusiasm and the spirit that had made these records possible, and therefore Jascha has flatly refused, despite any and all inducements, to undertake further recordings of this kind.

The preparation for the chamber-music records had put everyone under considerable strain. The players had slaved for months to perfect themselves in interpretation and ensemble. The actual recording took its toll of everyone's nervous energy. When the last record had been made satisfactorily, an impromptu party was arranged, and I understand it was quite a party. I did not join it because my own nerves had been rubbed raw from morning to night for too many days in the studio, and I honestly feared that the reaction which might come about at a gay party could lead me to indiscretions of speech that I might later regret. I have celebrated more than once with Jascha, however, and he himself has been host at some notable fiestas. When I first knew him he occupied an enormous apartment at 247 Park Avenue—an apartment so big that two full concert Steinways standing at one end of it looked, from the other end, like miniature grands. I am sure that room was a hundred feet long, and it was a marvelous place for entertaining. I have seen well over a hundred people seated in it, and nobody was crowded. I remember this particular occasion because I had the pleasure of seeing a copy of the first edition of my book, *The Victor Book of the Symphony*,[4] auctioned off by Albert Spalding for $18.50.

The room was filled with magnificent pictures, French furniture, rugs, and tapestries. Behind one of the rarest of these tapestries was a little door, and if you pushed the tapestry aside

[4] *The Victor Book of the Symphony* by Charles O'Connell, Simon and Schuster, New York.

and went in through this little door you were in an old-fashioned barroom, complete to the soap painting on the mirror, the sixteen-inch brass spittoon on the floor, and a bartender's license, issued to Jascha Heifetz, framed on the wall. There was also a working cash register, and I mean to say it worked, for Jascha demanded some contribution, whether it was a penny or a twenty-dollar goldpiece, for each and every drink he served. He would ring up your money with a flourish, and I know a certain charity that profited very handsomely.

Jascha likes a party as well as anyone else. When he has work to do, however, nothing will tempt him to gaiety and he lives the life of an anchorite. I do not believe he has ever been intemperate in anything. He loves good food and drink, indulges in them moderately, and loves good company the while. He is fond of the theater and likes music well enough to go to concerts other than his own. His house in Connecticut was an old one, remodeled and enlarged, and this had been done in such taste that the exquisite simplicity of the original house had not in any way been compromised. His home in Balboa, California was somewhat more to my taste. It was designed in accordance with the Frank Lloyd Wright school of modern architecture, largely of native materials. It was beautiful, practical, and *gemütlich*, which is enough for any house to be. But I think Harbor Island at Balboa is little better than a mud-flat. Jascha's interest in boats, of course, led him there, and doubtless for him it was an eminently satisfying location, since his yacht was anchored practically in the living-room.

Heifetz preserves his youth of body and spirit very remarkably, I think. He is about my age, and that is our affair; and he has been before the public since he was a child. His face is yet unlined, his bow arm strong and firm, his left hand knows no error, and his nerves, though acutely sensitive, are under rigid and utterly perfect control. I remember when Jascha used to get himself pinched for speeding once in a while, and there are those who know of gay escapades in Paris and elsewhere. But these are a tale that is told.

PIERRE
MONTEUX

∞§ Pierre Monteux ১◦

"His wise, rare smile is sweet with certainties,

And seems in all his patients to compel

Such love and faith as failure cannot quell."

WILLIAM ERNEST HENLEY: *In Hospital*

THESE LINES were written of the great physician Lister, and it seems to me that they apply with equal aptness to Pierre Monteux. It has been suggested that a great conductor should be a teacher and a philosopher, and I think that also he must be a doctor, which, after all, is but another way of saying "teacher." Monteux, one of the half-dozen great conductors and the peer of any of them, is a philosopher, a teacher, and a doctor—a doctor of preventive musical medicine. As a teacher prevents error by inculcating truth, as a philosopher extracts most from life by his primary assumption that human beings are human and sinners will sin, as a doctor thwarts illness and pain by preventing them before he has to cure them, so this modest, happy, profound, genial man makes beautiful music, and makes music beautiful by excluding from it in advance every trace of error, of ugliness. He prevents wrong so that it is not necessary to correct it, he passes music through his own clear mind and warm heart so that it flows between him and his instrument—his orchestra—in a shining stream by which even the dullest are enlightened, of such gently irresistible force that the most indolent are constrained to effort and the most enthusiastic are borne above their natural level.

The most sophisticated orchestra in the world glows with new luster in the reflection of his smile—a smile that is by no means the painfully ingratiating smirk of the typical guest conductor but an expression of serenity and confidence and love of life, of music, of work, of being, that is utterly irresistible. "Smile, Charlie, smile when you conduct. Don't you love music? Don't you love to conduct the orchestra? Aren't you happy when you do? Then you must make your musicians know this. Music usually smiles; you must smile too, and you must first smile inside of yourself and then it will come out all right."

If one knows Monteux as a man of the most profound and flawless musicianship and encyclopedic musical knowledge, fastidious taste, almost miraculous technique, and orchestral experience beyond that of any living conductor, it seems absurd to refer to his smile as one of his important assets. Yet it is no less than this, for somehow bound up in it are all the musical and human qualities of the man that combine to make him a noble soul and a sensitive musician. The smile can be reproving too, as well as genial. It can, and does, express gentle ridicule, incredulity, amazement, mockery, sympathy, or praise. It can signal a humor that is pointed but never barbed. It can silently praise a man when he has done his best, and as silently and emphatically make him feel small when he has fallen short. It can and does hide disappointments and such griefs as few men are called upon to bear, and it must indeed hide both the contempt and pity that so great a soul must feel for the little ones that have harmed him. It is true that "one may smile, and smile, and be a villain." It is equally true, I think, that one may smile and be a hero.

When I say of Monteux that he has a sense of humor I mean something more than ability to make a joke or laugh at one; I mean an acute and tolerant perception of the incongruousness of human life and living, a genial contempt for fatuousness, pretentiousness and fake, a Gallic awareness of human frailty that can express itself in a wit as broad as his smile or as refined as his music. I remember an incident of a few seasons ago when his wit was Gallic enough but not precisely *raffiné*. Mr. Monteux had graciously invited me to conduct a pair of concerts with his orchestra at San Francisco, an opportunity that I eagerly accepted. Of course it was an occasion of the highest importance to me, and while, after my ample and gratifying rehearsals with the friendly San Francisco Orchestra, I felt reasonably sure of myself, nevertheless I could not face such a test with complete equanimity. I was pacing restlessly off stage waiting for the signal to go on, very tense, no doubt pale and shivering with "nerves" and impatience, full of Tristan's agonies and Schubert's dolor. Suddenly, just as the bell rang to go on, I was seized from behind. A fat knee collided vigorously not once but thrice with my posterior portions and a very French voice said, "*Trois fois merde! Allons-y!*" It was *mon mâitre*, of course, who delivered this *coup de pied au queue* not only in conformity with the rowdy custom of the French theater, but, more shrewdly and kindly, to distract me and relax the very obvious nervous tension I was suffering. I was startled, but I think I must have been smiling and at ease as he almost violently propelled me out onto the stage. Even a kick in the pants can be helpful. The concert went well.

It should be clear that Mr. Monteux is an amiable man, but it should not be inferred that his blood lacks iron in its composition. One must know him long and well to perceive how fierce a rage, how deep a hurt he can sustain without revealing it. He is a happy man in the truest and broadest sense, but he is at the same time a man of sorrows and acquainted with grief.

The war brought him agonizing personal tragedy, the more bitter because the dreadful news came to him when the battle was almost over and the exaltation of imminent victory was in the air. The word came that his closest and dearest relatives, _en famille_, had been shamefully tormented and then coldly murdered for their activities in the French underground forces of resistance, and the more shamefully tortured, the more wickedly slain, because they were Jews. Monteux asked no sympathy, advertised no grief, publicized no political beliefs, but bore his agony with fortitude and in silence. He remembers that he is a Frenchman, but never forgets that he is an American, and if his personal tragedy made any difference in his behavior or his wife's (she is a down-East Yankee), it was only to intensify their efforts in every department of patriotic activity accessible to them. Here is a man "of ancient race by birth, but nobler yet in his own worth."

The minor tragedies in Monteux's career have been almost as numerous as the major triumphs. To this day I do not understand why, after the departure of Karl Muck and the opportunity to retain Monteux, the Boston Symphony Orchestra failed to do so. Here was a man who, because he was recognized the world over as one of the greatest living masters of the orchestra, would have brought sorely needed authority and prestige to the Boston Symphony Orchestra. Here was a man who had the affection and respect of all the world's great musicians for a generation, who was admired by Brahms, by Widor, by Saint-Saëns, by Debussy, a man who had brought into being under his own hands the greatest music of Stravinsky, of Ravel—the world _premières_ of _Petrouchka, Le Sacre du Printemps, Le Rossignol, Daphnis et Chloé_, and countless others. Yet the Boston Symphony dallied with well-meaning but inferior men like Henri Rabaud and various others, and after Muck's departure never reoriented itself until the fortunate arrival of Koussevitzky. Again, in Philadelphia when Stokowski began to take vacations half a season long, Monteux came and revealed what the Philadelphia Orchestra could be under his hands. Contrary to remarks I heard at the time, I believe his tailoring was quite as good as Stokowski's, but he did not return until comparatively recently to Philadelphia.

When, out of ennui, dwindling audiences, and other reasons, Toscanini departed the Philharmonic, and Bruno Walter failed utterly to resuscitate it from its moribund state, the directors sought a German conductor with imputed Nazi connections, though Monteux might have been available. When the enskied and sainted Toscanini permitted a guest conductor at NBC, Monteux was indeed chosen for a pair of concerts, and was extraordinarily successful. He has not been there since. I have never discussed these matters with Monteux, and it seems improbable that he would discuss them. Anyone knowing the man's stature as a conductor and his history of achievement, his sensitiveness, and his worth would know that these and similar dealings must have touched him painfully and deeply; but he is a man who bears his hurts proudly, nobly, silently.

Monteux looks almost exactly as, thirty years ago, we would have expected a typical Frenchman to look. He is rather short, rather stout, with contours suggesting those of both the penguin and the pigeon. The famous smile finds its way through, and indeed involves certain oscillations of, a luxuriant mustache, at last quite gray, but his hair is abundant, curly and, let us say, remarkably black. He has the merriest eyes in the world, I think. He speaks with a pronounced French accent imposed upon a very American and extensive vocabulary, including slang. In the more serious moments of a rehearsal he is quite likely to interrupt with the latest catch word of the bobby-soxers, and very much to the point too. He has a lamentable fondness for puns, palindromes, and plays on words. He loves good living and when he comes to the table is happily uninhibited by any considerations of a boyish figure. He is a princely host and a delightful guest, a raconteur of rare charm, and so unaffectedly simple that he is completely at ease in any company, however urbane, however naïve. He is regarded by his neighbors in Hancock, Maine (the home town of Doris Hodgkins, his wife), with the same warm affection that greets him in Paris or Amsterdam or Philadelphia or San Francisco. He professes a certain indifference to parties, but I think he secretly enjoys them, and he will participate in any kind of fun, whether it be playing Santa Claus in costume or picking up a viola to join in a reading of difficult modern quartets—and he will do this with the most innocent and genuine gusto, without losing a particle of dignity and without asserting any. Chronologically he is a contemporary of Toscanini; mentally and spiritually he is forty years younger.

Musicians love Monteux. They love him first, I think, as a musician—for his profound knowledge of the score in hand, his utterly convincing, sound, and sometimes intuitive readings, his penetrating but never precious or finicky analysis of the music, his happy faculty of making his wishes clear with the strictest economy of words and gestures, not to mention the resulting economy of rehearsal time. His attitude at rehearsal is paternal rather than magisterial. Somehow without obvious effort he makes it very clear that he expects full cooperation and honest effort, and these he invariably gets. He will often lighten a dull moment with a jest, and invariably a relevant jest, and one easily appreciated by everyone in the orchestra. Not long ago he rehearsed with the Philadelphia Orchestra, among other things, *Till Eulenspiegel*. At the first playing things did not go too well, but this did not disturb Monteux. Knowing that the orchestra has played the piece for years and is perhaps bored with it, he stopped in the middle of the music and said, "Gentlemen, I know that you know this piece backwards, but please do not let us play it that way." At another point in the same piece it happens that Mr. Ormandy inserts a trill for a certain instrument. The musician, having just played the interpolated and unorthodox ornament, asked: "Do you want me to play that trill?" Monteux replied: "Trill? Did you play a trill? I thought it was only that you had a very rapid vibrato. No, my dear, no trill."

Orchestra musicians are toil-hardened, cynical men, but at heart most of them are truly artists and render to a master a remarkably warm and loyal devotion. In Monteux they find not only a master, but a man who, without compromising for a moment his authority or his dignity, establishes the relation of a colleague and friend. The men of the San Francisco Orchestra and the children on the streets of Hancock, Maine, call him Pierre. Paradoxically perhaps, this is affectionate without being familiar.

Discipline in Mr. Monteux's own orchestra is rather easy, which can be disconcerting to a guest conductor, though it never relaxes to the point where there is any real disturbance. I am afraid, however, that some sly tricks have been played by the San Francisco Orchestra. I know of one instance when Stokowski was conducting as guest, and the rehearsal was dealing with Stokowski's orchestration of *Pictures at an Exhibition.* There are as many music critics in a symphony orchestra as there are players, and the gentlemen of San Francisco, having been thoroughly trained in Ravel's orchestral setting of this work, were somewhat scornful of Stokowski's. In the midst of the rehearsal one of the second violins, whom I shall mercifully allow to remain anonymous, busied himself with some of the more brilliant passages of the Mendelssohn Violin Concerto, which his colleagues in the immediate vicinity could hear, but in a great orchestral *tutti* Stokowski apparently could not hear. This went on for some minutes, to the half-consternation, half-amusement of the violin section. Stokowski, noting a certain psychic storm in the violin choir, suddenly stopped, but our mischievous friend, not having his eye on the conductor at the moment, went on for several bars of his Mendelssohn cadenza after the rest of the orchestra had become silent. Stokowski—I don't know whether he really appreciated the situation or not—quickly saved everybody's face, except possibly his own, by remarking, "There, gentlemen, there is the kind of enthusiasm I want."

During the same rehearsals Mr. Stokowski worked out with the orchestra the B minor ("Unfinished") Symphony of Schubert, using his own orchestral parts into which he had inserted a part for bass clarinet. It happens that at the time the San Francisco Orchestra rejoiced in a bass clarinetist who was a quite temperamental gentleman, and a composer as well as a virtuoso on his particular instrument. When he took his place at rehearsal and saw a bass clarinet part for the Schubert "Unfinished" he was possessed by a fury, for naturally he knew that Schubert never wrote it. He swore in several languages that he would be damned to hell if he would play a bass clarinet in a Schubert symphony, because Schubert had not put it there. He made such a disturbance that Howard Skinner, manager of the orchestra, trying to avert a serious situation, persuaded the bass clarinet to sit through the symphony and go through the motions of playing, but excused him from actually sounding a note. This compromise was effected and effective—Mr. Stokowski didn't notice.

It is a matter of some regret that on Mr. Monteux's visits as guest conductor in the East his programs tend to be either somewhat stylized or somewhat heterogeneous. I suppose the reason for this is that the resident conductor naturally reserves to himself so much of the orchestral repertoire that the guest conductor has no great freedom of choice except, of course, in the field of contemporary music. Monteux, because he is a Frenchman, is expected to do little but French music. He does French music with singular conviction, naturally, but he is likewise a master of the classics. His Beethoven and Mozart are delicious, his Brahms revealing, and he is hospitable to modern composers. It should be added that he is discriminating in the modern music he elects to perform, and this was true long before it was fashionable to play contemporary music; true, too, when Monteux gave first performances to Ravel, Stravinsky, Honegger, Bloch, and many others. What is more remarkable, however, is that Monteux will play modern works even if they are not dedicated to him, even if his is not a first performance. That is so rare as to be almost unique, and testifies to degrees of sincerity and artistic integrity that one could wish were qualities common to all conductors.

Monteux wears his honors lightly, though his expansive bosom could be heavily decked with decorations if he chose to display them. He is almost the only conductor I have known who at one time or another, directly or indirectly, has not indulged in a little boasting. Indeed, I can recall an occasion when even Monteux was guilty in a minor degree; his boasting was not for himself but rather for his countrymen as musicians. A good many years ago he organized and played (viola) in a string quartet. It happened that during a tour of Germany the quartet played in Hamburg, where Brahms was living at the time. Doubting that the gruff old fellow would come to their concert, the quartet made arrangements to go to his house and play one of his quartets for him. Brahms was delighted, and Monteux loves to tell that the taciturn old man said: "It takes Frenchmen to play my quartets. The Germans and the Austrians who play them are much too heavy-handed and too slow."

Some of Monteux's colleagues and all of his friends entertain a certain resentment on his behalf because they feel that Monteux has not been accorded proper recognition as one of the greatest living musicians. It is true that in some small matters, such as the organization and training of the NBC Symphony, Monteux has not been given due credit, but this man, who is almost as innocent and in many ways as unworldly as César Franck, is utterly unconcerned with, and very likely unconscious of, some of the slights that have been put upon him. New York, Philadelphia, and other parts of the incorrigibly provincial East think of Monteux as having been banished to a kind of musical Siberia, not knowing that the most civilized, urbane, beautiful, and charming of American cities has taken him to its heart; a city where all the arts are more lively, involve the interest and participation of more people, and are less commercialized than in any other community in the United States. In music as in other arts, San Francisco is highly sophisticated, fastidious, and quite intolerant of second-rate things, second-rate artists, and second-rate people. It would be embarrassing, though pitifully easy, to count the number of conductors who could successfully occupy the post there; and if, in the parochial belief of the Atlantic seaboard, to be excluded from New York means death and obscurity, then to be accepted in San Francisco is a heavenly exile. Everyone in San Francisco knows Monteux, everyone is interested in the orchestra, and everyone helps to pay for it.[1] San Francisco's memorial to her sons fallen in World War I is the magnificent War Memorial Opera House, home of the San Francisco Opera Company and the San Francisco Symphony. Neither of these is maintained as a luxurious plaything of society or of the rich. Both are operated so as to bring their services within the reach of everyone.

I once spent four hours in traveling eight hundred miles to have lunch with a lady of San Francisco, and with that luncheon began several of the most precious friendships I shall ever know. I had for quite some time been considering ways and means of recording the San Francisco Symphony.[2] I was not familiar with it, but I knew that any orchestra that had worked for years under Monteux must necessarily be a fine orchestra, and I wanted to record Monteux. The problem was more than ordinarily difficult because Victor had no portable recording equipment available to the West Coast, and to transport material from New York would have meant heavy expense, considerable risk, and the disruption of recording schedules in the East. There were also, as ever, the question of expense, and a certain lack of enthusiasm among my colleagues. When other matters took me to California I determined to do something about the situation in spite of its

---

[1] A tiny fraction of the San Francisco tax rate is earmarked for the support of the orchestra and the opera company.

[2] A few unimportant records had been made, in the 1920's, under Alfred Hertz.

difficulties, and so arranged to meet Mrs. Leonora Wood Armsby, managing director of the orchestra. I telephoned her from Hollywood one morning and she invited me for lunch the same day. I was both startled and pleased with her directness and friendliness and promised to be in Burlingame, just outside of San Francisco, for lunch. I was there on time and found that while my plane was winging four hundred miles from Burbank to Burlingame, Mrs. Armsby had assembled a quite fascinating luncheon table: there were Pierre Monteux and his wife, José Iturbi, Raymond Armsby, Arthur Brown, Jr., Miss Nancy Scott (now Mrs. Roger Lapham, Jr.), Howard Skinner, devoted and able manager of the orchestra, and Peter Heyes, leader of the second violins, Harry Meyerson of Victor's Hollywood staff, Mrs. Armsby's son, and certain other charming people, all of them interested in the orchestra and all of them, I found, regarding me as a much more important person than I was or am, and keen to hear what I had to say about the possibility of recording the orchestra.

I did have a plan: one that would resolve both the technical and financial difficulties of recording the San Francisco orchestra if I could have the active co-operation of our technical staff in Hollywood, and of Mrs. Armsby, Mr. Monteux, and others directly concerned with the fortunes of the orchestra. Before leaving Hollywood I had had several long discussions with our engineering staff, and I was well prepared as far as the technical situation was concerned. After putting my financial plans before Mrs. Armsby and her friends, I found them immediately enthusiastic, and they gave me their pledge of co-operation. My plan released the Victor Company from any immediate financial obligations. The cost of recording, so far as it involved payment to the musicians, was to be assumed by Mrs. Armsby's group, eventually to be amortized by royalties from the records. Mr. Monteux's compensation was to be similarly arranged. As for the technical difficulties and the absence of portable recording equipment it was decided that we would record simultaneously in two ways—first, over an equalized telephone circuit between the War Memorial Opera House in San Francisco and our studios in Hollywood, four hundred miles away, where the actual cutting of the discs would be done. This special telephone line was already in existence, and was often used by the National Broadcasting Company. We therefore could use it only at such times as it was not needed for broadcasting, which meant recording could not begin until midnight. Then, as a safety measure, we arranged to record simultaneously on sound film, bringing a sound truck from Hollywood and driving it directly onto the stage of the War Memorial Opera House. I considered this precaution necessary because of the possibilities of interruption to the telephone circuit which, however momentary they might be, would utterly ruin any recording. As matters turned out there were a few interruptions, though they did not seriously discommode us, but to my surprise and pleasure I found that the film recording, when transferred to disc, was distinctly superior to the direct recording made via telephone line. The first recordings of the San Francisco Orchestra, therefore (César Franck's Symphony, D'Indy's *Symphony on a French Mountain Air*, Rimsky-Korsakoff's *Scheherazade*, and several other works), were the first symphonic recordings issued by Victor that were primarily made on sound-film and later transferred to disc records.

The phonograph critics discovered what every musician had long known—that the great orchestras and conductors are not confined to the Atlantic seaboard. The critics found the records distinctly superior both in performance and in reproduction. With surprise and gleeful cries they discovered a conductor who has been a musical figure of world importance since before any of them was born. Victor, with its nerve center in the accounting department, presently experienced the revelation that the San Francisco Orchestra records were also financially successful, and in a very short period the talent cost had been amortized and the company was sending handsome five-figure royalty checks to Mrs. Armsby.

At the risk of offending her genuine and very touching modesty, I must add my inconsequential word to the many that have been uttered in praise of this great and gracious lady. Mrs. Armsby is not only a patron, but a real friend of music. I do not believe she is extraordinarily wealthy. I do know that she has made generous financial contributions to the orchestra. However large these must have been, they are unimportant compared with the devotion, the sagacity, the wisdom, counsel, and understanding that she has loyally, tirelessly, freely given. Her interests extend into every phase of the orchestra's activity, and her judgment and advice have been applied wherever her interests have led, invariably to the advantage of the orchestra and the human beings who constitute it. If her judgments are shrewd and farsighted, her greatness of heart and nobility of spirit are still superior, and every citizen of San Francisco, from her friend, Mayor Roger Dearborn Lapham, to a modest young Italian from Fisherman's Wharf, is in her debt and knows it. Through her the strongest cultural force, in a city where cultural forces are strong, lives and has its being, and through the records that her foresight made possible, the contribution of Pierre Monteux and the San Francisco Orchestra to American musical life has made itself felt in ever-widening circles.

ARTUR
RUBINSTEIN

◆§ Artur Rubinstein §◆

"There is an evil which I have seen under the sun, and it is common among men. A man to whom God hath given riches, wealth, and honour, so that he wanteth nothing for his soul of all that he desireth, yet God giveth him not power to eat thereof, but a stranger eateth it; this is vanity, and it is an evil disease."

ECCLESIASTES vi: 1-2.

IF THIS QUOTATION is apposite with respect to most musicians, it is opposite in the case of Rubinstein. It has been suggested in these pages that musicians are not only as dull, vicious, and, generally, as fallible as other humans, but also that they are usually polarized personalities whose thoughts and efforts through every hour of their lives are directed upon their art and ego. That is why they are so often provincial as citizens, circumscribed as artists, and uninteresting as people. They do not permit themselves to enjoy even the very wealth for which they strive with such aquiline ferocity. They desperately seek publicity and desperately fear it. They crave the comforts that their success puts within their reach and fear to take them lest somehow in the taking they neglect an opportunity for more "success." Even their loves are, more often than not, furtive, ephemeral, and essentially no more dignified or important than the satisfaction of any other physiological function—except, of course, when a publicized courtship properly climaxed by marriage can bring more "success," more money, more fame, and more publicity. Musical artists are forever on guard—against the malice of rivals, the first ominous success of the upstart, the machinations of the manager, the fickleness of the public, and a thousand other real or imaginary perils. Few of them know how to enjoy life; few have any real life to enjoy.

Artur Rubinstein is a sane man. If this seems no compliment, let me add that to be sane is a rare thing among geniuses and rarest among musicians. Rubinstein is sane in the sense that he is a sound and rounded personality; a wit, a linguist, a raconteur par excellence, a gourmet, a bon vivant, a chivalrous husband, and a devoted father—and primate of all living priests of the piano. He knows that to play the piano is his reason for being, but it is not his being; it is his living, but not his life. He looks upon his art with reverence, and serves it with passionate devotion. He likewise makes it serve him as the source of opportunities for cultivation of the humanities that are greater than any art. He thoroughly enjoys his work, as any honest worker will. He profoundly respects his talent, as any true artist must. He likewise has the intelligence and the perception to appreciate life, and the capacity to enjoy it. I have spent an age-long evening with him in the Stork Club—an evening that would have been an eternity of vulgar music, garish light, clumsy dancing, and too much Scotch, except for my pleasure in Rubinstein's conversation with Charles Boyer and myself, and his obvious pleasure in the commonplace delights of that famous institution. Again, I have spent days and weeks with him while he, alone or with others, exhausted his ultimate impulse of nervous and physical energy in wringing from his instrument the secrets of Beethoven and Brahms and Mozart. I testify that his pleasure in degree, if not in kind, was as keen in one instance as in the other.

"Behold, that which I have seen to be good and to be comely is for one to eat and to drink, and to enjoy good in all his labour . . . all the days of his life which God has given him: for this is his portion . . . this is the gift of God . . ."

Rubinstein is in every way an attractive man, but I should hesitate to call him handsome. His face has neither prettiness nor regularity nor the meretricious dark, brooding look of the artistic poseur. It is exceedingly mobile and expressive, and when Rubinstein tells a story he somehow makes his face look like one of his characters. He can at will resemble a satyr, a simpleton, a Semite—or anything else that occurs to his humor. His eyes have a rather terrifying light in them at times, attributable, I suspect, more to a slight degree of exophthalmia than to any particular workings of the spirit within. His hair, as it recedes from his front, seems to be correspondingly extended at the rear, which tends to give his fine cranium the contour of a prolate ellipsoid.[1] As a matter of fact, when Mr. Rubinstein sits at the piano his silhouette is very much like that of two prolate ellipsoids, one on top of the other; with the major axis of the upper one at right angles to that of the lower. He is powerful in the shoulders, deep-chested, and expanding in circumference from there on—in short, the figure of a pianist and a gourmet.

He enjoys a good story and can tell some of the best. A good play, a pretty girl, a clever dance tune, a genial host, alike give him keen and innocent pleasure. When he is not immediately engaged upon serious work he looks Demon Rum straight in the eye without a qualm. His taste in food is fastidious, and so, naturally, is his taste in wine. He loves fine per-

---

[1] Egg-shaped, if you prefer.

sonal linen, and sometimes is "perfumed like a milliner," having the weakness for strongly scented colognes that I have noticed quite frequently among European musicians. He likes games, books, conversation, and generally a good time, when the time is available. To be sure, this doesn't happen often, for he is much in demand; the point is that he lives with gusto for work and for play.

Prior to his sensational success in America before World War II, Mr. Rubinstein had no very extensive audience here. In Europe and in South America, however, he was appreciated to a degree paralleling his present popularity here, and held a recording contract with Victor's European affiliate, "His Master's Voice." Through this arrangement his records were available here, and they enjoyed great popularity among record collectors. I should point out that the records of all artists under contract to HMV are available through Victor in North and South America. When Rubinstein did score his initial success in the United States it was not necessary to have a contract with him, as we could record him under the terms of his HMV arrangement. This was fortunate for the Victor people, who were able thus to obtain the services of a very distinguished artist and a group of highly commercial records with the minimum of effort and expense—a situation that always had a strong appeal. Under this arrangement the royalties on Rubinstein's American sales were paid him not through Victor but through "His Master's Voice," which was responsible for the original contractual obligation. This worked out very well until war conditions developed and the export of funds was prohibited by law.

The most successful recording Mr. Rubinstein ever made, and one that established the particular composition recorded as the most popular of its type in all the world of music, was his Tchaikovsky B-flat minor piano concerto. The sales of this recording in America had earned very substantial royalties for Mr. Rubinstein when, in accordance with wartime law, these royalties, which would ordinarily have been paid him through "His Master's Voice," were sequestered in a New York bank. The artist was both irritated and inconvenienced. Today he commands top fees, but for a very considerable period, because of contractual arrangements and other factors, his fees did not parallel his artistic stature or his power at the box office. His status as a musician, his standard of living, and his financial obligations were, however, equivalent to those of other top-flight artists who had been collecting enormous fees in America for years. Mr. Rubinstein didn't join this elect group, financially speaking, until the tax situation had begun to take most of the cream off the top fees. Consequently, knowing that his records were earning substantial sums—probably more than his concert appearances—and yet these sums were not available to him, he felt a certain resentment and, I dare say, financial embarrassment. Not without asperity, he called on me to do something about this condition, and no explanation I could give him could mollify him in the least. Since I did appreciate his situation, and did feel that a certain injustice was being done him, I took measures calculated to ingratiate the company and myself with the artist, and by exercising some persuasion in divers high places, I was able to arrange for the release of a very large sum of Mr. Rubinstein's money, most of which represented accrued royalties on his recording of the Tchaikovsky concerto. I was naïve enough to be surprised that Mr. Rubinstein was not particularly appreciative, but I attributed this to his ignorance of the facts in the case rather than to any ill-humor. He felt that since the money was his and under his contract was due him, there was no reason why it should not be paid; he had no interest whatever in my recital of the technical and legal difficulties involved.

It has been unfortunate for Mr. Rubinstein that his American success was so long delayed. His colleagues, some of them younger and with shorter careers behind them, have been able to amass fortunes in America during the period when it was

possible to make long-term, and very profitable, solid investments. When the tax situation developed to what it is now,
these artists already had incomes from invested money probably equal to, if not greater than, incomes from their active
concertizing. Meanwhile, Rubinstein commanded top fees in
Europe and South America, but these were by no means as
large as those he could earn in the United States. When he
did finally exploit his American market, he was instantly recognized as one of the greatest of all pianists, but because of
prior commitments his fees, while far from small, were not
comparable with those of Heifetz, Horowitz, Menuhin, Rachmaninoff and others with whom Rubinstein rightly ranked.
His arrangements with his manager were such that he was
not able to raise his fee for several seasons. This circumstance
made him highly profitable to local managers and no doubt to
his own managers and booking agents, Sol Hurok and the
NBC Artists Bureau. In spite of his Tchaikovsky, everybody
made money but Rubinstein.

To aggravate this situation, ordinary income and surtaxes
made ever more serious inroads upon the artist's resources; his
family increased and the necessity for security became more
and more exigent. Furthermore, the accumulation of wealth
and the ability to demand large fees are often to an artist
quite as much matters of pride as of acquisitiveness; Rubinstein, who ranked with the very greatest artists musically, was
irked because he could accomplish neither. He continued
to look to his recording of the Tchaikovsky concerto as a main
source of income, and a second time I was obliged to scheme
out a way whereby he could collect some of his royalties from
this recording.

I recount the details of this matter because it has a direct
bearing upon the interruption of my friendly relations with
Rubinstein. To me this was very painful and embarrassing.
Personally I felt a warm affection and a profound admiration
for him; officially it was my duty to maintain amicable relations between Victor and all recording artists. This was some-

times attended with considerable difficulty because whatever went wrong in an artist's recording affairs, whether it had to do with poor sales, advertising, frequency of record issues, or indeed, any and every matter connected with the making, promotion, and sale of records, I was held responsible by the artist. Indeed, I was responsible for many details—too many—and even in such a matter as the use in Victor advertising of a photograph which the artist felt was not sufficiently flattering, I was the sacrificial lamb. I was Victor to the artists, and the only contact they ever had with the company. They did not know that the musical aspects of Victor's business were the last and the least to be considered by the powers. They did not know that their success as recording artists was often controlled by various "personages with long ears," by ignorant, officious, correspondence-school sales experts whose acquaintance with and interest in music were limited to the occasional use of a free concert ticket. They did not know that for nearly twenty years Victor had no established advertising policy, that such advertising as it did was conditioned by intra-company politics and financial expediency, rather than by intelligent planning based upon the essential nature and need of the record business. I never controlled Victor's advertising, though I often did influence individual advertisements. Ultimately, in sheer desperation I did present and accomplish the adoption of a long-range and, I thought, well-planned advertising policy, but it died aborning in the depths of an economy wave. I did for a long time control the monthly releases of Red Seal records, and I wonder with all modesty if it was merely coincidence that during this period we had no serious difficulties with any artist, and Victor record sales and profits reached their highest point to then in the company's history.

My troubles, not only with Rubinstein but with others, as well as a sharp decline in Red Seal record popularity, began when a crackpot sales organization was permitted to encroach upon my field and even was given certain powers relating to the repertoire to be recorded. Their first and most egregious error in this direction was their insistence upon making a new record of the Tchaikovsky concerto with Vladimir Horowitz and his father-in-law, Arturo Toscanini. I had for some time been trying to arrange some recording by these two volatile personalities, and had chosen repertoire that I felt would be artistically satisfying to them (it was) and to the public, as well as commercially successful. Meanwhile, the sales department had been eying the mounting popularity of Rubinstein's Tchaikovsky, which had been in our catalog for some years. It occurred to them that a new recording of this music, by Horowitz and Toscanini, would amplify and accelerate the sales of this title. It was never the policy of the sales department to put pressure and promotion behind recordings that did not sell voluminously; they always took the path of least resistance and put their sales effort, such as it was, into increasing the sales of those records that were already touching their peak. The salesmen saw that Rubinstein's Tchaikovsky was doing really well; I had already proved by recording a Brahms concerto that the Horowitz-Toscanini combination would appeal to the public with tremendous force. Therefore, it was reasoned that the ideal combination would be Tchaikovsky and Horowitz and Toscanini. This reasoning was not wrong as far as it went, and certainly included no malicious intent respecting Rubinstein or his records, but I could not see the profit in a feverish flurry of sales at the expense of a great and important artist's good will, and at the cost of making obsolescent a recording already in our catalog and highly profitable. Walter Toscanini, who had been employed in the record division at the command of David Sarnoff as a kind of statistician and general handyman, and who on his part seemed to conceive his job as one of observation and special investigation for his father, naturally supported the sales department. Canny little man that he is, the projected recording doubtless looked like Golconda to him. He announced his willingness to persuade his father and his sister's husband to undertake the Tchaikovsky recording.

The procedure was to be: Walter would prepare the way with Horowitz and Toscanini and I would apply the finishing touches and get them to contract for the Tchaikovsky recording. This was clever, for the private conversations between Walter and his relatives that softened them up and made them receptive to a project they were actually panting to carry out were not matters of record and cannot be proved, whereas it could be proved, for example to Rubinstein, that it was I who actually brought about the recording.

The records were made, and after certain difficulties, approved; and then began a series of alarums and excursions that brought about another Toscanini crisis. This eventually involved Horowitz and Rubinstein as well as the maestro. In the first place, Horowitz was dissatisfied with one of the records because in a certain passage he had omitted one note. This omission could not be detected, without advance notice, by one person in a hundred, and indeed, was not observed at the time the record was made, by Horowitz, Toscanini, or myself. For various reasons we had no opportunity to make the record again, so Horowitz persuaded me to combine two records, substituting a part of one to cover the defective passage in the other. This was a matter of very considerable difficulty, but it was accomplished to Horowitz's satisfaction and the set of records put into production. Through a tragic error in our matrix manufacturing department a master record of this repaired disc—not the one approved by Horowitz—was used in production, and to pile Pelion on Ossa, this particular record was slightly out of tune with the rest of the concerto. More than forty thousand sets of the concerto reached the public, and apparently no one, not even the omniscient record reviewers, noticed this defect.

Naturally, the set had been scheduled for quite large production and shipped out as fast as possible, and though steps were taken immediately to substitute the correct master, by the time it had been located and identified the public was in possession of a quite substantial number of sets. This infuriated the Toscaninis and Horowitz, and quite justifiably; but the fact that no one aside from the performers had detected the flaws, and that the correct master was substituted as soon as possible, did nothing to ameliorate their feeling of outrage and resentment. The whole matter was reported to his father and Horowitz by Walter. Actually the error was purely a manufacturing one and could not have been accomplished by me even if I had had the inclination to do it. Walter knew this. My relations with Toscanini deteriorated from that time forward. *"There be six things which the Lord hateth: . . . haughty eyes, a lying tongue, a heart that deviseth wicked imaginations, feet that be swift in running to mischief; a false witness that uttereth lies, and he that soweth discord among brethren."*

Our troubles with the Tchaikovsky concerto did not end with the correction of the mechanical errors in the recording. Rubinstein's attitude respecting the publication of the Horowitz record was precisely what I had anticipated, and of which I had warned Victor. He felt that when his recording of the work was doing sensationally well its successful course should not have been interrupted. Either the piece should not have been re-recorded, or if it were to be given a more modern recording, Rubinstein should be the soloist. He resented a certain diminution of prestige that he felt might result from superseding his record, and he entertained the painful conviction that his income from his record would be drastically reduced. He was further exacerbated by the fact that in various cities he visited on tour, he was informed by record sales people that Victor had withdrawn from circulation his Tchaikovsky and substituted the Horowitz performance. This was not true and still isn't. In spite of such stupidity on the part of sales people, the sales of Rubinstein's recording actually were accelerated by the injection of new interest in the piece brought about by the Horowitz-Toscanini recording, and even the sales department was not stupid enough to withdraw any recording that was doing such handsome business. Many people, attracted to record shops by the noisy bally-hoo for the Horowitz-Toscanini record, were discriminating enough to compare it with the Rubinstein version, usually to the advantage of the latter; for indeed, apart from certain details of recording technique, Rubinstein's is far more poetic and musical. He invests the superficial brilliance of the concerto with his own imaginative concept, giving it warmth and virility infinitely more satisfying than the meretricious glitter, inflexible rhythms, and unnatural pace of the Horowitz-Toscanini recording.

Rubinstein never uttered a word in criticism of Horowitz or of his performance, but he did feel that we were unjust if we withdrew his recording from our catalog, which we did not; or if we failed to give it the flamboyant advertising and promotion which we had given the Horowitz recording—which we could not. As I had foreseen, I was the personification of all Victor's shortcomings and I was the object of Rubinstein's resentment.

I could not undo what had been done. I could, however, and did propose constructive reparations in the form of a project that I hoped would compensate Rubinstein for any wrong that might have been done him. It happened that Freddy Martin, the band leader, unquestionably inspired by Rubinstein's concerto and its popularity, had evolved a dance tune based on themes from the concerto which not only had enormous popularity itself but contributed to public interest, first in Rubinstein's records and later in Horowitz's. I suggested, with the approval and later the co-operation of my then boss, Mr. Frank B. Walker, that Rubinstein record the Grieg concerto with the Philadelphia Orchestra; and that if he would do this I would see to it that Freddy Martin would treat in a dance arrangement the themes of the Grieg exactly as he had done with the Tchaikovsky, record it, and give it equal prominence on all his radio and other programs. Victor would give the recording a promotion similar to that given to Horowitz's.

I found it necessary to discuss this with Mr. Rubinstein over the long-distance telephone when he was in Chicago, which did not make matters any easier. He received the proposal very coldly and intimated that he was not interested in making any more records for Victor. I then enlisted the co-operation of Mr. Walker, whose irresistible persuasiveness and unique skill as a pacifier and negotiator brought about a successful conclusion of this project. Rubinstein said that he had never played the Grieg concerto, which seems rather improbable, but he recorded a magnificent performance with Ormandy and the Philadelphia Orchestra. Freddy Martin carried out his part of the bargain to his own great profit and to the advantage of Rubinstein's record, and the melodies of Grieg, chiefly those of the concerto, have hardly been out of hearing since. These records furthermore provided, I believe, the spark that animated the producers of *Song of Norway*, records of which are not only popular in themselves but also contribute to the sustained interest in Mr. Rubinstein's Grieg concerto.

Even this happy denouement did not reinstate me in Mr. Rubinstein's good graces. Certain friends of mine, grieved by this situation, without my knowledge undertook to clarify the situation to Rubinstein. Since he is a fair and intelligent man, he acknowledged his error; in the course of a three-hour luncheon à *deux* at my favorite restaurant in New York—La Chaumière—we enjoyed a gratifying *rapprochement*. Later, when the time came for a renewal of his arrangement with Victor, the pianist was able to extract from the company a highly advantageous contract based on my advice to him—an agreement which, while exacting, was not onerous to the company, and provided at least a fair chance of Rubinstein's getting a square deal.

Jascha Heifetz was primarily responsible for bringing together the group of superlative artists who, in the summer of 1942, undertook a series of records of certain chamber music. When some time previously the Budapest Quartet had left

Victor, the company lost caste with devotees of chamber music and could no longer boast of leadership in this field. There was no permanently organized quartet that could compete with the Budapest in public acceptance. There were other quartets, such as the Pro Arte, the Musical Art, the Roth, and the Coolidge, which had fair claims to some share of public support, but they got very little. The Budapest Quartet, composed, oddly enough, of Russians exclusively, had the inside track, and was worshipfully regarded in those esoteric circles where chamber music is esteemed as the only music worthy of an intelligent man's attention, circles composed largely of bloodless snobs who regard any music involving more than five players as grossly overblown, whose tastes are so refined and aristocratic that they don't like even a program of chamber music if their neighbor does, and who think that anything popular is necessarily vulgar. These precious folks had grown in such number as to make chamber music not only important to Victor from an artistic point of view, but commercially profitable as well. It was evident that it would take mighty musicians indeed to compete with the Budapest Quartet or to regain for Victor the position in the field of chamber music that it had lost.

There was no one at Victor sufficiently expert to choose such a group, and for this reason I asked the aid of Jascha Heifetz. I did not debate his selection of Primrose, Feuermann, Rubinstein, Sanromá, and the Musical Art Quartet headed by Sascha Jacobsen, to carry out the program I had in mind. I was, however, a little uncertain about Rubinstein. I knew him as a great virtuoso, a man of aggressive and even dominating personality, a master of the heroic style, and a player whose technique is more than adequate to any pianistic difficulties ever conceived by any composer. I knew him as an artist of rare perception, imagination, taste, and skill in the matter of piano tone, but I was faintly dubious, not as to his ability, but as to his willingness to become part of an intimate ensemble. I knew Primrose and the others, as well as their work in this field, much more intimately. I discussed my doubts with Jascha and found him completely reassuring; so in the summer of 1942, which Heifetz, Rubinstein, Feuermann, and Primrose had arranged to spend under the balmy California skies, we set to work preparing and recording peerless performances of the Beethoven Trio No. 7 in B-flat ("Archduke"); the Dohnanyi Serenade for Violin, Viola, and Cello in C major; the Brahms Trio for Piano, Violin, and Cello in B major; the Schubert Trio for Piano, Violin, and Cello in B-flat major; the Mozart Divertimento for Violin, Viola, and Cello in E flat; the Beethoven Duet in E flat for Viola and Cello; and a Chausson concerto, which you can now enjoy on Victor records.[2]

Elsewhere I have intimated that Rubinstein is one of the few contemporary pianists who employ tone as a medium of expression, who employ it deliberately and with calculation, who have imagination enough to conceive it, skill enough to produce it. This conclusion again impressed itself on me during our recordings of chamber music in Hollywood. By some miracle, Rubinstein altered his musical personality completely. He not only adjusted the power of his tone to the proportions of the ensemble, but actually modified its quality and its variations of color to blend or contrast with violin and cello tone as occasion required. The masterful and somewhat arrogant personality that can and does dominate orchestras and conductors was merged into the composite personality of trio or quartet, the fine intricacies of chamber music were materialized under this man's hands with such justness, such a sense of proportion, such exquisite nuance, and above all, such complete rapport with his colleagues as to make them as well as myself frankly marvel.

One of these recordings provided the only occasion I ever

---

[2] The Concerto for Violin, Piano, and String Quartet of Chausson had been recorded previously in New York by Heifetz, Sanromá and the Musical Art Quartet. If my memory is accurate, it was the first Victor recording of a long and presently concluded series made in the Gallery of the Lotos Club at 110 West 57th Street.

had to practice any deception on Rubinstein and, incidentally, the only moment throughout these sessions when Rubinstein refused to make a concession to a colleague. We were recording the "Archduke" trio and at a certain point a low note in the cello is doubled in the piano part. Both are marked *fortissimo*. In this particular range the timbre of the cello and of the piano are not very dissimilar, but the piano tone is, of course, much more powerful. Rubinstein's *fortissimo* is a mighty sound, and here it completely blotted out Feuermann's corresponding *fortissimo*. "Munio" complained of this, and in the most comradely way endeavored to persuade Rubinstein to deliver a somewhat smaller volume of tone. Rubinstein refused, pointing out that his part said *fortissimo*, and *fortissimo* it was going to be. I did my best to compose the difficulty, but I had no success except in provoking the resentment of both men. We made record after record, and invariably at this particular point both artists would detonate their biggest explosions; and on hearing the record played back would turn away in anger and disgust. Finally, during a little intermission, I took Feuermann aside and asked him, as a friend, to stop arguing with Rubinstein; if they would try just once more I would see to it that his cello would be heard together with the piano in their proper relationship. It happened that we recorded this group with several microphones simultaneously in order that we could more easily adjust such discrepancies in balance as might develop because of the varying power of piano, violin, and cello. On the next attempt to make the record, when we came to the danger spot I simply had the recording engineer suppress the piano to a point where it was just possible to hear the cello tone cut through. Rubinstein knew nothing of this, and probably would not have permitted it, but when he heard the playback he said gleefully, "You see, Feuermann, I was right; you can be heard no matter how loudly I play if you just bear down a little harder and give us a real *fortissimo*." Feuermann was satisfied, and when and if ever Rubinstein reads these lines I don't think he will resent my little trick or like his records the less.

I have never heard Rubinstein play when he failed to provide excitement and pleasure and profound satisfaction. This has been true in the concert hall where I worshipped from afar, in the recording studio where I was in the middle of things; and it never mattered whether he played solo, with a little ensemble, or against the multicolored background of a symphony orchestra. I shall remember most vividly, however, one occasion when after hours of eating, drinking, and dancing indefatigably in a night club we adjourned with our lovely companions to the *salon* of one of them. Here Rubinstein, without having been asked, seated himself before an ancient Steinway not too well tuned, and released a flood of music that never ebbed until the dark waters of the East River were silvered by the morning.

Abruptly, then, there was silence. He said suddenly, "It is time to stop." So be it.

SERGE
KOUSSEVITZKY

⋖§ Serge Koussevitzky §⋗

"Fortiter in re, sed suaviter in modo." [1]

From the episcopal arms of the
late Rt. Rev. Thomas D. Beaven,
Bishop of Springfield, Mass.

WHEN KOUSSEVITZKY, austere, magisterial, and prepossessed, walks out on the platform to conduct his orchestra, he suggests to me not so much an individual as a procession—one of those magnificent ecclesiastical processions in which the personage of greatest importance comes at the end. Indeed he suggests the very end of the procession itself when, a veritable high priest of art, holding within himself as in a monstrance the spiritual essence of the host of mighty musicians who have gone before him, with solemn mien and pace he approaches the podium and the sacred rite. The bow is grave and slow, and with unfailing precision timed to that fleeting moment when the ocean of salutatory applause begins its premonitory ebb—whereupon an extra wave is generated; and on its crest the master, as if unwilling to interrupt a courteous and enthusiastic greeting yet impatient of it, turns to his orchestra. An atmosphere of anticipation has been created, a conviction that momentous events are presently to transpire has been

---
[1] Unflinching in principle, but gracious in method.

fixed in the audience's mind, and only the stage-wise and the cynical observe that here is showmanship—skillful, legitimate, and unfailing; here with a single gesture three thousand people have been rendered, without a word or a sound from the stage, "*attentos, benevolos et dociles.*"

The profound gravity with which Koussevitzky habitually invests himself in public might well, in a lesser man, be evidence of a humorless, self-important, and egoistic personality. In him it rather is an expression of his concept of decency, dignity, and decorum, coupled with a lively appreciation of its effect upon a stranger or an audience. As my acquaintance with him developed into a warm and confiding friendliness it was a relief and a delight to discover too that, almost alone among the notable conductors, he is sensitive to humor and quite capable of exercising a shrewd, sometimes acrid, but seldom cruel wit. He can divest himself of gravity, though not necessarily of dignity. More, he will do what few musicians dare or can: he will laugh at himself.

One night at dinner in Serge Koussevitzky's home, then in Brookline, the conversation turned, as it will among conductors, to the subject of conductors. Perhaps I should say it turned *around* the subject of conductors, for, in fact, it never got very far from that (to conductors) inexhaustible topic. Another guest, a Russian who has a particularly warm devotion to Koussevitzky, rather unctuously held forth on the thesis that Koussevitzky is a conductor of integrity, of intellectual honesty—in a word, not only an honest musician, but the *only* honest conductor. As the panegyric progressed in length and fulsomeness I could see our host's embarrassment. Such a tribute delivered privately from one uninhibited Russian extrovert to another might have been acceptable and even welcome; but poured out within the hearing of one who was on intimate terms with Koussevitzky, his colleagues, rivals, friends, and enemies—myself—it could have been dangerous and certainly was painful both to the conductor and to me.

Koussevitzky finally and with some difficulty interrupted the eulogy and said: "No, my dear, you are wrong. There are *many* honest conductors." His worshipper indignantly inquired: "But Uncle Serge, who are they then?" Koussevitzky answered: "Well, there is—now let me see; first of all, we can certainly name—now let me think a moment—." Then, preparing to count on his fingers, Koussevitzky said: "I will name them for you; ha, an honest conductor, eh? *Da.* Their names would be—Natachok," (to his wife, with an innocent air) "who, beside me, is an honest conductor?" The point of this story is not the one that our flattering friend so gleefully emphasizes on any and all occasions as evidence of the egocentricity of Koussevitzky. Rather, judging by the malicious gleam in our host's eye, it was evident that his apparently innocent question was a rather subtle bit of mockery directed at all conductors, including himself.

Dining with Koussevitzky has always been a pleasant experience, especially when after the first few occasions we abandoned the strictest formality and a certain reserve on either side, and particularly after I had overcome my awe of the late Mrs. Koussevitzky. Russian entertainment at table is sumptuous. I think Koussevitzky would like to indulge himself and his guests in this direction, but he observes a rather strict regimen for reasons of health and seldom violates it. I remember one occasion at my home in Philadelphia where he did commit a mischievous but, as it turned out, harmless sin against his doctor's commandments. The conductor and Mr. John Burk, program editor of the Boston Symphony Orchestra, called one afternoon to discuss certain musical matters. These matters lay mostly between Mr. Burk and myself. While we discussed them, Dr. Koussevitzky accomplished the total annihilation of approximately a hundred licorice jelly beans, and at the end of my discussion with Mr. Burk I found that the conductor had abandoned us entirely and was in earnest consultation with my wife on the subject of licorice jelly beans and where the best ones could be had. Dinner with the Koussevitzkys would have a not too emphatic Russian accent, perhaps noticeable only in a pre-prandial tall glass of hot water and lemon juice; and then, freely translating the Scriptural injunction to "take a little wine for thy stomach's sake," he would pour out for himself and his guests gigantic beakers of rye or bourbon. Now brandy for breakfast may be a distressing thought, but whisky for dinner is, I think, an absolute horror; and among the many painful sacrifices I made in the interest of amicable relations with musical artists, the ingestion of Dr. Koussevitzky's potent spirits just before dinner was the most heroic. Dry sherry may be pleasantly stimulating; even a cocktail is useful for bright-ening dull appetites or dull people; but *spiritus frumenti* anesthetizes the taste buds and is likely to do as much for the brain cells. Nevertheless, it was always rather amusing to observe this fastidious Russian gentleman toss off his quarter pint of bourbon with all the matter-of-factness of a Missouri politician, and he never failed to tease me about my attempts to postpone the fatal moment myself. Lest I be accused of attempting to undermine a noble American institution, let me add that I have a proper respect for 100 proof American whisky, but to me, four ounces of it as an *apéritif* is practically lethal.

Usually when I dined with Koussevitzky, or on those few occasions when he visited my home, there were important musical matters to be discussed, but they were delicately avoided during dinner or any other purely social moment we might have. He is one of the few musicians who can converse on subjects other than himself and music, and his dinner-table talk, whether we have been alone or *en famille*, has been invariably bright and witty, sometimes profound, and always interesting. He can also listen, a faculty that is rare and charming in a musician or a Russian. More engaging still is the fact that he can and will sit with you and the inevitable tea before his fireside and actually enjoy, with neither boredom nor uneasiness on your part or his, long periods of complete silence and relaxation. He has a lively appreciation of the arts other than music, and from him I have heard more than one illuminating discourse upon the theater, upon modern architecture, serious literature, the science of advertising, the economic determination of history, the difference between a democracy and a republic. He has an extraordinarily keen political sense, particularly with respect to international affairs, but though his experience and achievement in many lands would qualify him as a world citizen, he is sincerely, warmly and intelligently American in his viewpoint and in his citizenship. In one of his dinner conversations he made it clear that he foresaw World War II more clearly than almost anyone I know, and in the course of a long evening with him he forecast not only the war itself but detailed military operations with an accuracy which, in retrospect, seems utterly fantastic. He loathed and resented the idea of war and passionately hated the necessity for our becoming involved in it—not, I think, from particularly humanitarian motives, but rather because war interferes with the arts and war particularly interfered with his art, and because to a fastidious patrician, war is intolerably vile, stupid, and unnecessary. He seemed to feel, notwithstanding his European birth and background, a certain contempt for the European nations whose lusts and greeds and ambitions provoked them to mass murder.

After a decent period of dinner-table conversation we would withdraw to the library before the fire or walk for hours on the terrace. The moment for serious matters had arrived. On one such occasion when I had come to Boston full of enthusiastic plans, I noticed at once the conductor's melancholy abstraction and an apparent unwillingness to respond to any conversational gambit bearing upon music. I knew that the denouement could not be long in coming and so discreetly waited; but I was not prepared for what did come. "I cannot make plans beyond next season, Mr. Charlie, because I have resigned." I was startled, but observing no sudden engorgement of the vein that beats in Koussevitzky's temple when he is excited, no thickening of his accent, or exaggeration of the slight lisp that also are signs of emotional tensity, I decided that somewhere in the background there was a mental reservation. This, I thought, was pure Russian dramatization, the final bold feint in the campaign the conductor had undertaken to enforce his will upon the board and management of the Boston Symphony Orchestra. I am sure I looked properly distressed, nevertheless, and so Dr. Koussevitzky presently and mercifully informed me that his contract stipulated that when and if he should resign, his renunciation of the orchestra should not be effective until a year after its date. The fears that he had instantaneously generated in me quite as suddenly subsided. I felt hopeful that in a year whatever difficulties existed between Koussevitzky and the powers of the Boston Symphony would certainly be resolved.

Nevertheless, the moment was a dangerous one, because it came when both Koussevitzky and the Boston Symphony management were dissatisfied with their recording situation; the New York Philharmonic had been laid at Koussevitzky's feet; the Philharmonic was under contract to the Columbia Broadcasting System, and Columbia Broadcasting System controlled the Columbia Recording Corporation, which was prowling about seeking whom, especially among major artists, it might devour. It is probable that Koussevitzky's threat of resignation was a menacing gesture and nothing more, but he was, in fact, required to make two decisions, both of which were of vital importance to my employers and therefore to me.

The Boston Symphony Orchestra had for some time been proscribed by the American Federation of Musicians. This prevented both broadcasting and recording, a condition that intolerably distressed Koussevitzky. He had noted the frequent broadcasts of the Philharmonic and the NBC Orchestra and was quietly enraged to reflect that his own orchestra, which he rightly considers superior to either of these, was barred from the air. He believed too that he and his orchestra were capable of definitive performances of certain works and because the performances were definitive he was morally obligated to record them. He felt so deeply on the subject of recording that in an effort to satisfy his passionate demand for certain of his performances to be preserved, union or no union, the orchestra bought and installed in Symphony Hall elaborate and costly recording equipment; and many of its performances were made permanent.

This did not satisfy Koussevitzky. It seemed to him that the viewpoint of the trustees and management with respect to the musicians' union was stiff-necked and old-fashioned, and he was in favor of making peace with Petrillo on Petrillo's own terms. With both Koussevitzky and the management the musical well-being of the orchestra was the first consideration, but their viewpoints were widely divergent. Music was, I think, Koussevitzky's *only* consideration, whereas the trustees and the management had to consider the material welfare of the orchestra as well. The management was as eager as Koussevitzky to record his great performances, not only for the artistic reasons entertained by the conductor, but for the reason that recording has supplied a large and indeed a critical part of the orchestra's income. The orchestra had been fortunate in having as a trustee for many years Mr. Ernest B. Dane, who annually made good a deficit running between forty thousand dollars and sixty thousand dollars. At this troubled time the orchestra's generous benefactor died, leaving in his will no provision for the orchestra. To have this annual gift discontinued, and record income materially reduced, was serious indeed. To have the orchestra barred from both recording and broadcasting at this same time was catastrophic.

Koussevitzky therefore was for making an agreement with the musicians' union in order that sources of income might be exploited and the orchestra's budget balanced. The trustees and the management were firmly against this proposal, and,

strangely enough, for reasons that should have appealed more
to an artist than to a group of conservative businessmen. The
objection of those opposed to the union was not that a union
orchestra would cost more to operate, but rather, very simply
stated, that no one had proved or even proposed that unionization of the orchestra would add anything to its artistic
stature. An interesting paradox, this—a musician taking one
side of an argument for business reasons, and businessmen
taking the opposite side for musical reasons. Or was it a paradox?

Koussevitzky's dissatisfaction was by no means mitigated
when, because of the rationing of gasoline and perhaps because of other considerations, it was decided to suspend the
Berkshire Festival, to which he had given such unremitting
labor, such imagination, enterprise, and daring, and which had
achieved in the space of only two or three years a resounding
success.[2] The wisdom of the decision to interrupt the
sequence of the Berkshire Festival need not be discussed here,
but it should be pointed out that the Music Shed at Tanglewood can be reached only by motor; that in wartime there
was no public transportation to serve it; and that probably
more than half of the audience travels at least twenty miles
to and from the concerts. In the end the implacable determination of Koussevitzky kept the Festival alive even during the
troubled years of the war, though its activities had to be drastically contracted.

I think Koussevitzky seriously, though perhaps briefly, entertained the idea of resigning. Indeed, he told me explicitly
that he had actually dispatched a letter of resignation. Later,
when he had expended his anger and was more amenable to

2 It is usually assumed that Koussevitzky was the founder of the Berkshire
Festival, but this is not true. The Festival was founded by the late Dr. Henry
Hadley, one of the most distinguished musicians and one of the most lovable
men the profession has produced in America. Under Dr. Hadley the Festival
never approached the artistic dimensions that it has reached under Koussevitzky, but the idea of the Berkshire Festival was originally conceived and
realized with the most limited resources by Dr. Hadley.

sympathy and suggestion, he assured me almost tearfully that he would never, as long as he lived, regularly conduct any but the Boston Symphony Orchestra, which indeed is his creature and his monument. He added that one of the reasons why he did not immediately accept an offer from the Columbia Recording Corporation was his interest in the quality of Boston Symphony Orchestra records, for which he felt I was in some degree responsible, and he mentioned unwillingness to dissociate himself from myself because he had a certain confidence in my ability, taste, and technical knowledge. He asserted that he would never make a record unless I were present.[3] This was gratifying to me, but I reflected that even if he forbore to use the weapon of resignation, the situation was full of peril for my company.

He was considering several possibilities. He could accept the conductorship of the Philharmonic, in which case he would be lost to Victor for recording and to NBC for broadcasting. He could accept an offer more tempting than the Philharmonic—an exceedingly generous proposition from the Columbia Broadcasting System, which involved not only broadcasting on a sustaining basis, but also a very agreeable arrangement with the subsidiary Columbia Recording Corporation.

Our pusillanimous behavior with respect to the union problem as it affected the Boston Symphony had not endeared us to the orchestra authorities, who felt that the long and profitable association of the orchestra and ourselves should dictate and fortify a defiant attitude on our part. We had a contract to record the orchestra; there was nothing in it originally that made its execution contingent upon any dictate of the American Federation of Musicians; yet we refused to carry out the contract and as time went on were forced to reduce and delay

---

[3] After I had resigned from Victor, Mr. Koussevitzky and Mr. Judd agreed with the company that when and if the Boston Symphony Orchestra made records, it would be on the condition that I would be in charge. My subsequent connection with Columbia Records made this impossible.

issues of Boston Symphony Orchestra records, with the consequence that revenue to the orchestra declined.

In this situation it required no great degree of perspicacity
to see that Koussevitzky and the Boston management were
seriously tempted to accept the joint proposals of Columbia
Broadcasting and Columbia Recording. Surely this was a crisis,
and since it involved matters other than recording I felt
obliged to put the facts before the highest authorities. I suggested that Mr. David Sarnoff would meet with the Boston
people and see whether or not some kind of arrangement
mutually satisfactory could be made. I have learned that at
this meeting Mr. Sarnoff influenced the orchestra management toward joining the union, thus partly solving our problem and their own. At the same time NBC was frantically
promoting the NBC Orchestra and Toscanini, and was not
interested in engaging any other orchestra to compete with
them. The price offered by the Columbia people was an impressive one and well beyond anything Victor would offer. I
described the situation candidly and in detail to Mr. Frank
B. Walker, then vice-president of Victor in charge of all recording activities, and he presented it just as candidly to Mr.
Sarnoff. The president of RCA then took drastic steps and
made possible an agreeable broadcasting arrangement between the Boston Symphony Orchestra and the then Blue
Network of NBC.

Mr. Walker, who, when a subordinate was involved, was
always as quick to accept unmerited blame as to reject deserved credit, was generous enough to report in writing to Mr.
Sarnoff that I was largely responsible for the happy solution
of the Boston problem, and both Koussevitzky and Mr.
George E. Judd, manager of the orchestra, concurred. The
truth is that Frank Walker's management, his resourceful-
ness, patience, skill as a negotiator, and kindly shrewdness,
complementing similar qualities ard warm goodwill on the
part of Mr. Judd, actually were responsible. The active co-
operation of Mr. Mark Woods, president of the Blue Net-

work (now the American Broadcasting Company), was a factor minus which the satisfactory solution could not have been reached. Not to weary you with details, let me but add that a sustaining broadcast contract[4] at a figure well within the means of the Blue Network of NBC, and a recording contract quite satisfactory to Boston and to Victor were arranged. Of course these were contingent upon the unionization of the Boston Symphony, and this presently was accomplished, as Sarnoff had urged. It was rather dreadfully ironical that after all these excursions and alarums Mr. Petrillo's ultimatum of 1942 put Victor in the ridiculous position of having first refused to record Boston because it was non-union and then for two years refusing to record because it had become union.

All through these maneuvers Koussevitzky held firmly to his every point and principle without hysterics, without publicity, without recriminations, without for a moment modifying his determination or compromising his dignity. He was really the ultimate winner in all his controversies, and he was the winner because he sensed the nature and weakness of every opponent, whether that opponent was a Boston Brahmin, a Harvard overseer, or a labor overlord, and with each and every one he was always "*fortiter in re, sed suaviter in modo.*"

MAN AND MUSICIAN

When I first knew Koussevitzky he was a man of full habit, of a comfortable rotundity, by no means tall but giving the impression of tallness, adroitly if not conspicuously tailored, and with a countenance as handsome, as deceptively open, as mobile and expressive as an upper-class politician's. Indeed, in a general way, with respect to conformation of facial and cranial bones he was not unlike our late President, but feature for feature he was and is even more handsome. His eyes, of

---

[4] This has since been put on a commercial basis much more profitable to both the orchestra and the American Broadcasting Company.

a curious and definitely topaz color, are set well apart under
an impressive forehead, rather than disconcertingly close together as Mr. Roosevelt's were. The lower part of his face,
beneath an aristocratic nose, is rather delicately boned and
his jaw has the firmness of Mr. Roosevelt's without the heavy
prognathous contour that made the President a delight to the
caricaturist. It is curious to note, however, that while in ordinary circumstances his face has normally firm lines, in conversational moments when he wishes to be emphatic or feels
belligerent, his jaw is strongly thrust forward; whereas when
he is conducting especially moving passages the jaw is re-
tracted to a point where its bones seem to dissolve and disappear. In moments of stress the veins and arteries in
Koussevitzky's head and face become noticeably engorged
and chlorotic and his face is likely to assume an alarming shade
of purple. His eyes, ordinarily of a liquid brightness because
of a chronic rheum, become congested with blood. These
effects, it seems to me, are entirely the accompaniment of the
expenditure of nervous energy rather than physical.

His conducting manner does not involve violent, elaborate,
or even very many gestures, but even after his most vigorous
performance his temperature is as always subnormal; his hands
are gelid. Whereas most men tend to soften and increase in
weight after middle age, Koussevitzky has become leaner, more
tense, and somehow smaller. When I first knew him he seemed
vigorous, well fed, serene; more recently, and especially since
the death of his wife, it seems to me that his physical vigor
has declined while his nervous energy has greatly increased;
and sometimes I think that in his unfaltering devotion to his
work, his unsparing and constant demands upon his own resources of physical and nervous strength, he is actually con-
suming his own being. It is as if little by little everything but
his spiritual force is being burned away.

Koussevitzky, in his personal life, is neither Sybarite nor
ascetic. He loves beautiful clothes and fine tailoring, but is
neither foppish nor freakish in his sartorial tastes. I think he

has a moderate love of luxury, which finds its most notable expression in a truly Russian appreciation of beautiful furs. He has several coats that would make even a fashionable 52nd Street doxy squeal with envy, and one fabulous ermine-lined coat that is regal. The last time I saw this coat was when I helped Koussevitzky get into it on March 17, 1945. This happened in his suite at the Savoy-Plaza Hotel. The outside temperature officially on that date in New York was an unseasonable 86 degrees, and I wondered how the conductor could bear the warmth of ermine. Further to increase his suffering, a St. Patrick's Day parade was in progress along Fifth Avenue, and it was necessary for us to cross in order to get Koussevitzky to Carnegie Hall for an afternoon concert. The ermine coat is exceedingly light, unbelievably warm, but it was the only overcoat Koussevitzky had with him and he would not go without it. I had, therefore, to pilot him afoot a distance of at least a hundred yards through the tremendous crush of people on the sidewalks, through the ranks of fifty thousand Irishmen, through the sweltering street—and I thought, I feared, he would collapse. I had forgotten for the moment that Koussevitzky is always cold, and when I finally bestowed him in his car within minutes of curtain time for his concert, it was I, not he, who was hot and bothered.

Koussevitzky often seems cold, austere, reserved, and unapproachable, and indeed at times he is. This, I think, is no more than a defense in depth, to give him time and opportunity to estimate, to assay, to evaluate the person he is facing. He is shrewd, wise, and practical; observant, intuitive, and kindly. When I first went to him a good many years ago I was warned that my chances of success were faint, that Serge Koussevitzky and Judge Cabot and George Judd were difficult to approach, impossible to influence. For quite some time my employers had been indifferent in their relations with the Boston Symphony, and such an attitude, though it might be accepted with well-bred calm and outward equanimity, is not ingratiating with the powers that direct the orchestra's destiny. Years had passed and no move had been made to record with Boston. Contracts had lapsed, through neglect, and indeed the orchestra made the first step toward a definite breach in its relations with the company when it permitted the recording by Columbia of an early symphony of Roy Harris. This was alarming, but not sufficiently alarming, to Victor, for if it had been, no one such as I, so naïve, so unversed in the protocol of artist relations, so devoted to music and so ignorant of commerce, would have been dispatched to repair the damage. I think Koussevitzky sensed my ignorance, innocence, and uneasiness, for from the very beginning he was understanding, kindly, and helpful.

Koussevitzky can be a loyal friend or a bitter, unforgiving enemy, an implacable and merciless antagonist. In the areas of activity where political, social, and other skills are of more import than musicianship—and every conductor must operate in such areas—Koussevitzky has few peers and no superiors. His advantage lies in a shrewd estimate of human nature and his ability so to adjust and color his own personality as to make him irresistible to the personality he would subdue. He can be the imperious patrician, the suave diplomat, the genial friend, the absolute dictator, the accommodating colleague, the daring young man, or the venerable patriarch— as circumstances and occasions indicate. Nor in this may one impute to him any lack of sincerity, for everything he does is done for the furthering of the principle that rules his life: the advancement of music.

He has evaluated Boston spirit much more accurately than some Bostonians have done. He knows that the attitude slyly mocked by Emerson—

> What care though rival cities soar
> Along the stormy coast,
> Penn's town, New York, and Baltimore,
> If Boston knew the most!

—is no longer an important force in Boston. Boston is not complacent, ultra-conservative, culturally backward, in music or anything else. Boston is determined to have the best, whether it be new or old. Boston has its failings, certainly, but Koussevitzky has been keen enough to sense that Boston is dissatisfied, uneasy, and restive because of its failings. Bostonians do not enjoy being regarded as backward, and they are not; nor could they endure either the static backwardness and corruption of cities like Philadelphia or the noisy determination to expand and progress that one finds in New York or Chicago or Atlanta.

Koussevitzky's acquaintance with the present-day attitude of cultivated Boston doubtless has a bearing on his enthusiasm for contemporary music in general and American music in particular. He has probably played more American music than any other conductor of a first-rank orchestra, and he has made Boston like it. What is more important, he has, I think, exercised more discriminating taste in choosing what American music shall be played than has any other conductor who emphasizes contemporary music. This, in spite of the fact that he has been influenced by the coterie of composers that is headed, guided, and dominated by Aaron Copland—a coterie which tends to exclude all outsiders. Koussevitzky, however, is not a man to be dominated completely or for very long by anyone, and composers definitely outside the pale of Mr. Copland's clique, such as Roy Harris, Harl McDonald, and Howard Hanson, have managed to get their music played by the Boston Symphony Orchestra.

Koussevitzky's interest in present-day music and particularly American music can be, and has been, on occasion, tempered to the point where it dissolves completely if he is not offered a first performance, and here some reservation as to his sincerity might be entertained. But almost every conductor has this failing, and I still believe in this conductor's integrity with respect to music made in America. True, it has been questioned by certain American composers, and particularly by those who haven't had a first or any other performance of their work by Koussevitzky. Their questioning grows more querulous when the conductor's sometimes ephemeral enthusiasm for a new piece leads him to hint future performances that are improbable or impossible. I have one composer-friend who reproached Koussevitzky when an anticipated performance failed to materialize. This composer, who is on good terms with the master and furthermore is not noted for reticence, cried indignantly, "But Maestro, you said you would play my piece this season. You promised. You know you have a terrible weakness for making promises." "Yes, my dear," suavely, "but thank God I have the strength not to keep them."

I remember quite well the passionate determination of Koussevitzky to give the first American performance of the Ravel *Bolero*, which two other conductors were to perform on the same date. I have been told that the hour of the Boston concert was advanced a few minutes to make sure that the Koussevitzky performance would be the first, as indeed it was. Again, Koussevitzky was involved in the rather undignified squabble among Stokowski, Toscanini, and himself over the first performance of the Shostakovich Seventh. I was involved in this because a first recording was considered equally important with a first public performance. Long before there was any talk of the Shostakovich Seventh in this country I had learned in detail of the work from Stokowski, who had discussed it with the composer himself, and I had agreed that Stokowski should be the conductor to record it. Now with three conductors harassing me, I was in a somewhat difficult situation, which I resolved in collaboration with the publishers of Shostakovich by agreeing that Toscanini should have the first radio performance, Koussevitzky, the first public performance, and Stokowski, the first recording. I think this satisfied no one, because the recording was highly desirable for historic and documentary reasons [5] and was considered by all three conductors as actually more important than any other kind of performance. Toscanini was furious because he was not permitted to record the work, and for quite some time I roasted in the hell of his displeasure, but my employers stoutly supported me in my decision, knowing that I had given my word to Stokowski. Toscanini even proposed to record the work for his private use and at his own expense, but quickly abandoned the idea when he discovered what the expense would be. Stokowski was displeased because, though I sustained my agreement to assign the recording to him, recording at the time was impossible under the prohibition imposed by the musicians' union, and he sensed that before Petrillo's ban could be lifted interest in the Shostakovich symphony would have evaporated. To this moment I do not believe the Shostakovich Seventh has been recorded by anyone, nor do I believe anyone wants to record it. I have often regretted that such bitterness should develop over a work that at the time of its publication I believed and declared to be an insignificant, bombastic, and vacuous fake; a work that I thought every orchestra in the United States would try to play once during its first season and never thereafter.

Mr. Koussevitzky has been less kind to American conductors than to American composers. Most of his guest conductors have been Europeans—Sir Adrian Boult, Paul Paray, Hannikainen, and others. He has had in his classes at Tanglewood

---

[5] The purported historic connotations of this piece of music are as spurious and fraudulent as the hysterical and wholly factitious publicity that preceded its first performance. The work was supposed to have been written during the siege of Leningrad and to celebrate the German defeat before that citadel. On these premises it was promoted as not only an art work of first importance, but as a specimen of Russian heroism under fire and as an historic document. Actually the greater part of the work was written long before the siege of Leningrad, and I am reliably informed that none of it was written within the confines of that city. The title "Leningrad Symphony" and associations with the siege are purely adventitious.

a number of young Americans, some of them, like Ifor Jones, Richard Korn, and Leonard Bernstein, musicians of extraordinary talent and already of notable achievement. None of them, so far as I can ascertain, was ever permitted to conduct the full Boston Symphony Orchestra at Tanglewood, though subsequently Bernstein conducted some of his own works at a Boston Symphony concert in Boston and still later in New York. Koussevitzky admires Dr. Jones so warmly that he has more than once traveled to Bethlehem, Pennsylvania, to hear the incomparable Bach Choir of which Jones, with his gifts of British scholarship and Gaelic fire, is the conductor and the vitalizing spirit. Koussevitzky regards the gifted Bernstein as a protégé and is highly enthusiastic about him. I think the master must have deeply influenced and inspired Bernstein, but actually the young genius acquired his knowledge of conducting from that indisputable authority, Fritz Reiner. Richard Korn has conducted a half-concert of the Boston "Pops" and has made some admirable recordings, but, like the other talented young men whose conducting abilities Koussevitzky well knows, he has not been given opportunities by the maestro.

To speak for a moment about teaching: I think there is really very little that can be taught about conducting, and for that little I should not seek Koussevitzky as a master. I believe Koussevitzky could teach musicians how to think about music, but I do not believe he can teach them to conduct it. Koussevitzky's eminence as a conductor is not to be accounted for by any notable technical skill—by which I mean what musicians call "stick technique." He simply proves that one may succeed as a conductor without it, particularly if one has unlimited musical resources, absolute authority, several decades of tenure, and superb musicianship. The fact that Koussevitzky succeeded notably as guest conductor of the Philharmonic Symphony of New York is adduced as evidence disproving the foregoing statement, but his success with the Philharmonic proves and disproves nothing. Certainly he infused vitality and spirit and imagination and enthusiasm into that orchestra, but the performances resembled those of the Boston Symphony Orchestra only in the occasional uncertainty of attack and release, the sometimes tentative rhythmic pulse, and other details that are among the less admirable characteristics of Koussevitzky's own orchestra.

Koussevitzky has little more enthusiasm for his colleagues than for his young disciples. He rightly thinks a conductor should be, in relation to the orchestra, a philosopher and an exponent of the philosophy, the thinking, of certain great minds. In this sense he himself is unquestionably one of the greatest of conductors, in spite of his indifference to formalized conducting technique, and for kindred reasons he looks down with paternal, almost patriarchal tolerance, indulgence, and sometimes disdain on such men as Ormandy, Golschmann, and Barbirolli. Toscanini he considers one who is concerned only with a photo-phonetic reproduction of what a printed score indicates. Stokowski he assays as a singularly clever craftsman concerned with the basic and base appeal of sheer eroticism. A certain supercilious attitude toward animal passion may contribute to the soundness, profundity, and conviction of Koussevitzky's interpretations. It contributes little, however, to the sensuous appeal of his music.

Koussevitzky rehearses and conducts with his eyes and his mouth rather than with his hands. His indifference to baton technique—I might almost say his innocence of it—makes his rehearsals long and difficult for himself and his orchestra. The caliber of his players, the illuminating quality of his explanations, and the vehemence of his exhortations assure him, nevertheless, the response he demands; only rarely do the eccentricity and indefiniteness of his beat bring about a contretemps. Such minor tragedies do occur, however, and I witnessed one not so long ago when the Boston Symphony played in Philadelphia. There was a moment in the first movement of Beethoven's Fifth—a measure that is indeed a trap for the unwary—wherein various sections of the orchestra were at odds with each other and with the conductor. I met him as he came off stage at the end of the symphony, white and quivering with rage at his orchestra. This was unjust; the fault was distinctly and exclusively his and he knew it. One positive downbeat would have prevented the accident.

Boston Symphony rehearsals are not open to the public, nor even to occasional visitors. Curiously enough, this exclusiveness has been brought about by the action of the orchestra men and not by the conductor. Usually permission to attend a rehearsal is asked of the conductor. In Boston it is asked of the chairman of the orchestra, and even the conductor himself must ask this permission. I discovered this in rehearsing a Boston "Pops" concert in the summer of 1945 when a friend of mine wanted to attend. I readily acquiesced, but found that my position as guest conductor was not sufficient to assure my friend's admittance. Upon inquiring into the reason for this I learned that in the past when rehearsal spectators had reported on Koussevitzky's outbursts at rehearsal, there was acute embarrassment to some of the players. The conductor might, for instance, say to one of his men, "You are a stupid man. You do not know even how to hold your instrument. I do not want you to play with me any more." Now the man might be a distinguished virtuoso and perhaps the head of a department at the Longy School or the New England Conservatory of Music. Such remarks as I have quoted are not necessarily offensive to the player when he is among his colleagues at rehearsal, for he understands perfectly well that the conductor doesn't for a moment mean what he says, but merely exaggerates a momentary impatience in the hope of shocking a player into greater effort. Such remarks, however, put into laymen's mouths and circulated outside the rehearsal hall may cause serious damage. Through the Boston local of the American Federation of Musicians the men of the Boston Symphony, in defense of their personal dignity and private interests, enforced the rule—a wise one, I think— against visitors to rehearsal.

Koussevitzky's attitudes are sometimes as carefully studied as his scores. I would never accuse him of being a poseur; every conductor must be, to a considerable degree, an actor—and an actor cannot always forget that he is one. When Koussevitzky's real beliefs and feelings are touched he ceases to be an actor or even a great artist; he becomes a great man. I shall not soon forget a performance of the Ninth Symphony, which he had by sheer chance programmed for the night of the false V-E Day. I am quite certain that had the rumors of the peace not developed this performance would have been soundly conceived, exquisitely polished, and quite satisfying. Actually it was the most disorderly, passionately sincere, exciting, and convincing performance of the Ninth I have heard. Koussevitzky, I know, had considered himself an American soldier with music as his weapon, enlisted on the side of the more decent part of humanity. Here then, he thought, was the victory, and the thought excited him beyond control. The noble fury that possessed him communicated itself through the frantic music of Beethoven to the orchestra, to the chorus, and even to some radio listeners. Such a performance, undisciplined and technically faulty though it was, seemed like an unpremeditated outpouring of the man's most sacred beliefs. It seemed to me infinitely superior and more happily to be remembered than the polished and precious perfectness of the Mozart he gave a few weeks later at Tanglewood—for the self-conscious sophisticates and simpering sycophants whom Olin Downes regards as "the elite." No, this Ninth Symphony of Koussevitzky was no fare for Petronius. It was Whitman's barbaric yawp incontinently bellowed into the high heaven that looks down on free men and brothers. Mozart's courtesans and Koussevitzky's courtiers would not admire the uncouth, imperative *sursum corda* of this Beethoven, but I think Beethoven would.

LEOPOLD
STOKOWSKI

❧ Leopold Stokowski ❧

"There is one that is alone, and he hath not a second,
yea, he hath neither son nor brother; yet is there no
end of all his labour, neither are his eyes satisfied
with riches."

Ecclesiastes

"Nunquam se minus otiosum esse, quam quum
otiosus, nec minus solum, quam quum solus esset." [1]

Cicero: *De Officiis*

"No, Charlie, I am never lonely, never tired, never bored, never sick, never idle." More than a dozen years have passed since Mr. Stokowski made this assertion; at least half of them passed before I could fully understand and believe the essential truth of Mr. Stokowski's bold and apparently boastful statement. Most of us find it necessary to share the burdens, the trials, the disillusionments, and the little triumphs of life with friends or mates or children. Most of us occasionally look for distraction from reality to the theater or to music, or in solitude turn for companionship to books old and beloved or

---

[1] "He is never busier than when at leisure, never less lonely than when he is alone."

new and fascinating. Mr. Stokowski has nothing and nowhere to escape, and for him no escape is ever desirable or necessary. He has the constant companionship of a person who utterly absorbs his interest, one whose mind is forever stimulating, every aspect of whose spiritual and physical life is of the most intense and imperative interest, whose devotion is constant, exclusive, unquestioning, and unquestioned. Stokowski's wonderful friend and companion is himself, and he needs no other.

His life proceeds precisely in every detail as he has planned it. He wants nothing that he cannot have, accepts nothing that he does not want, follows with silken, suave, and savage determination the dictates of his own will an'! these only. He has no impulses; his every thought and word and action are calculated and directed by a brilliant intelligence to the accomplishment of some definite if often ephemeral purpose. His egocentricity is seldom obvious, never offensive. It is not congenital, but acquired. I believe he is naturally gentle, considerate, kindly, emotionally responsive; but observing how a man is often made vulnerable through these very virtues, he has steeled himself against them; but has employed them—or convincing images of them—to his purposes. I do not believe he has ever failed in anything he has undertaken, first, because he would not undertake anything in which failure was possible; second, because he shrewdly calculates every factor in every project and eliminates the sources of possible failure before he undertakes the work. He is not an inhuman man, but rather one who by the exercise of a superb intelligence has extirpated from within himself what he considers human faults and frailties. His fierce pride could not tolerate failure; therefore, he has schooled himself to control, to employ, or to eliminate every process, every avenue by which failure could come to him, and every person who ceases to be of use, who actively or passively obstructs his purpose is, without either malice or mercy, deftly, quietly, and finally removed from his orbit.

Many a crocodile tear has been shed for Stokowski of late, particularly among those who for one reason or other have been disqualified from association with him; they weep, they say, to observe the deterioration and distortion of a career so brilliant in its progress, so founded upon singular natural gifts, so sadly arrested at its zenith. The truth is that Stokowski, in all his dealings with the Cleveland Orchestra, the Philadelphia Orchestra, the Philharmonic Orchestra, the NBC Orchestra, the motion picture industry, and radio, has contrived exactly what he wanted. *"He did according to his will and became great."* He is, according to his own standards and his own plans, completely in control of his own destiny, completely successful, completely happy.

Stokowski has been a subject of controversy almost from the very beginning of his career in America more than a generation ago, and in most cases all parties to the arguments were wrong. Even his name has been a matter of dispute. Why this should be of particular interest I can not explain, except that some unfriendly and envious people could find little else with which to embarrass him. In the world of entertainment artists often use names other than their own, and I know some whose right even to their father's name has been questioned. Name-changing is a long-established convention in the theater world. Why the acute interest in Stokowski's name? Olga Samaroff, the first Mrs. Stokowski, was born Hickenlooper; Judy Garland was born to a family named Gumm; Bruno Walter's name is Schlesinger; Paul Muni's, Weisenfreund; Frank Black's, Schwartz; and we have had musicians claiming such unlikely patronymics as Paul Musikonsky and Mischa Violin. Nobody has made issue of these. I know more than one musician who knew him as a student in England and will swear that his name is Leo Stokes. This is a matter I never cared to discuss with Mr. Stokowski, as he is extremely reluctant to talk about himself or to reveal any biographical data whatsoever. He did, nevertheless, tell me unequivocally and with certain genealogical references that his name is Leopold Antonin Stanislaus Stokowski. I believe this. After years of close association, professional and personal, I cannot convince myself that Stokowski is capable of uttering an untruth. I do think he reserved some of the facts in the case, since several of those who have told me his name is Stokes are also people of veracity. Why, then, the apparent contradiction? I believe it comes about because Stokowski must have been known as Stokes, perhaps during his student days. For some years he had as patron a wealthy and powerful lady of the English nobility, and it is credible that she may have preferred at that particular time to have her protégé an English boy with an English name. This is pure speculation on my part and I do not vouch for it; but if correct it would, I think, lay the ghost of "Leo Stokes."

Perhaps Mr. Stokowski's curious accent, which I must concede is an affectation, has encouraged speculation about his origin, for his sometimes curious intonation, syntax, and pronunciation are not definitely to be associated with any country that I know. This manner of speaking, which he assumes or discards at will, is Slavic in its elimination of the definite article and certain other characteristics; Germanic in other respects and, according to William Primrose, Ifor Jones, and other British-born friends of mine, it is occasionally cockney. Mr. Stokowski is rather humorless in his employment of this peculiar speech. I remember that when, as associate conductor, I was with him and the Philadelphia Orchestra in the town of Holdredge, Nebraska, he had no difficulty whatever in pronouncing the name of the place, but not long afterward at a dinner for the orchestra in Philadelphia, he repeatedly referred to this community as "Holdrrray-ga." The orchestra was unexpectedly amused.

As for the corporeal Stokowski—he is a miracle. I had occasion recently to look at some photographs about thirty years old that reveal a tall man of Byronic comeliness, "pard-like, beautiful and swift"; a body erect, tense, yet suggesting a feline quickness, suppleness, and grace, and in these details I can see little difference wrought by the years from 35 to 65. The bright mane, certainly thinner and whiter, nevertheless frames his face and handsome cranium with the same shining aureole. The broad brow, ice-blue eyes, heroic but finely sculptured nose, and sensual mouth combine as ever in a face of imperious beauty. Stokowski is about six feet tall, exceedingly well proportioned, with the strength and agility, but not the contours, of an athlete. It is said that he was at one time an amateur boxer, but either this is untrue or he was an extraordinary champion; otherwise, I cannot understand how his classic nose escaped injury. His physique is not that of a boxer or of any other kind of athlete. The skeletal structure is male enough, but there are no knotted and bunching muscles—rather, the pale, smooth hide under which long, flat muscles extend themselves like serpents. He shows no surplus adipose tissue, but rather only enough to overlay a somewhat massive bone structure with a certain almost feminine roundness. His celebrated hands, to which he pays no particular attention and concerning which he has no vanity, are actually not, in the usual sense of the word, beautiful. In the first place, they are disproportionately large, powerful, and thick-fingered. The illusion of beauty that they give comes from the instinctive grace with which they are used. I had never noticed the unusually large bones of his ankles until he himself once called my attention to them under rather curious circumstances. We were riding in a taxicab and, perhaps with one eye on the meter, I was complaining about the disadvantages of poverty and the corresponding advantages of wealth. Stokowski said, "Charlie, I don't think you want to get rich, and I hope you never do. I like you much better being poor." To this I answered, perhaps with a little asperity, "You wouldn't say that if you had ever been poor." He pulled up his trouser leg and said, exposing an ankle, "Look at that. Do you know how that came about?" I said, "Well, it looks very much to me like the result of malnutrition or rickets." Stokowski smiled rather grimly and said, "That's exactly what it is, so perhaps you will not say again that I don't know what it is to be poor."

I have often wondered that Stokowski could keep in such

superb condition without any apparent effort. He has a tigerish ability to relax completely and to spring into co-ordinated, graceful action in a second; and he has a catlike aversion from exercise for exercise's sake. Apparently he needs none other than that supplied by conducting, which these days is so infrequent as to be an insignificant factor in his physical condition. In fifteen years I have not known him to cough, sneeze, or use a handkerchief. Contrary to the many silly stories that have been printed, he is not a food faddist, he does not diet, he is not a total abstainer, and he does smoke. He is unlikely to drink and certain not to smoke during a period, whether it be days, weeks, or months, during which he has conducting engagements, but he permits himself moderate indulgence in these minor vices when he has leisure. He professes to abhor ardent spirits such as whisky, but will sometimes drink much more potent waters: vodka, Demerara rum, and on one vividly remembered occasion, absinthe frappé. I think he really prefers wines, however, but I cannot agree with him in his choice, for he loves muscatel, port, and a certain heavy, spicy, sweet wine from the island of Cyprus. On occasion he will mingle these, and the result is something no real wine-bibber could possibly tolerate.

I recall one strange example of Mr. Stokowski's singular tastes with respect to alcohol. Mrs. Stokowski (Evangeline Johnson), the conductor, and myself had attended a weird performance of the first indigenous African opera, given in an obscure second-floor theater in downtown New York. About three hundred people were packed into a room too small for a hundred, and between their aggregate weight and the furious stamping of dozens of gigantic Negro dancers on the stage, the floor of the place sagged and vibrated noticeably. Mrs. Stokowski was frankly quite terrified. We stayed to the end, but I will confess it was a relief to escape. We hurried uptown to Mr. Stokowski's Park Avenue apartment where upon our arrival Mrs. Stokowski immediately took to her bed. My host felt that a drink would be in order and trundled into the room a little wagon on which I suppose was every kind of liquor civilized men have ever imbibed. I was content with a simple Scotch-and-soda, but Mr. Stokowski insisted on mixing a drink for himself and invited me to the butler's pantry to see how it was done. He took a measure of heavy cream, a portion of pineapple juice, about an ounce of honey, stirred them up vigorously and then, with the expression of a boy stealing jam, slyly extracted from his coat pocket a six-ounce bottle of pure grain alcohol which he added to the mixture. I do not know what this drink was called, or indeed, what it could be called in polite language. He drank it.

Mr. Stokowski does like exotic flavors and fragrances, particularly when they are the natural flavors and aromas of flowers, fruits, spices, and vegetables, but aside from curiosity about the new and the exotic I have never noticed any peculiarities in his diet.

When he came to our house for dinner, which he has done countless times in the last fifteen years, we ordinarily made no special arrangements other than to provide the best in raw material and preparation that our resources permitted. The lady of the house, who makes an entry in her diary once every five-and-a-half years, did, however, make note of the first dinner we gave Stokowski, and I think you will agree that it wasn't for a man who was concerned about dietary matters. We had some sherry, a *boula gratinée*,[2] roast guinea hen with wild rice and celery, a salad of greens, whole giant peaches preserved in brandy, Puerto Rican coffee. Stokowski did full justice to this and every other dinner he ever had at our house. He hadn't come to us often before we noticed his curious habit of making a synthesis of all the flavors possible. He would get as many different items as possible onto his dinner plate and make a kind of pâté of them, and then eat his whole dinner with a spoon. Our limited silver didn't provide a spoon of exactly the

---

[2] Highly recommended. It is simply a blending in equal proportions of green pea and clear turtle soup slowly and carefully heated, topped with beaten cream and put under the broiler for a few minutes. Sherry with discretion.

right size so we had one made for him by Mr. George Stieff of Baltimore—an implement of heroic size and ponderous, very simple in design, but with a tiny and vaguely obscene figure of the little god Pan engraved on the handle. We thought we were making a double-edged pun, for Pan is not only regarded sometimes as a god of music, but the word "*pan*" in Polish corresponds with our English word "esquire." Mr. Stokowski appreciated the musical connotations and the exquisite little engraving, but the Polish meaning of the word never occurred to him.

He loves to investigate obscure and exotic restaurants, and together we have explored many interesting ones from New York to Mexico to California. I remember a noisome little hole in Juárez, but the enchiladas were good. I remember, too, Stokowski pre-empting the barman's job in a bar and grill at Urbana, Illinois, and shaking up terrifying cocktails called, fetchingly, a "Pirate's Breakfast" at 10:30 in the morning. Then there are fragrant recollections of La Chaumière and the personal ministrations of its presiding deity, M. Henri Massé. M. Massé at 163 East 56th Street provides provincial, but not too provincial, French cooking as well as an unpretentious and civilized atmosphere; but beware *quart d'heure de Rabelais*. Not, perhaps, such an adventure, but on the whole most satisfying of all public dining rooms we have discovered is the Three Threes at 333 South Smedley Street in Philadelphia. It is possible to find more sophisticated food, but a more courtly and engaging boniface than Gino I have yet to meet; the soundness of his cuisine and the quiet charm of his establishment provide a pleasant background for talk and companionship. The most amusing experience I ever had, however, occurred in New York when Mr. Stokowski decided that he wanted to dine at a Greek restaurant. He consulted a little book and chose a restaurant called the Apollo located somewhere far down on the East Side, I believe on Avenue "A." Something told me that this was not a café attending to exotic tastes, but I said nothing until, after a long taxi ride, we drew up in front of the place. One could see at a glance that it was an average white-top restaurant, decent, and no doubt operated by a pure Hellene, but not precisely a source of delicate egg-lemon soup, or the curious resinous wine of Greece. Mr. Stokowski was not to be dissuaded from entering and ordering—not even when the waitress, upon being asked what was particularly good, pointed to the blackboard on which were chalked such fascinating items as clam chowder, 10¢; ham and eggs, 35¢; coffee, 5¢; Shredded Wheat, 15¢. Undeterred by this rather uninspiring overture, Mr. Stokowski asked: "Do you have any of that lovely Greek wine?" to which the response was, "No, we ain't got no liquor license." He was determined, nevertheless, that we should have something to eat in the place and finally ordered some clam chowder. This was, I believe, the only time when I have dined with Stokowski and paid the check—20 cents.

Stokowski has a passion for color that is quite precisely parallel, I think, to his sensitiveness to taste, to sound, to scents, and everything else that appeals to the senses. Yet he lives very simply indeed. For many years he occupied the second and third floors of a rather decrepit ancient house in Philadelphia where he had a bedroom not too luxurious for an anchorite, a very pleasant studio room with nothing much in it but a piano, a desk, a couple of chairs, and a very handsome fireplace built by Mr. Stokowski with his own hands, and a room for his secretary's papers and files. Most people with one-tenth of Stokowski's income live much more luxuriously. He surrounds himself with color, and his studio apartment in Philadelphia was painted in a very beautiful shade of chartreuse—or perhaps it was between chartreuse and lime green—against which the vivid blues, burnt orange, and magenta of his lounging pajamas, shirts, hose, and other accessories made startling but by no means unpleasant contrasts. Aside from color, however, he has never been abnormally concerned with smart clothes or tailoring. If his tailcoat fit him and became a part of his every movement, it was not because, as some hard-

pressed reporters have claimed, the garment was complicated
in its interior by a system of straps and buttons and belts, but
rather because of the inborn grace and superb physique of the
man. I have known him to buy thirty-five dollar ready-made
suits with such satisfaction to himself that he wondered why
he had ever paid a London tailor five or six times as much for
suits that were no better. True enough, he gave away these
clothes to an elevator man a few weeks later. I do remember a
dark blue topcoat of fine English wool weighing but a few
ounces and yet very warm and wonderfully tailored, of which
Stokowski was a little vain. One night when he arrived at our
house for dinner he wore this coat and as I took it from him I
nearly dropped it for it weighed, instead of a few feathery
ounces, at least ten pounds. Stokowski noticed that I was
startled and, reaching into the two side pockets of the coat he
brought out, to my momentary dismay, two .45-caliber Colt
automatic pistols. It must be explained that at the time I lived
in perhaps the least respectable section of Philadelphia, and
furthermore, it was during the period when kidnapping was not
uncommon; it had been reported that Stokowski had received
threats involving his children. Consequently, he came to our
neighborhood prepared to sell his life dearly. However, he
couldn't have considered his own neighborhood any too respectable because I noticed not long after this incident that
he slept with the same pieces of ordnance on the floor within
arm's length.

Stokowski's preoccupation with human beings is perhaps
his greatest interest; it likewise contributes enormously to the
powerful magnetism of his personality. Business potentates
regard him at first with awe or even with fear, but eventually
with a fraternal attitude; artists, with love or hate or envy;
lawyers, with grudging admiration; engineers, with surprised
understanding; women, with delicious trepidation; children,
with uninhibited friendliness; dogs, with suspicion. At any
gathering he is automatically the center of interest, but this he

skillfully dissipates, and at the same time more firmly establishes himself in the attentions of those about him, by his extraordinary ability to speak anybody's language and, what is
more important, his stimulation of other people's talk and his
willingness to listen and to learn. With the banker he can discuss with intelligence and penetration the possible increment
of debentures, the coffee futures, or the current earnings of
Bell Telephone. He will listen also to the banker's opinion on
the same subjects and will profit thereby, but what is most important of all, socially, is that he knows when to talk music to
the banker and finances to the musician. He can astound the
engineer in acoustics, electronics, and related matters. The
man is not astounded that as a musician Stokowski knows so
much about engineering, but that he knows anything at all
about it. He confounds and delights the lawyers because of the
simplicity, clarity, directness, and completeness of his mental
processes, for these are qualities in a client to which lawyers
are unaccustomed and which render their own maneuvers
easier and more successful. He subdues women with flattery
and will chivalrously expend his most charming compli-
ments, sometimes, on the most unattractive; persuading each,
whether she be princess or pariah, that for the moment at
least she is the only existing female; leaving her with that
touch of glamour which few women can resist. It is touch and
go, however; these are purely drawing-room conquests, and if
he has pursued them farther I know nothing of it.

It is somehow curious that children are immediately and
uninhibitedly friendly with Stokowski. I do not believe that
he is interested in them other than as biological experiments.
He has an acute curiosity about all the processes, all the products of human life, and certainly children are the product of
an interesting process. I recall my own Puritanical shock when
he described to me with the utmost candor, with a kind of
dreadful naïveté, the pangs of parturition preceding the birth
of one of his children, which he witnessed; the fierce determination of the mother to satisfy nature's wanton demands for

the last measure of energy, blood, and pain, and the final cli-
mactic moment when the surgeon held aloft like a triumphant
banner the naked and whimpering infant. In retrospect I could
not attribute to morbidity Mr. Stokowski's fascinated interest
in this grim yet glorious affair, and I have cause to think, on
reflection, that it was not his utter lack of tenderness or sympathy, but the average man's excess of these emotions, that is
morbid.

If Stokowski worships any god, that god is nature. He was
baptized a Roman Catholic, but I have heard him declare
himself at various times an adherent of various faiths. He has
been, as expediency or his humor suggested, a Theosophist, a
Buddhist, a Greek Catholic, a Quaker, an Episcopalian, an
Anglican, and an agnostic, but he believes only, I think, in
nature and the inevitable processes of nature. Even here,
though, he has reservations. While he boldly insists upon, demands, and admires growth, he cannot accept with equanimity, nor can he even bear to contemplate, the corollary of
growth which is age, or its climacteric which is death.

Old people often take their lives or perish of sheer loneliness
and boredom because they have survived their friends and
families. Mr. Stokowski will never find himself in this sad situation, for his psychological and even to some extent his physical
contemporaries are in their teens and twenties. He has a vam-
pirine appetite for youth, and nothing so stimulates him or
calls forth to so high a degree his own engaging charm and
powerful magnetism as the proximity of young people and the
opportunity to study, to direct, to influence, and vicariously to
participate in their thoughts, their wild imaginings, their for-
ward-moving ambitions, their erratic eroticism. This he does
with quite impersonal detachment. Let there be no cry of
"wolf," for while his life is not precisely that of an ascetic, it is,
to my knowledge, morally aseptic. The psychological implications seem clear and obvious, however. It is as if he were eager

to believe that by a kind of homeopathic or contagious magic [3] he can see himself fixed in the stream of youth that surrounds yet rushes past him, as one gazing into flowing waters sees his image immovable in their depths, though the waters themselves move ever onward. Thus he has always immersed himself in youth and comeliness. His secretaries for the last eighteen years—and he has had as many as three at a time—while chosen primarily for efficiency were, nevertheless, invariably young and lovely; and those who agitate for fair employment practices with respect to race, color, and creed would have no quarrel with Mr. Stokowski. The concerts for youth of nubile age which he inaugurated in Philadelphia were uniquely successful, solely because of Stokowski's profound understanding of young people and uncanny skill in stirring—and controlling—their imaginations and emotions. The All-American Youth Orchestra, discounting for the moment the number of fathers and grandfathers it included, was another example of Stokowski's singular skill in dominating and manipulating for his purposes the plastic spirits of young people. He is interested in modern composers, but more particularly in young modern composers. Recently he has given final affirmation to his belief in this devotion to youth; and his friends, I think, prefer to accept the miracle of his indifference to the mounting years, rather than to entertain any other possible explanation of his perennial adolescence.

STOKOWSKI AS MUSICIAN

Stokowski asserts that the art of conducting, aside from a few rudiments of time-beating that almost anyone can learn in half an hour, cannot be formally taught, and he himself is the best proof of this theory, for as a conductor he is his own pupil. Prior to his engagement by the Cincinnati Symphony Or-

---

[3] See Sir James Frazer's *The Golden Bough*.

chestra he had conducted twice, and then only hastily assembled and previously unorganized orchestras in Europe.
This information was sent to the Cincinnati Orchestra board
and management by Herman Thumann, then music critic of
the *Cincinnati Enquirer*, who had been dispatched to London
at the instance of the Taft family to prospect for a conductor.
Mr. Thumann emphatically recommended Stokowski, notwithstanding his inexperience, and with the Taft influence and
that of Mrs. Christian Holmes (neé Betty Fleischman), Stokowski was engaged. The late Leonard Liebling, a few days
before his death, recalled in detail Stokowski's early experi-
ences with the Cincinnati Orchestra as well as the circumstances surrounding his engagement. His education as a
conductor there began and is still in progress; meanwhile, he
has reached, it seems to me, an eminence in his profession not
approached by anyone else.

Comparisons between Stokowski and Toscanini are inevitable. Comparison, however, implies the existence of common
qualities, and in my experience with these conductors I can
find little that they have in common. "Contrast" would be a
better word than "comparison." Toscanini is old and Stokowski, however factitiously, is young. One is concerned with the
frozen, the fossilized past; the other, with the plastic future.
Toscanini is literal; Stokowski, imaginative. The Italian re-
sponds passionately to a musical stimulus; the American is
sensual without passion. One enforces the musical discipline
developed by years of tradition; the other devises a discipline of
his own no less real but far less rigid. One finds the ultimate
beauty of music in the organization of its sound; the other, in
the character of the sound itself. One regards the metronome
as the ultimate authority over tempo; the other adjusts tempo
to the beat and pulse of his own life and feeling.One is a
meticulous etcher; one, a painter of vast murals. One is simple,
primitive, yet cunning; the other, complex, civilized, direct.
One, in living with music, would withdraw from life; the
other would live it.

I think of Stokowski as a musician mostly in relation to the Philadelphia Orchestra, where I knew him longest and most intimately, where in developing himself he simultaneously created that wonderful orchestral instrument. It was fortunate for him as well as for Philadelphia that in his early days with the orchestra he had the moral and material support of such men as Alexander Van Rensselaer and Edward Bok. The first necessity of a great orchestra is money, and lack of it was never among Stokowski's difficulties. An aggregation of great musicians does not make an orchestra. Money will buy great players but even they, if they are great, can sicken of their jobs and leave the orchestra if it fails them. Money, plus a great musician as leader, plus determination, plus skill, plus patience, plus art of the highest and most complex character can make a great orchestra, and with Stokowski a great orchestra—one of the greatest the world has ever known—was made.

I am told that Stokowski had periods of being a martinet, of being one of "the boys," of being an amiable friend or a remote and Olympian deity. I never have witnessed any of these manifestations during the last eighteen years. With his men he is pleasant, slightly aloof, impersonal, and correct in his rehearsal deportment and quite insistent upon the incompatibility of mercy and justice. He will not for one moment tolerate inattention or stupidity, and at any manifestation of these he could and would punish the offender with a few icy but polite words. I have never heard him raise his voice in anger or use a profane or vulgar word. I have seen him cruelly bait an inept player whose days in the orchestra were already numbered, and coolly and pleasantly torment the poor fellow into such embarrassment that he was utterly helpless and unable to play a note.

On the whole the orchestra profoundly admired Stokowski, and most of the musicians had a real affection for him. He always knew precisely what he wanted, how to explain to the orchestra what he wanted, and how to get what he wanted. In these respects and in others he is, I think, the most expert of all conductors; and because of these things he wasted neither his own time nor that of his musicians, a virtue that promotes regard for any conductor. His rehearsals, any Philadelphia man would tell you, were always and to the last minute interesting. He worked with the orchestra under the fiercest tension, but knew how and when to relax this tension and permit a new influx of interest and energy. On purely musical grounds, too, it was a joy to play with Stokowski, for he always left to the individual considerable freedom of expression as well as of technique. I do not believe that Mr. Stokowski ever cared how a man would bow or blow if the tone and phrase were of the precise kind of beauty the conductor wanted. The superb, the incredible legato of which the Philadelphia Orchestra alone seems capable is the result of Stokowski's insistence on free bowing; that is, the players were not obliged to follow the bowing of the section leader, but handled their instruments in the way that was most natural and easy for them in producing the effect the conductor demanded. The late J. Walter Guetter, for years first bassoon of the Philadelphia Orchestra, and without a rival among players of that instrument, did everything wrong technically in handling his instrument; but out of it came the loveliest phrasing and the most beautiful tone I have ever heard. Robert Bloom became the greatest of all English horn players not because he wanted to, but because Stokowski actually compelled him to do things with his instrument that violated every technical rule he had ever learned; but thereby the potentialities of the cor anglais were extended and amplified. William M. Kincaid, solo flute, and Marcel Tabuteau, solo oboe, were given, within limits imposed by the conductor, such liberty of interpretation as led to their recognition as peerless virtuosos; and there were others like Samuel Mayes, first cello; Anton Torello, first contrabass; Saul Caston, the incomparable first trumpet; Alexander Hilsberg—I must end this list or name half of Stokowski's Philadelphia Orchestra.

Stokowski never wore the orchestra out in rehearsal or exacted from it, until the concert itself, the ultimate degree of passionate expressiveness that he alone could evoke. In a sense he never led the orchestra, but rather made it an extension of himself, and he reserved for actual public performance the last full measure of tonal beauty and emotional expressiveness. His control of the orchestra was, and is, delicate and sensitive and complete, and a hundred times I have seen him change the whole contour of a phrase and the timbre of a tone by a sudden and apparently unpremeditated glance toward one of the orchestral choirs. The passionate expressiveness of Stokowski's orchestra was always, as far as he was concerned, calculated with mathematical nicety. While exacting preternatural effort and almost intolerable intensity from his players, he himself, as a great artist—and particularly a great actor—must be, was cool, detached, and perfectly poised. I shall never forget one occasion during a broadcast of the Philadelphia Orchestra when he included in the program his arrangement of the Love Music from the second act of *Tristan*—music the erotic content of which he emphasized to the point of indecent emotional exposure. For certain technical reasons Mr. Stokowski had me sit immediately in front of him and check up on the time, minute by minute. He honestly could not tell the broadcasting men how long the music would be, since he knew that according to his own mood his timing might vary by several minutes in this twenty-two-minute orgasm. I was not a very good timekeeper, and neglected to keep him informed of the passing minutes because I became so absorbed in the score and in the fascinating succession of expressions that passed over his countenance while he, apparently lost in ecstasy, drew from the orchestra the painful beauty of this music. I was startled and embarrassed, then, when in the middle of a passage of fiercest rapture, I heard a perfectly controlled, calm whisper: "Charlie, what time is it?"

Stokowski understands, at least from the psychological as distinguished from the intellectual viewpoint, the essential meaning of music. I think he would agree with Paul Elmer More [4] that: "Great music is a psychical storm, agitating to fathomless depths the mystery of the past within us. Or we might say that it is a prodigious incantation. There are tones that call up all ghosts of youth and joy and tenderness;—there are tones that evoke all phantom pains of perished passion;— there are tones that revive all dead sensations of majesty and might and glory,—all expired exultations,—all forgotten magnanimities. Well may the influence of music seem inexplicable to the man who idly dreams that his life began less than a hundred years ago! He who has been initiated into the truth knows that to every ripple of melody, to every billow of harmony, there answers within him, out of the Sea of Death and Birth, some eddying immeasurable of ancient pleasure and pain."

Music composed by Johann Sebastian Bach, and transcribed for the modern symphony orchestra by Leopold Stokowski, has become a definite part of the symphonic repertoire. Bach, in many respects the greatest of all musicians, wrote relatively little for orchestra; nothing for the orchestra as we know it. Most of his music was written for the church; much of it for chamber orchestra, for the organ, and for the clavier. Yet there are among his works things which, in grandeur of conception, richness of detail, beauty of form, and emotional value, transcend by far the limitations imposed by the instruments for which they were written. Stokowski, as an organist, naturally has studied intimately and for many years the music of Bach. He has perceived the peculiarly adaptable features of much of Bach's music, and has virtually rewritten for the orchestra not only several of the mightiest works, such as the Passacaglia in C minor, the great Chaconne, and the Toccata and Fugue in D minor, but also many obscure and relatively unknown smaller works.

Stokowski has brought to bear upon this music a vastly

---

greater force than the scholar's studiousness or the pedantry of the musicologist. The conventional blind worship of Bach and his music as it was left to us has not been a factor in the conductor's transcriptions. He has been able to see that the flawless formalism of so much of Bach's music, with its endless striving for color and variety within rigidly disciplined boundaries, is not the foolish and footless pleasure of a musical mathematician of almost superhuman ingenuity, but perhaps the sublimation of much warmer and more human feelings—an infinite refinement and elaboration of very sound and healthy and human impulses. No chilly ascetic ever had twenty children, as Bach did; and no man who has written great music or made great art in any form has been able to divorce his own emotional nature from it. Stokowski with extraordinary keenness of perception has recognized in much of Bach's music his joy in the act of creation, his passion for color and ornament, his sensitiveness to pure melody; and these things are likewise recognized in the orchestrations. Yet some of them are chaste as ice, and accomplish with amazing economy of means climaxes and effects of grandeur that would doubtless please, and certainly do credit to, Bach himself. Bach's humors are always taken into consideration, and in Stokowski's transcriptions the old master appears in as many guises as he doubtless assumed in the flesh. Sometimes, certainly, he is the pious organist; sometimes the sensitive lover of beauty; sometimes the virile figure of a manly man. But he is always Bach; Stokowski has perceived and penetrated his spirit, not perverted it.

The critics have not been unanimous in their enthusiasm for these Bach transcriptions. Indeed, some have taken the transcriber to task for having brought to brilliant and vigorous life some of the organ pieces. Yet here are works, fundamentally perhaps the most perfect and expressive in all the treasury of music, which but for Stokowski might today still languish in the fusty gloom and barrenness of the organ loft and the choir room. It was not by altering their spirit that he has made them the most thrilling and uplifting of all his or-

chestra's great utterances, but rather by translating that spirit
into terms of modern orchestration, by investing them with
all the tonal glories that today's superb orchestral instrument
makes available—resources that Bach himself, with his love for
variety and intimacy and magnificence and climax, would have
been the first to employ had they been within his reach or
knowledge.

Some commentators have resented the richness of the color
that Stokowski applies to the convolutions of a Bach fugue,
and indignantly quote (sic) the conductor as having said,
"Bach is just a sleepy old man." That is exactly what Bach is to
many people—and no wonder. His interpreters for the most
part forget, or perhaps never have realized, that music is a
sensuous as well as an intellectual pleasure, and, engrossed
with the mathematical and architectural perfections of Bach,
they have usually allowed the tonal possibilities of his music to
go by the board. Of course, transcriptions are frowned upon,
and often with justification, by the musician. What is written
for one instrument is seldom played upon another without distortion of meaning and loss of effectiveness, but this is not
always the case. Bach is often dull and sleepy to modern audiences because he has fallen into the hands of scholars and
purists.

As Stokowski himself remarks of one of his transcriptions:
"The most free and sublime instrumental expressions of Bach
are his greater organ works, and of these the greatest is the
Passacaglia in C minor. Unfortunately one does not often
enough have opportunity to hear it, and so, to bring it nearer
to those who love Bach's music, I have made it for orchestra.
I have transcribed it simply, adding one instrument to the
usual orchestra—a small tuba—which plays in octaves with the
larger tuba in the final entry of the theme in the fugue, just as
the 8 and 16 feet pedal stops sound in octaves on the organ.
*The Passacaglia is one of those works whose content is so full
and significant that its medium of expression is of relative un-
importance; whether played on the organ, or on the greatest of*

all instruments—the orchestra—it is one of the most divinely inspired contrapuntal works ever conceived."

This would seem to be an opportunity to scotch the ridiculous gossip to the effect that Stokowski's Bach transcriptions were not his work, but the work of Mr. Lucien Cailliet. During Stokowski's tenure at Philadelphia, Cailliet was bass clarinet and copyist for the orchestra, and an orchestrator of truly remarkable gifts. It has been, and still is, common gossip among orchestra players in Philadelphia and elsewhere, whose musicianship is by no means equal to their malice, that Cailliet actually made Stokowski's orchestrations. I know that this is false, and anyone owning a slight degree of musical perception would likewise know it to be false. Mr. Cailliet has made many orchestrations and transcriptions of Bach and other composers, and it is necessary only to compare any one of his works with any one of Stokowski's to know that they could not have been produced by the same hand. It is true that Mr. Cailliet copied out parts for Stokowski, and very possibly worked from Stokowski's orchestral sketches, filling in harmonies and otherwise attending to the laborious detail of orchestral transcription. But that he contributed to Stokowski's transcriptions any more than these details is absolutely untrue. I have spent many an hour with Stokowski as he worked on these scores, and I have seen the more important of them set down on paper with his own hand, out of his own mind. They are his and his only. Nothing here should be regarded as disparaging of Cailliet, whose work I warmly admire and have used to my own satisfaction and profit, and whose talents in the field of orchestration are truly remarkable even if they have no resemblance whatever to those of Stokowski. Mr. Cailliet's transcriptions, from Jerome Kern all the way back to Bach, are agreeable, viable, worthy works, but they hardly compare with, for example, the Stokowski transcription of the C minor Passacaglia, which is as great a service to Bach as Mendelssohn's first performance of the *St. Matthew Passion* and would, I believe, make Stokowski deathless if he had made no other contribution to music. Other arrangements by Stokowski of music not originally intended for orchestra alone, have given the critics, most of whom dislike him, an opportunity to get at him. These arrangements and transcriptions are called "symphonic syntheses," a term that I must confess I invented. Stokowski has made a number of these, involving music from *Die Walküre*, *Götterdämmerung, Rheingold, Parsifal, Tristan and Isolde*, and *Boris Godunov*. In them he has attempted, with extraordinary success so far as the public is concerned, to cast into rhapsodic or sometimes into almost strict symphonic form the most interesting music of the operatic works I have named. In doing so he disregarded, rightly and necessarily, the sequence of the music as it appears in the opera, and this alone was enough to infuriate the omniscient reviewers. These precious gentry chose to ignore completely the purpose of Stokowski's work, which never was to interpret operatic action through the orchestra alone, but rather to substitute a logical dramatic sequence roughly in symphonic form, taking the music of the opera subjectively, not objectively, and imposing upon it a new, logical, and convincing dramatic scheme. One may suppose that the rage of the critics was the more furious because, without exception, these syntheses were successful with the public. The most exciting of all was Stokowski's arrangement of the *Vorspiel, Liebesnacht*, and *Liebestod* from *Tristan*. This piece was damned to fame because, as the critics said, it extracted from *Tristan* all that was sensual and erotic, all that expressed the irresistible imperative of carnal love—its ferocity, its tremulous beauty, and its frightful penalty. It is difficult for some people, knowing the motivation of the plot of *Tristan*, to see wherein Stokowski has done violence to Wagner's central idea; whether he has done so or not, he has made of this music an orchestral song of songs that no one who has heard it will soon forget. Even the critics, or at least that proportion of them who are capable of normal sexual feelings, by implication admitted the power and conviction of Stokowski's performance of this music, but to establish publicly their devotion to the Wagnerian *Urtext*, felt obligated to damn the piece because it did not follow Wagner's cumbersome, labored, and sluggish dramatic sequence. They committed the sin that inferior critics are prone to commit—the sin of daring to criticize while deliberately closing their eyes and ears to what the artist is trying to do. They criticize on their premises, not on his. They commit, as Saintsbury pointed out, "one of the commonest but most uncritical faults of criticism—the refusal to consider what it is that the author intended to give us."

In recording, it was always a joy to work with Stokowski. Much has been said and written of the excellence of records made by the Philadelphia Orchestra and their tonal superiority to other orchestral records. This superiority has been attributed to almost every circumstance except the really causative one—the acoustic properties of the Academy of Music in Philadelphia, the curiously designed shell or setting or acoustic resonator that Stokowski helped to build, the participation of Stokowski in the electro-mechanical part of recording, and various other factors. The truth of the matter is that Stokowski understands the recording of sound and conducts his orchestra accordingly. To begin with, he was always more interested in orchestral tone than any other conductor and knew more about it—how to produce it, how to employ it, and how to make it register on a record. Secondly, he decided that, given sympathetic co-operation in the recording room, he could accomplish more by manipulation of the orchestra than by revolving a rheostat, and he rightly concluded that having learned the limitations of recording, he could register more convincing music on records by operating in his own way, within those limitations, than by applying to so plastic and sensitive an instrument as the orchestra the artificialities that are possible in any recording system. He accomplished his results, therefore, through conducting technique; leaving entirely to me the adjustment of the electronic-mechanical factors. In his last several seasons with the Philadelphia Orchestra we had become so completely *en rapport*—even to the extent that I would use an extra microphone to pick out details in the orchestra that I knew he would want to hear—that we could go through a recording session from start to finish, from ppp to fff without the necessity for the recording engineers to touch their instruments. I have never worked with any other musician who could do this.

Mr. Stokowski's services to American music and to music in America have been many, varied, and important. He has sought tirelessly and has succeeded in bringing about radical improvement in the quality of radio broadcasting of symphony orchestras and likewise has contributed mightily to the improvement of recorded music. He made his Philadelphia Orchestra records the most beautiful musically and technically that anyone has ever heard; therefore, they were the most popular. The transcontinental tours of the Philadelphia Orchestra, and particularly the first one in 1936, were his idea and through them he brought great orchestral music to many communities which, though prepared for it to some extent by radio and phonograph, had in many instances never actually seen a symphony orchestra. When he first proposed the tour to me I was skeptical, not of its feasibility, but of the co-operation of Victor, whose enthusiastic support, financial and other, would be necessary. I reckoned without the imagination, enterprise, and courage of Thomas F. Joyce, then the head of Victor advertising activities, who fell in with the plan with his characteristic vigor and enthusiasm; in most ways other than musical he was responsible for its success. I am afraid that Stokowski and Joyce will have to accept responsibility also for my public debut as a conductor.

The itinerary of the tour required that we play seven concerts a week, usually in seven different cities, each separated from the other by three to six hundred miles. This would be extremely wearing on any conductor, and particularly on one who in making music would completely exhaust himself of nervous energy, as Stokowski does. He suggested that he conduct but five concerts a week and that we should find someone else to do the other two. Naturally we turned to Saul Caston, then associate conductor of the Philadelphia Orchestra and now conducting the Denver Symphony, who was to do one of the two extra concerts, but since Saul could not be replaced as first trumpet, it was thought inadvisable to have him conduct more than once a week. Stokowski then suggested that I conduct the second of the two extra concerts. I did not take him seriously at first, for the reason that my conducting had not extended beyond a few informal and semi-private concerts with a student orchestra in Paris; a few rehearsals, more for fun than anything else, with a "scratch" orchestra of Philadelphia men, and some painfully incompetent recording performances with the Minneapolis Orchestra.[5] Therefore I declined the honor, but the more firmly I refused, the more insistent Stokowski became. He finally enlisted the authority of Mr. Joyce, then a vice president of Victor, and in fear and trembling I accepted the post of associate conductor for the tour. Few conductors have ever made a public debut with an orchestra of the stature of the Philadelphia, and Stokowski knew, of course, that however inept I might be the orchestra would save my neck. Actually there was no occasion for any rescue, and I had gratifying success in Springfield, Massachusetts, Little Rock, Arkansas, the festival at Ann Arbor, Michigan, and elsewhere. These concerts also were the occasion for Stokowski's only appearances as an orchestra player. It happened that the final work on my program was Arnold Zemachson's Chorale and Fugue for Organ and Orchestra. In the Municipal Auditorium at Springfield there is a magnificent organ. There is a similar instrument in the Hill Auditorium at the University of Michigan, where the Ann Arbor festival is played. Stokowski, out of a combination of

---

[5] Happily, my position at Victor enabled me to suppress the evidence of these.

kindness and shrewd showmanship, suggested that he play the organ part in this work, but only on condition that I would pay not the slightest attention to him, proffer him no applause, and as far as possible ignore him entirely. Furthermore, there was to be no advance publicity respecting Stokowski's playing in the orchestra when I conducted. I eagerly accepted these conditions and carried them out as far as possible. Naturally the unexpected appearance of Stokowski drew forth thunders of surprised applause, which he with generous hypocrisy directed toward the conductor.

At Ann Arbor there was an amusing incident growing out of Stokowski's love of mischief. We went to the hall some hours before the concert to rehearse with the organ, as he was not familiar with it. We found it a fine, large instrument of really enormous power; Stokowski privately made a wager with me that at the concert he could and would drown me out. I was willing to take him up on this and privately informed the men of the orchestra about our bet, knowing that they would take malicious pleasure in blotting out the organ if they could possibly do it. Incidentally, I assured myself of a rather overwhelming climax to Mr. Zemachson's piece.

At the concert I observed Stokowski's injunction against so much as looking at him, but as the climax of the piece approached something told me all was not well. I stole a glance at him, observed that his normally pale face was decidedly pink, and deduced—accurately as it turned out—that he had lost his place in the score. This would have been easy to do because the organ is *tacet* from the end of the chorale, which forms the introduction of the piece, to the *stretto* of the fugue eight minutes later. In those eight minutes Mr. Stokowski had apparently been busy drawing every stop on the organ, and had become so absorbed in this that he forgot to count bars. When the moment for his entrance occurred, then, I was obliged to violate his command to ignore him, and I gave him an exaggerated cue for his entrance. The rest of the orchestra fully appreciated the situation and were so tormented by their restrained laughter that they could not give me the sonority I had fondly hoped for; with the result that Stokowski collected our bet.

I am not certain that Stokowski is either satisfied or successful as a free lance, and it seems doubtful to me that he has been artistically happy at any time since he left the Philadelphia Orchestra. He is living his life according to a definite plan he entertained as long as twelve years ago. He told me then in considerable detail what he expected to do, year by year, and he has proceeded on schedule with almost unfailing precision. He wanted gradually to withdraw from the strenuous labor of thirty weeks of concerts per year; he wanted time for research, for travel, for musical activities in fields other than the concert hall, and for relaxation. He said that he looked forward to the time when he could conduct four or six concerts a year, make a sound film annually, and conduct a few important broadcasts; for the rest of his time he would enjoy living. Years ago I could see this program taking shape. I knew that Stokowski was impatient for it to materialize; I knew, too, that with his characteristic intolerance of control and unwillingness to subordinate himself to any circumstances, to any man or group of men, the situation at Philadelphia was becoming intolerable to him. The series of difficulties with his board of directors that presently developed there would, I was certain, lead to a complete break, with the onus of the divorce deftly placed upon the board, though in fact the separation actually was Stokowski's own doing and in conformity with his own wishes. The Hollywood adventures, 100 Men and a Girl and more particularly *Fantasia*, completed further steps in Stokowski's plan for himself as it had long existed in his mind. The New York City Symphony was to provide opportunity and audience for the few superb concerts he planned to do each season, and finally the NBC Symphony Orchestra fitted perfectly into the picture as the vehicle for the projection of the most beautiful and technically advanced radio broadcasts. Here Stokowski's plans completely went to pieces, for after a season he was not re-engaged.

The reasons for this were many, but they were not the reasons that have been publicized. It has been given out that to have more than one conductor (Toscanini) was damaging to the orchestra, and particularly to have a conductor with ideas other than those of Toscanini was especially bad. This cannot be true, for Toscanini has permitted and in some cases dictated the engagement of other conductors. Eugene Ormandy, Dimitri Mitropoulos, and others, even including myself, have been engaged to conduct the NBC Orchestra. Frank Black conducts it dozens of times through the year and, what is even more important, the orchestra has frequently been broken up into units of various sizes to play under all kinds of conductors and on all kinds of commercial and sustaining broadcasts. Apparently there has been no objection from Maestro Toscanini.

The argument has been advanced that Mr. Stokowski played too much American music on his programs and that this was disagreeable to the sponsor of the broadcasts and to the National Broadcasting Company. This argument will not hold water. It is true that the sponsors were afraid of programs entirely of American music, and it was suggested to Stokowski that he should not overemphasize native contemporary works. He actually played programs consisting of about two-thirds music from the standard orchestral repertoire and one-third new music. It was intimated to him that General Motors was opposed to the broadcasting of American music, but no one representing General Motors ever said anything of the kind to Stokowski; and he continued to play a fair proportion of new music. This brought about unusually extended comment in the newspapers each week, and naturally the sponsor was pleased. An important executive of General Motors did warn Stokowski that *too much* American music might cause the sponsor to lose enthusiasm for the broadcasts, but there would be no complaint (and there was none) if the conductor proportioned his programs as he was then doing. Mr. Niles Trammell, president of the National Broadcasting Company, did not set his face against Mr. Stokowski's programs, though he suggested, as General Motors did, that the relative proportion of American music to standard repertoire be maintained within definite limits. This, of course, was exactly what Stokowski was doing. Who, then, objected to hearing some of our own music played by the NBC Orchestra? As far as I can discover, only the Toscaninis, father and son, and Samuel Chotzinoff, musical adviser of NBC. Why did they object? Actually there was a definite agreement with Toscanini and Stokowski: the maestro would confine himself to the classical repertoire; Stokowski would emphasize the modern. Notwithstanding this, however, when a piece of modern music with unprecedented opportunities for promotion and advertising came along, it was the classic-minded Toscanini who first broadcast it. Under the rules of the game it should have been Stokowski's. I refer, of course, to the Seventh Symphony of Shostakovich.

No, I think the objection was not to Stokowski's American music so much as it was to Stokowski as a rival. Stokowski saw in his engagement with NBC an opportunity to expand the latent powers of broadcasting, to improve the musical quality of transmitted sound, and in doing this to employ the unmatched facilities of the greatest broadcasting company toward the establishment of unquestioned leadership and in improving radio. To this end he reseated the NBC Symphony in conformity with his very extensive knowledge of microphone technique and of acoustics. He eliminated the orchestral rigidity imposed by uniform bowing because, as he has demonstrated over a period of years, uniform bowing destroys *legato*; insistence upon it wastes rehearsal time that could better be employed for purely musical matters; when the string players are commanded to bow together they concentrate too much upon this and too little on feeling for the music; and finally, players have individuality and differences, and the incorporation of these into the music, Stokowski believes, is of definite value.

Toscanini does not like Stokowski's conducting methods. He neither understands nor knows the reasons for them, and what he does not know and understand he fears and hates. One would suppose that with the evidence of the success of Stokowski's methods available in the form of records—records that the maestro admired, at least for their beauty of sound —he would be inclined to adopt some of these methods himself. On the contrary, habits and practices that have grown up through years of orchestral history, often quite without reason, seem to Toscanini to have the force and rightness of Mosaic law. An orchestra must be seated today as it was in Mozart's day, notwithstanding the fact that every acoustic condition, not to mention broadcasting and recording techniques, has completely changed or eliminated the reasons that originally dictated orchestral seating. Toscanini not only lives in the past, thinks in the past, and feels in the past, but insists on putting the past before the present, with the consequent *rigor mortis* that inevitably must ensue.

Stokowski really and wholeheartedly and enthusiastically believes in his own principles, and will not modify them at the dictate of any man living. He knew that he was giving the Toscanini group grounds for resentment, and he knew too that resentment or fear or envy among this group is very likely to be followed by action. He persisted, nevertheless, in seating the orchestra as he thought best, in permitting free bowing, in playing the best of American music in reasonable amounts, and, in general, arranging circumstances in such a manner that he could give his best—which indeed he was engaged and paid to do. He knew, I think, that this would result in no re-engagement, but his deep feelings and beliefs had been touched and he has the courage to defend and to promote his convictions. I think his sense of justice was outraged and his patriotism—a very marked quality in the man

—offended that everything American—American music, American scientific advancement, American improvements in the science of sound, and even in effect the money of the American public, which ultimately pays for NBC Orchestra concerts—should be thrust aside, discouraged, ignored, or proscribed by a non-American musician, however eminent. He did not rage, for he is much too poised and intelligent a man for that; and besides "there is no sport in hate when all the rage is on one side." But he has said, in connection with the NBC Orchestra affair, "If I am an acceptable American conductor who enjoys bringing music of American composers to the American public, it would seem fair that I should have the same consideration as a conductor who has not made himself an American citizen and who very seldom plays American music and who ignores the inventions and new methods of broadcasting, which have mainly developed in the United States. In one sentence, it is the *old* trying to stop the *new* —Europe trying to dominate America. There is a great principle involved in all this. The people of the United States have the right to hear the music being composed by young talented Americans as well as all the great music of all countries composed by great masters. The radio stations are permitted by the Government to use certain wave lengths. This gives the radio stations *privileges* and also demands of them to fulfill their *responsibilities* to the American people. No one is saying that I do not know how to conduct—they are only saying that I use methods different from the old European traditions formed in pre-radio days."

It does seem unjust that RCA, which occasionally boasts in the public prints of the time, money, and equipment it so nobly devotes to research, would coldly dispense with the services of a man whose researches in music, the reproduction and transmission of music, have already accomplished so much —so much too that RCA itself has capitalized and by which RCA, through its creatures NBC and RCA Victor, has profited. This, to conform with the iron whims of a man whose genius, however great, is an expression of archaic concepts and outmoded thinking, whose mental processes have become polarized, and who looks forward only to more of the past.

The NBC contretemps, I think, has caused a fundamental fissure in the plan of life which Stokowski has so carefully and firmly erected for himself. Knowing him as I do, I cannot agree with those perhaps hopeful ones who, the wish being father to the thought, do not hesitate to assert that his career is completed. Stokowski has never yet subordinated himself to man or circumstance. He will not do so now. When he feels that his work is done, no conductor, no corporation, no indifference of dullards or influence of dollars, no thing and no man but Stokowski himself will say *"Es ist vollbracht."*

THE ORGANISTS

❧ The Organists ❧

Make us a wind

To shake the world out of this sleepy sickness

. . . a full organ swell

Through our throats welling wild

Of angers in unison arise. . . .

CECIL DAY LEWIS: *The Magnetic Mountain*

ON THOSE rare occasions when the Pope, the Bishop of Rome, the Vicar of Christ on earth, issues a pronouncement bearing upon music, he usually says something of import and of influence. There are nevertheless people of invincible ignorance, of incorrigible perversity or unregenerate skepticism, who find difficulty in accepting all papal pronouncements on the subject of music or any other. For example, I know stubborn heretics who find it incompatible with decency and humanity to honor the dictum that it is "ad maiorem Dei gloriam," as well as to the benefit of the Sistine Choir, to manufacture sopranos by emasculating boys, as one of the Pontiffs asserted under the seal of the Bull. On the other hand, that most marvelously beautiful, reverent, decorous, and above all things, practical system of music for the Church, designed, promulgated, and sanctioned by the great Gregory, as well as the admirable regulations laid down by His Holiness, Pius X, in the encyclical *Motu Proprio*, are regarded with profound respect even by the heathen, the heretic, and the infidel; and indeed, often are observed in letter and in spirit by a multitude of dissident sects, excepting, of course, those who are bound to respect and obey them—the Roman Catholics.

Occasionally, however, the Holy See delivers itself of a declaration that is universally recognized as an ultimate distillate of the Church's centuries of observation and toleration, and of a wisdom hardly less divine than human; for example, the recent pronouncement of His Holiness, Pius XII, quoted in the newspapers as follows: "Like every human invention, the radio can be used as an instrument for evil as well as of good."

The protagonists of radio are numerous, vociferous, and of compelling influence, and they can prove at least to their satisfaction the force for good that makes itself felt through radio. I am not at the moment concerned with radio's influence for good because, being untrained in scientific investigation generally and in histology particularly, I have not been able to detect in radio much that is good; but I am profoundly concerned with some of the things radio has done and is doing that are evil. The Holy Father has indicated that it is possible for radio to do wrong; so very humbly, and with no encouragement from His Holiness, I dare to adduce certain evidence pointing to radio's influence for evil. The gravamen of my indictment lies in radio's treatment of the unsceptred and outcast king of instruments, the organ.

The Church has fostered the organ, its development and that of its music, and the art of organ-playing too. This was more particularly true up to the first part of the twentieth century than it has been since. Nowadays the Church provides little more than a mortuary for an art that has almost died, and an economic sanctuary for organists whose musicianship, personalities, and enterprise disqualify them from competition in a fiercely competitive world. The odor of dry rot that pervades so many a choir loft is too often mistaken for the odor of sanctity, and the almost exclusive association of the organ with the Church and with ecclesiastical music has not contributed to the popularity of the instrument. The position of the average church organist is that of an inferior kind of cleric, inhibited by sanctimonious conventions, desperately clinging to the meager degree of security provided by his job, and too often not a musician but a mechanic.

What surges of popularity the organ has enjoyed have been energized not by the Church but by distinctly secular influences. Huge pipe organs were built and were made centers of interest at various fairs and expositions of the late nineteenth and early twentieth centuries. Visitors to these were mightily impressed and carried home with them a new idea of the beauty and power of great organ music. John Wanamaker purchased from one of the expositions the nucleus of the organ now in the Philadelphia Wanamaker Store—possibly the largest and I think certainly the most beautiful instrument in the world. Another organ was built in the New York Wanamaker's. Such instruments as those in the Mormon Tabernacle in Salt Lake City, the Municipal Auditorium in Springfield, Massachusetts, Constitution Hall in Washington, D. C., the Northrup Auditorium in Minneapolis, at Yale, and many others came into being and into fame. Mr. Wanamaker was not content with providing merely the instruments but also had to do with bringing to this country such giants of the organ world as Charles M. Courboin from Antwerp Cathedral, Marcel Dupré from Notre-Dame, Joseph Bonnet from St. Eustache, Günther Ramin from Bach's own Thomaskirche in Leipzig, Marco Enrico Bossi from Italy. Church organists, yes, but by their revelation of the possibilities of the organ as a concert instrument these masters brought life and interest to organ art and won for themselves enthusiastic audiences of impressive size. Charles Courboin, and later Dupré could, and did, have several highly successful transcontinental concert tours. William Churchill Hammond at the Skinner

Memorial in Holyoke, Massachusetts, and Samuel Baldwin in the Great Hall of City College in New York could, and did, give not hundreds but literally thousands of recitals to house-filling audiences. Walter Piston, Alexander Russell, Leo Sowerby, Rollo Maitland, Robert Bedell, and other Americans dared to write successful American music for the pipe organ.

While the organ was making progress in the concert field it was being perverted and prostituted in the theater. Owners and operators of motion-picture houses, noting both the growing popularity of the organ and the economy of substituting it for an orchestra, rushed to install hundred-thousand-dollar pipe organs often costing as much as six thousand dollars, and for the familiar aura of holiness that for so long had surrounded the organ they substituted the inescapable fragrances of camphor, paradichlorocide, and vermifuge—the characteristic odor of movie houses before air-conditioning. Theater pianists, exhumed from the darkness of the pit, leaped to the benches of theater organs—for the most part bastardized contraptions mechanically miraculous and musically monstrous. These players were even "featured," and presently achieved a standard of technical virtuosity that fully flowered in such geniuses as Jesse Crawford, Lew White, and later Ethel Smith. The versatility and color of the organ, multiplied by "effects" of fiendish ingenuity, lent themselves effectively to the braying out of popular tunes or to supplying a lush musical background to the movies' tensest dramaturgical triumphs. The organ had a brief heyday, but presently the sound film accomplished its extinction as an appurtenance of the theater. Sound film carried its own music, composed and directed especially for the picture, automatically cued to the picture and, it must be conceded, quite often enhancing the emotional appeal of the picture with appropriate music. Further, it made the screen characters talk. So, the mightiest of musical voices was silenced by the shadow of a sound on a film. Theater organists, after an unprecedented brief prosperity, returned to the oblivion from which they had come and in which they should decently have remained. For reasons that I do not understand the concert business similarly declined, and for a space of years only two or three concert organists could follow their profession with any degree of success. The organ was again almost entirely in the hands of the most inept, complacent, sanctimonious, and, worst of all, the most unmusical of musicians, the church organists. The king of instruments again sought asylum in the church and nearly died there. Most of the great concert organs were allowed to lapse into desuetude and neglect.

But the end was not yet: if concert management and the recorded-music industry insulted the quasi-corpse by ignoring it, radio went further: it degraded the corpse by abusing it. Here I do not overlook the many broadcast organ recitals given by Dr. Courboin from the American Academy of Arts and Letters as a "sustaining" program by NBC; nor do I ignore the several seasons of magnificent broadcasts given by E. Power Biggs, first under the auspices of the Columbia Broadcasting System and presently with the joint sponsorship of CBS and of that valiant enthusiast for music, Elizabeth Sprague Coolidge. All of these were superbly done, though, being given during Sunday morning hours, they reached the smallest possible daytime audience that the radio chains could find, and occupied only such time as local stations could not sell. It is the use of the organ as a mere "sound effect," as a "filler-in," as an occupier of unpremeditated blank moments, as an accompaniment of airy venery and murder and famous jury trials—this is what hurts the lover of the organ, makes his "angers in unison arise," alienates the interest of the average listener, and perverts his understanding of the instrument. But it saves money for advertisers.

Radio has actually very little respect for the organ. I remember the shock felt at NBC when, having been engaged to conduct the Philadelphia Orchestra in the RCA broadcast then known as "The Magic Key," I insisted on the engagement of Charles Courboin as soloist at a fee of seven hundred and fifty dollars. The NBC people were horrified and, I am sure, thought I was quite mad to suppose that any organist could possibly be entitled to such a fee. "Why, Charlie," they told me, "we can get an organist over at the studio to do this job for twenty-four dollars, the union scale." I replied that however true that might be, one could not buy for less than a crooner's fee the services of one of the world's most distinguished organists, a Victor Red Seal artist, and one whom I, as musical director for Victor, felt bound to promote through every possible facility. Dr. Courboin got his fee, but I am sure that never before nor since has any organist been paid for a broadcast anything approximating this sum. The truth is that radio's sole interest in the organ is purely economic. An organ can, for radio purposes, simulate and even rival a full orchestra. The orchestra involves a varying number of players, always a considerable number, and is correspondingly expensive. An organ requires but one player, who can be maintained to do "standby" music and other tricks at relatively little expense. Some broadcasting studios actually built small pipe organs, all of them of quite inferior quality, and the expense of building them plus the salary of the player was, in relation to the service performed, really trivial. Then, to make matters better for the broadcaster and worse for the listener, someone surely inspired by Beelzebub invented a thing called the Hammond organ, which further reduced the cost of music by producing electronically from an extremely compact and inexpensive instrument a variety of sounds, all of them hideous and all of them catalogued under various divisions of organ tone. It was bad enough for the organ as a valid musical instrument when it was cast out even from such a musical bawdyhouse as the motion picture theater. Its final abasement was not reached until radio employed it, and then added insult to injury by substituting for it an electrified hideousness which, until restricted by law, dared to use the name "pipe organ"; a creature conceived by clockmakers, vivified by tubes and oscillators, tonally designed by electricians:

a toy, a machine, a monster, an abomination. With the development of this implement, "organ" music became in some ways the darling of radio—cheap to produce, to buy, to use, to hear: and therefore dear.

The deterioration of organ-playing and of the organ itself was a matter of moment and of deep concern to me. I have known, and learned from, such men as Charles-Marie Widor, William Churchill Hammond, Alexander Russell, Arthur Turner, Joseph Bonnet. I loved and admired the art of the organ and bitterly resented the condition in which it stood. I decided that in my position as musical director for Victor I could, should, and would do something about it. I did.

Until comparatively recently the record catalogs of both Columbia and Victor were almost bare of organ recordings. It happens that I myself played the organ for the first successful electrically recorded disc of this type—more than twenty years ago. But aside from this and a few other insignificant records and still fewer imported discs, Victor offered the organ-loving public abolutely nothing. Columbia was in a somewhat better situation: its catalog listed a number of recordings by Albert Schweitzer. These records were made from European matrices, and Columbia did no organ recording whatever in this country. Furthermore, Dr. Schweitzer, a noble man, a humanitarian, a profound scholar, is not and never was a great organist, nor did he pretend to be.

It seemed to me that the best of the organ literature—classical, romantic, and modern—performed by the most distinguished organists in the world and recorded by the most modern techniques, could not fail to find a public. Even if they did fail, it seemed to me that Victor's artistic conscience would require that such recordings be made regardless of their commercial success. One day while I was in the midst of such deliberations and pondering how I should persuade Victor to undertake such a project, there appeared at my office a certain concert manager. He was burning with enthusiasm for a new coloratura soprano named, with clumsy suggestiveness, Galli-Campi. I have no doubt she was a very worthy artist, but at the time I did not feel Victor required her services. While we were discussing the matter I noticed that the manager had left in my anteroom a companion whose face looked familiar though I hadn't seen it for upward of ten years. The manager had not mentioned him, but I could not forget and I said: "Surely that is Charles Courboin." My visitor informed me that it was and that Courboin also was under his management. On an impulse I said, "Well, I can't engage Galli-Campi, but I will sign a contract with that man this afternoon." There was a jolly reunion on the spot and a contract was signed.

This happy coincidence inaugurated a period extending to the present during which organ music, so far as the record public is concerned, became of vital and widespread interest. It was a fortunate accident that Courboin was the first organist I engaged for Victor because his style and repertoire were, and are, calculated to reach the widest section of the public. He is the great master of romantic organ music, and particularly that of Widor, Guilmant, and Mailly. Widor and Mailly were his teachers, and the former dedicated his greatest organ work—his Sixth Symphony—to Courboin.

Courboin, the successor of Pietro Yon as organist of St. Patrick's Cathedral, is a vividly glowing and quite irresistible personality. He in no way resembles the saintly priest's underling suggested by so many church organists. He wears his multitude of decorations lightly. He is genial, jovial, amiable, and able; his work is a joy to him, as he is to his family, friends, and colleagues. He is a graduate engineer and organ architect as well as a virtuoso: he has designed many noble instruments. His lightheartedness conceals a profound knowledge of his instrument and a feeling for it that amounts almost to reverence. Apparently he is given a free hand in musical affairs at the Cathedral, and even in the short period he has served Dr.

Courboin has influenced and conspicuously improved the quality of music at that great church.

The emphatic success of the first Courboin recordings [1] gave me assurance that other kinds of organ music could be equally acceptable to the record public. By this time I had the full co-operation of my superiors at Victor, and thus emboldened, I decided to record the complete organ works of Bach, the Handel and other concertos, and similar works. It seemed desirable to me that an instrument as nearly as possible like Bach's own should be employed. The modern organ, with its tremendous accretion of mechanical gadgets, swell pedals, crescendo pedals, combination pistons, compound and imitative stops, and other elaborations, is far removed from the mechanical simplicity and tonal purity of the organ of Bach's day. We are fortunate to have in this country one instrument, and only one, that truly approximates the instrument on which Bach played. This is the baroque organ in the Germanic Museum at Harvard University, designed by G. Donald Harrison. It is not the little practice organ on which Carl Weinrich had made a few records for Musicraft.

By a most fortunate coincidence the organist who had access to the Germanic Museum instrument is a man who combines poetry and scholarship, faultless technique, and musical taste in his playing. I speak of E. Power Biggs. One can believe that Bach himself was such an organist; certainly one cannot believe that the old man played with the wooden inexpressiveness, insecure and yet mechanical rhythm, unimaginative registration, and feeble dynamics that are characteristic of the pedantic purist who lurks in the usual organ loft.

I had heard of Mr. Biggs, but was not at this time acquainted with his playing. When he approached me in an interval of a recording session with the Boston Symphony Orchestra with

---

[1] His royalties came to exceed those of certain "popular" entertainers before whom radio made genuflections.

an invitation to hear the baroque organ, I was candidly more interested in the instrument than I was in Mr. Biggs. I readily accepted his invitation, after which I was more interested in Mr. Biggs than in the instrument. We made arrangements then and there to record with him and the Germanic Museum organ, and shortly afterward I put before the artist certain long-range projects which I am happy to see are being moved forward. Mr. Biggs is rather diffident, very affable and merry, but he has in him a fierce determination to put the organ in its proper place and he has accomplished giant strides in this direction. His playing of such works as the great Reubke Sonata and contemporary music by Walter Piston, Leo Sowerby, and others demonstrates an extraordinary versatility and, what is equally important, a demonstrable conviction that the organ need not, should not, and must not be relegated to the church or the museum. Mr. Biggs's appearances as soloist with the Boston Symphony and other first-rate orchestras have established him as a scholar, a virtuoso, and an artist of the first rank.

Virgil Fox is the most brilliant organ-player I have ever heard. He has the facility and agility of Horowitz, Stokowski's sense of theater, and musical taste just sufficiently vulgar to make him eventually the most popular of concert organists. I say nothing in disparagement, and I use the word "vulgar" in the sense of that which appeals to the multitude.

When Mr. Fox was engaged for recording, the company wanted to know why, when we had Courboin and Biggs, we should need another organist. Organ recording involves the transportation of much equipment, and this the recording companies always do with a certain reluctance, for it is expensive and troublesome. It seemed to me that we should record Mr. Fox as well as Courboin and Biggs for much the same reasons we had for recording the Boston "Pops" in addition to the Philadelphia and Boston Orchestras. Mr. Fox's métier lies in the virtuoso performance of the better-known, the popular "classics," and this he accomplishes sensationally. Before the war Virgil Fox had studied somewhat with Courboin and later headed the organ department at the Peabody Institute in Baltimore—a really distinguished achievement for a very young man. The fact that he is a young man, however, also brought about the interruption of his career both on records and in concert: recently the United States Army had need of young men, and Mr. Fox exchanged his crimson-lined cape for the army's olive drab. He has survived, and he will be heard from in the future.

It seemed to me that with Courboin, Biggs, and Fox we would be able eventually to cover the whole organ repertoire, or at least that part of it worth recording. To this end we had put definite plans in operation, and did not expect to engage other organists; but I calculated without Mr. John Hays Hammond, Jr. Let me say at once that Mr. Hammond, though intimately concerned with electronics, with music, and with improvements in certain musical instruments, has never at any time had anything to do with the Hammond organ—except to regard it with utter horror. Mr. Hammond is an organ enthusiast, though not a musician, and that is only one of the ways in which he is a very remarkable man. Mr. Hammond is cynical, superior, cruelly witty, shrewdly acquisitive; he regards human failings, human passion, and most human mentalities with unpitying scorn. In addition to money he collects medieval tapestries, stained glass, furniture, house-fronts, and ecclesiastical architecture. Celebrities too—especially musicians.

Mr. Hammond is a director of the Radio Corporation of America. Some time ago he had as his house guest, and I believe was responsible for bringing to this country, the eminent French organist Joseph Bonnet. He had also installed in his house, previously and somewhat more permanently, a pipe organ of several hundred stops—an extraordinary, interesting, but quite badly organized instrument. Mr. Hammond wrote to me and suggested that a discussion of recording at his place

with Mr. Bonnet might be in order. In view of the standing of
Bonnet as well as Hammond's position as an RCA director, I
was constrained to agree that it might; and soon set forth on a
journey to Gloucester, Massachusetts, where Mr. Hammond
maintains his establishment.

Mr. Hammond's house overlooks the reef called Norman's
Woe on which the ship *Hesperus* was wrecked. The living-
room, if one may call it so, is a chamber approximately one
hundred feet long, sixty feet high, and forty feet wide, done in
purest twelfth-century Gothic. It is actually the nave of a
church, and this impression is fortified by the crepuscular light
that filters through some lovely lancet windows of stained
glass, and by the innumerable objects of ecclesiastical art used
as decoration. Mr. Hammond's characteristic mockery finds
expression, I think, in the fact that one of the bays of this profane fane is a very luxurious cocktail lounge, one side giving
upon the chaste and heaven-soaring arches of the nave, the
other facing the grisly reaches of Norman's Woe. Numerous
emasculated cats flit surreptitiously through the shadows.
What would be the sacristy is a sumptuously appointed din-
ing-room. In the great hall itself one may encounter here and
there a touch of Mr. Hammond's macabre wit; as for example,
one is encouraged to examine, to open an exquisite armoire,
whereupon a light flashes on and a livid skull grins at you. Beyond the organ and concealed from the nave by a huge red
velvet curtain is a modern, completely equipped, and busy
workshop and laboratory where Mr. Hammond's assistants
materialize his mechanical, electrical, and electronic ideas. At
the opposite end of the great room a small door admits the
visitor to a patio in the middle of which is a lovely pool, green
as emerald. Surrounding it are a number of house-fronts, some
of them perhaps a thousand years old, which Mr. Hammond
imported intact from various parts of Europe. Behind them
are bedrooms quite as authentic. I slept in a cardinal's bedroom, which in every detail except the good spring on the bed
was straight out of the thirteenth century, even to the jewelled

miter that glittered darkly from the top of a chest of drawers. I was happy to observe that behind the worm-eaten Gothic door there was a very modern bathroom, and flattered on being informed that I was not the first O'Connell to sleep in this suite. For its last previous occupant had been a friend of my host, His Eminence, William Cardinal O'Connell of Boston.

I feel at liberty to describe this extraordinary home because Mr. Hammond spent a good many hours describing and showing it to me before he would discuss the matter that had brought me to Gloucester. We explored even the grim and massive mausoleum, half-concealed around a bend in the shore and approached by the most beautiful stair I have ever seen. Here in this lordly tomb, knelled by the never-silent bell buoy of Norman's Woe and the ceaseless winds that make an organ of the dark cypress trees, lie the bones of Mr. Hammond's favorite cat.

During our walk about the place I politely admired everything, particularly the catacomb and the really charming bedchambers. My host mentioned, rather surprisingly, that he never used them; indeed he usually slept aboard his yacht and worked at night while the world slumbered. He expressed the conviction that during the daytime when most people are busy about their affairs, their dull minds encumber the ether with inferior thoughts which, radiating and impinging upon the thought processes of better minds, hamper them. An interesting theory, but somewhat unflattering to the antipodes.

I think Mr. Hammond admired Bonnet because the great French organist was so simple, so saintlike, and so unsaintly. Bonnet was as meek as a medieval monk and looked like one; a valiant trencherman and prodigious tosspot too. I believe he had studied for the priesthood, but stopped at the lower plane of the organ loft. He was a truly great organist in the nineteenth-century French tradition, and mastered the unnecessary intricacies of Mr. Hammond's organ in a remarkably brief time. His musicianship was magnificent. Nevertheless, I felt obliged to tell Mr. Hammond privately that I personally felt that practical considerations should not permit us to undertake an extended series of recordings with Mr. Bonnet in view of the program we had planned and the organists already engaged; but that for artistic reasons and, more particularly, because Mr. Hammond himself wished it, we would undertake a limited number. We did so, successfully, and I rejoice that we did, for Bonnet made some really priceless recordings for us; and not long afterward died. I should not enjoy having been responsible for missing an opportunity to record him.

The records were made at Mr. Hammond's instance, not on my initiative, and perhaps would not have been made at all except for his prestige as a director of the Radio Corporation. I was surprised, then, when Mr. Hammond sent us a bill for the use of the organ and his home. The explanation for this, I learned, lay in the fact that his house is called the Hammond Museum. This explained too the occasional strange but reverent visitors who would wander in during the morning hours of certain days, at fifty cents per capita, and tiptoe breathlessly through the great nave where goings-on of a decidedly secular nature had transpired not twelve hours before. I suppose the small admission fee paid by these pious intruders as well as the charge against Victor for the use of Mr. Hammond's place bore little relation to the expense of maintaining so vast and luxurious an establishment. Perhaps it had something to do with taxes. It did seem strange that Mr. Hammond would levy a charge against his own company for the use of his house in making records that he particularly wanted and the company especially didn't. One might suppose that he would even be willing himself to pay a small charge to procure the records in which he had such interest.

> I'm ignorant of music, but still, in spite of that,
> I always drop a quarter in an organ-grinder's hat.

CODA

CODA.

ᴇᶘ Coda ɞᴗ

"*Let us now praise famous men . . . such as found out musical tunes . . . There be of them, that have left a name behind them, that their praises might be reported. And some there be, which have no memoriam. . . . We may speak much, and yet come short: There are yet hid greater things than these be.*"

APOCRYPHA, ECCLESIASTICUS, xliv

SOMEONE has written that the happiest nations have no history. Some artists' lives are so perfectly ordered and serene as to be completely dull, and could be recorded as adequately in numerals as in words. Hence they have no place in this chronicle. Of some musicians who are close and valued friends I have written not at all because even when our relations were most intimate they are not necessarily of interest to anyone but ourselves. If the purpose of this record were to make propaganda for or against anyone instead of inclining in the opposite direction, its content and the subjects discussed would be very different indeed. Furthermore, I have worked successfully for years with certain artists without establishing any relationship closer than the purely professional, and a report of such conventional contacts would be of little interest, I think. If this were a book concerned with musical criticism the situation would again be different, but I have preferred to avoid, on the whole, and to reserve for another time and place, strictly musical evaluations of performers with whom I have worked long and intimately. The fact that one artist is included and another not, or that one artist requires twice as much space as another is no index to my list of friends. There has been little or nothing said here about certain artists who have my admiration and affection and whose friendship I treasure, among them Richard Crooks, Lotte Lehmann, John Charles Thomas, Fritz Reiner, the late Frederick Stock, Alexander Brailowsky, Harl McDonald, Howard Hanson, Roy Harris, Gregor Piatigorsky, Rose Bampton, Rosa Ponselle, Wilfred Pelletier, Vladimir Golschmann, Eugene Goossens, Eleanor Steber, Marian Anderson, Fabien Sevitzky, Albert Spalding, Fritz Kreisler, Igor Gorin, Jeanette MacDonald, Claudio Arrau, Artur Rodzinski, John Barbirolli, Lawrence Tibbett, Josef Hofmann, E. Robert Schmitz, Joseph Szigeti, the lamented Emanuel Feuermann, Sir Thomas Beecham, Yehudi Menuhin, Gladys Swarthout, Amelita Galli-Curci, Dorothy Maynor, Mischa Elman, Paul Robeson, Reginald Stewart, Elisabeth Schumann, Nelson Eddy, Ezio Pinza, Dimitri Mitropoulos, Hans Kindler, Mack Harrell, Myra Hess, Alfred Wallenstein, Henrietta Schumann, Bruno Walter, James Melton, George Szell, Leonard Joy, Maurice van Praag, Dorothy Kirsten, Hulda Lashanska, Mischa Levitzki, Mario Chamlee, Efrem Zimbalist, Kerstin Thorborg, Carlos Salzedo, Sir Ernest MacMillan, Jarmila Novotná, William Primrose—this list can hardly be complete without including almost every notable musician of the last twenty years. With every one of these I have enjoyed friendliness in our collaboration, and I am proud to have contributed to the preservation of their art and the enlargement of their audiences.

I feel a particular glow of pride when I survey a list of to-day's recording artists and today's recorded repertoire, and reflect upon the privilege of helping the cause of the American artist and of American music that has been mine. Recognition of the importance of American music by Victor, which I brought about, has been generously acknowledged by a citation from the National Association of American Composers and Conductors. Long before they were established with the public I engaged for Victor Red Seal records such artists as Rose Bampton (actually while she was still a student at the Curtis Institute of Music as a contralto, and again in her reincarnation as a soprano); Leonard Warren, the magnificent American baritone who always sings in time because he is a watchmaker, and in tune because he is an artist; Norman Cordon, heroic in voice, appearance and exploits of one kind or another; Eleanor Steber, who possesses the loveliest lyric soprano since Alma Gluck; Dorothy Maynor, whom I heard and engaged before she had ever made a solo public appearance; Patrice Munsel, whom we engaged for Victor through the cooperation of Wilfred Pelletier and Earle Lewis of the Metropolitan before she was heard at the opera house or on the radio or anywhere else of importance, and whose possibilities as a radio attraction rather than my admiration for the coloratura brought about a contract; Ifor Jones and the Bach Choir of Bethlehem, incomparably the most beautiful and intelligently trained choral ensemble in America, whose value and possibilities have not been and will not be realized by Victor; Jeanne Behrend, pianist, whose accomplishments for American music, though yet to be fully recognized here, have only in the past few months caused a furore in South America's musical centers; John Jacob Niles, the unique American troubadour whom no imitator has yet successfully imitated; George Copeland, a neglected artist, an artist for the sophisticated, who plays Debussy like nobody else and, unfortunately, like he plays nothing else; Carlos Chávez, who has brought Mexico to music.

Though I actually brought about their engagement for Red Seal records, I must thank David Sarnoff and Samuel Chotzinoff for providing the initial stimulus that resulted in recording contracts with Jan Peerce and Nan Merriman. It is true that ultimately we would have recorded Peerce, particularly when he was engaged by the Metropolitan. At the time we were having difficulties in assigning repertoire for operatic tenors and I was reluctant to engage another one whose presence on the Victor list would complicate matters. When Peerce joined the Metropolitan and Mr. Sarnoff expressed his personal interest, there was no excuse for further delay in making arrangements with Peerce, and it was fortunate that this was so.

Nan Merriman is an artist of extraordinary versatility, superb vocal equipment, really thorough musicianship, and highly attractive personality. I do not believe that either she, her management, or Victor has exploited her possibilities to any appreciable degree, but I have to thank NBC and particularly Mr. Chotzinoff for making me acquainted with her. This young woman was doing nothing more important than obscure sustaining programs at the time; I risk the prophecy that she will. Her extraordinary talents and above all, her honesty, industry, and intelligence will make her not only a notable artist but a famous one.

The debt of American composers, and indeed of the American public, to Howard Hanson of Wahoo, Nebraska, and points east, is considerable. No one else has been so active and so effective in promoting American music. Howard Hanson accomplishes this in his own music, through his functions as head of the Eastman School at Rochester, New York, and through his annual festival of American music, where a full symphony orchestra of excellent quality and a conductor of conspicuous ability are placed at the disposal of American composers and devote themselves exclusively to American music. When I sought for means within my means for recording contemporary American music, it was Hanson, with his sympathy, enthusiasm, energy, and resources, who made much of the recording possible. The company naturally was unwilling to record more than the irreducible minimum of American music with the great expensive orchestras because of the dubious commercial value of such recordings. With Dr. Hanson's co-operation it was possible to make many really beautiful recordings of present-day compositions by Americans, with no cost to the company for orchestral talent. I am afraid that otherwise it would have been a long day before any of this music was recorded.

Jesús María Sanromá, notwithstanding his exotic name, is a native American. When I first knew him he was eating his heart out in Boston, as pianist of the Boston Symphony Orchestra and a distinguished teacher. True, his position with the orchestra gave him golden opportunities for concerto performances and premières, particularly of modern works like the Ravel Concerto, the Stravinsky *Capriccio*, and other important music. Contrarily, he played the Gershwin *Rhapsody in Blue* so many times with the Boston "Pops" Orchestra that his association with it was becoming too close for comfort. Above all, I thought his talents were far too broad and brilliant to be so confined; ultimately I was of some influence in persuading him to take the risks attendant upon an independent career, and to cut loose absolutely from Boston. This eventually he did; and after a season or two of difficulty the tide of public approbation and appreciation began to flow in his direction and has already carried him to an enviable place among the great pianists. Technically Sanromá is at least the equal of any practitioner of the pianistic art. This is impressive, but what really interests an intelligent listener is, I believe, the sensitive musicianship, the soundness and saneness of his interpretations, and his extraordinary versatility. He has absorbed the best that his two great teachers, Artur Schnabel and the late Antoinette Szumowska, could give him: Schnabel's scholarship, and the sense of color and tonal values that Szumowska, one of Paderewski's few pupils and the only one a woman, absorbed from her master.

A few years ago Victor was asked to produce certain recordings of both opera and symphonic works for a certain agency normally not connected in any way with the business of recorded music. These records were to be produced under a special label, and no indication given of the identity of the performers or of the producer. The symphonic records actually were made by personnel of the NBC Symphony, the Philharmonic Symphony of New York, the orchestra of the New Friends of Music, and of the Philadelphia Orchestra. The conductors were Eugene Ormandy, Fritz Reiner, Artur Rodzinski, Fritz Stiedry, Alexander Smallens, Wilfred Pelletier, Hans Wilhelm Steinberg, and Charles O'Connell. For the operatic records it was necessary to engage a company of artists capable of doing both German and Italian opera. This was accomplished with the very important co-operation of Wilfred Pelletier, conductor of the Metropolitan, and I engaged Pelletier, Smallens, and Hans Wilhelm Steinberg to conduct the opera records. The whole job had to be done very economically, and therefore it was necessary to employ in them singers of real ability but not necessarily with great names; in a word, singers who would sing for very little money. It was in the course of assembling these that I became acquainted with Eleanor Steber, Norman Cordon, and Leonard Warren, and as a result of their performances I quickly engaged them for Victor Red Seal records. They have since very emphatically justified my belief in them.

I did not always guess correctly in engaging young artists. There was the strange case of Lucy Monroe. Lucy, through the elaborate, persistent, and able operations of a publicity and promotion expert, had acquired the title of "The Star Spangled Soprano." A certain patriotic hysteria was beginning to develop—this was before World War II—and if you attended a convention of any importance, a national meeting of the American Legion, a World's Fair, a race-track opening, or any occasion where great numbers of people were gathered, you probably heard Lucy valiantly screaming. She has sung *The Star Spangled Banner* thousands of times on thousands of occasions, and has been prettily photographed with every notable from the late President Roosevelt all the way down, and I believe she is still busily engaged with the ungrateful music of *The Star Spangled Banner*. Surely if she ever finds the strain too great she may truthfully say, with Falstaff: "For my voice, I have lost it with hollaing and singing of anthems." Lucy hasn't lost her voice, as far as I know, but if she did it would be a small loss because it is a small voice; and not the most important of her charms. She is pretty, personable, gracious, and should have, I think, moving picture possibilities where her undeniable charm could be adequately presented.

However, though I know well from experience that records of *The Star Spangled Banner* do not interest the public, I was persuaded to engage Lucy for the purpose of making such a recording. Hans Kindler was kind enough to lend the company the National Symphony Orchestra; the record was made in Constitution Hall; wonderful photographs in full color recorded the momentous occasion; Victor helped with advertising; and Lucy's own manager sweated mightily at the job of selling the records, but they did not sell. Subsequent recordings of unimportant but charming trifles did a little better, but Lucy as a recording artist was one of my mistakes. Regardless of the failure of the records, Lucy was promoted into the job of director of patriotic music for RCA Victor, whatever that was, and spent her time for a year or so, at a good salary, traveling about the country singing at employees' meetings in industrial centers from coast to coast; and what do you think she sang?

I put this book aside with a certain satisfaction and relief, for it has been an effective anodyne for the accumulated irritations of years. I have "put nothing in in malice," I have omitted much in mercy, and if anywhere I have done violence to the truth it is only by suppressing the more unpleasant parts of it. I do feel guilty of sins of omission; perhaps there are those about whom I should tell you more, others about whom

I should tell you something. In extenuation and apology, let me quote [1] once more; a little more solemnly than the occasion warrants, perhaps, but nevertheless in words that to me are appealing. More than a thousand years ago an Irish scribe appended as a colophon to his manuscript, this: "The names enjoined on me to enter in this book, but omitted by carelessness, sloth or forgetfulness of mine, I commend to Thee, O Christ, to Thy Mother, and all the heavenly host, that here or in life eternal their happy memory be kept in honor."

[1] By permission of the British Museum.

INDEX

DATE DUE